MW00658282

A Kineño Remembers

Perspectives on South Texas
Sponsored by Texas A&M University–Kingsville
Timothy E. Fulbright, General Editor

My official photograph as U.S. secretary of education, 1990.
Courtesy U.S. Department of Education.

A Kineño Remembers

⚭

FROM THE KING RANCH
TO THE WHITE HOUSE

⚭

Lauro F. Cavazos

Texas A&M University Press
College Station

Copyright © 2006 by Lauro F. Cavazos
Manufactured in the United States of America
All rights reserved
Second printing, 2008
The paper used in this book meets the minimum requirements
of the American National Standard for Permanence
of Paper for Printed Library Materials, z39.48-1984.
Binding materials have been chosen for durability.

Library of Congress Cataloging-in-Publication Data

Cavazos, Lauro.
    A Kineño remembers : from the King Ranch to the White House /
Lauro F. Cavazos. — 1st ed.
        p. cm. — (Perspectives on south Texas)
    Includes index.
    ISBN-13: 978-1-58544-526-4 (cloth : alk. paper)
    ISBN-10: 1-58544-526-6 (cloth : alk. paper)
    1. Cavazos, Lauro.   2. Cabinet officers—United States—Biography.
3. United States. Dept. of Education—Officials and employees—Biography.
4. Hispanic Americans—Biography.   5. Bush, George, 1924–   —Friends
and associates.   6. King Ranch (Tex.)—Biography.   I. Title.   II. Series.
    E840.8.C385A3   2006
    370.92—dc22
    [B]
    ISBN 13: 978-1-60344-044-8 (pbk.)   2005034155
    ISBN 10: 1-60344-044-5 (pbk.)

For Peggy, our family,
y para los Kineños

Contents

Illustrations

My official photograph as U.S. secretary of education   *Frontispiece*

Preface

This book records my memories of a journey from the King Ranch in Texas to my work in Washington, D.C., as U.S. secretary of education. I had the honor and privilege to work for two presidents, Ronald Reagan and George H. W. Bush. In 1988, I was the first Hispanic appointed to the Cabinet in the history of the United States. I am pleased that, in the years since my service in the Cabinet, seven other Hispanics have followed. I am confident many more will be appointed in the years to come.

The journey from the King Ranch to the White House was long and took many turns, curves, and reverses. It commenced with my childhood years and education, took me to the academic world of teaching and research in two medical schools, to the deanship at Tufts University School of Medicine, to my selection as president of Texas Tech University and the Health Sciences Center, and subsequently to my appointment as secretary of education. In the pages of this book, I share many lessons I learned about education and public service.

In writing this memoir I have also attempted to give the reader a sense of my life as son, spouse, father, teacher, medical school dean, university president, and Cabinet officer.

The primary purpose of this book, however, is to document in some detail my life and my achievements. Some people consider my life extraordinary. Perhaps it has been extraordinary, considering that I was born on a ranch to Hispanic parents with limited resources and eventually attained a prestigious position in the U.S. government. I am certain that without loving parents insisting that I educate myself, I would have achieved little in life. I hope this book will encourage others, especially young minorities, of the importance and great necessity of education. Anyone who reads this book will see that education is critical to achieving one's highest potential.

My second purpose for writing this autobiography is a personal one rather than a public one. I wanted to leave for our ten children a document that explains their father's achievements and some of his failures. I wish my father had written his memoirs or at least left me audiotapes about his life. All I have from him are two letters—one written the day I was born and the other a few weeks before he died.

Writing this book was not a long-term goal of mine, but as the years went by and I thought about my life, I decided to chronicle that passage from Texas ranch to Washington's halls of government. I wanted to share the journey with others so they could understand that with an education, one can progress with pride from humble origins to a position of national leadership in education policy and governance. It took more than a year to write this book, and although it demanded much time and effort, I delighted in thinking back over the years. I ask forgiveness for any factual errors or for any dates, times, and places I may have gotten wrong. My only excuse is that any misstatements in this book are not intentional; time may simply have dimmed memory.

I hope you find this book a good read. Life has been an interesting and delightful journey, and I hope that I have shared that sense of pleasure in my description of it.

A Kineño Remembers

CHAPTER I

Lessons from the King Ranch

At a ceremony in the East Room of the White House, on September 20, 1988, Vice President George H. W. Bush swore me in as U.S. secretary of education. I was the first Hispanic appointed to the Cabinet in the history of the United States. A few weeks before, President Ronald Reagan had asked me to join his Cabinet, and I was unanimously confirmed by the U.S. Senate. My wife Peggy and I were very pleased that our ten children, most of their spouses, and one grandson—none of whom had visited the White House before—could be there. Their presence made the ceremony a family affair. They were so proud and pleased that I had been appointed to the Cabinet. Also present were many friends whom we had invited.

Also present were a number of Hispanics, including leaders of national Hispanic organizations, educators, and several of our friends. They must have been pleased there was a Hispanic in the president's Cabinet after more than two hundred years.

President Reagan looked on while Vice President Bush read the oath of office. Peggy held our family Bible, on which I rested my left hand while I raised my right one to repeat the oath. I felt great pride, not because of any personal accomplishment or achievement but because this event marked a new beginning for Hispanics in our nation.

During the swearing-in ceremony I remembered my parents. They would have been so proud to see their son at the White House on a beautiful day in September. I remember thinking how my parents spoke Spanish to each other and how I had started my education in a two-room schoolhouse. I tried to recall what events, circumstances, and good fortune had shaped my life in such a way as to result in my appointment as secretary of education.

I decided that the many excellent lessons I learned while growing up on the King Ranch had played a big part. It was on the ranch where I was taught the value of hard work, the importance of learning, the significance of commitment and dedication to worthy causes, how to make decisions, and the great value of family. Honesty, loyalty, integrity, and love of country were instilled in me. In other words, on the King Ranch I learned how to live. During my childhood years it was mostly my parents who fashioned my life, but the men and women working and living on the ranch were also my teachers. The wisdom about living I received on the King Ranch enormously shaped my being. This, in turn, impacted decisions I made and actions I took in my adult life, throughout my academic career, and during my service as secretary of education.

So my journey to the White House began on a ranch in Texas.

LOS KINEÑOS

I was born on January 4, 1927, on the 825,000-acre King Ranch in South Texas. The ranch is about the size of the state of Rhode Island, and at one time it comprised approximately 1,250,000 acres. The King Ranch has always been home to me, even though I have been away from it for many years. Just the thought of the King Ranch stirs grand memories in my mind. When I think about growing up there, I recall my childhood days, my parents, brothers and sister, relatives, and many of the fine people who worked on the ranch. It was a remarkable place, so it is not surprising that the lessons I learned there about life are still deeply ingrained in me.

In the late 1920s, '30s and '40s, my childhood years, the King Ranch was fertile ground for the growth and development of children. Parents and those who lived on the ranch stressed education. The Great Depression had slowed the nation's economy to a crawl. Money was short everywhere, and across the nation people were out of work. But on the ranch, in the face of these economic difficulties, the emphasis was on people. It was a caring place.

In those days, people who worked for the King Ranch and did their jobs well had work for life. They could expect the King Ranch to educate their children and provide health care, housing, money, and food for the entire family. They knew that when they died, the ranch would bury them.

One worked long hours helping to improve the ranch. People were born on it, worked there all of their lives, and died on it. Their children followed in their footsteps, and some families on the ranch, including mine, had been there for several generations. They were *Kineños*, King's People. I am a fourth-generation *Kineño*.

Running the ranch were members of the Kleberg family, the driving forces who eventually developed it into the greatest cattle ranch in the world. They instilled the tradition of caring and looking after those who worked there. This tradition of caring was in the spirit and commitment of the founder of the ranch, Capt. Richard King.

As a child, I remember seeing the Klebergs working side-by-side with the men on the ranch. All of the Klebergs were fluent in Spanish, had superior equestrian skills, and knew the cattle business. They cared so much about the people working there that to them the ranch was a family with many skills and talents. Some stayed on the ranch to help enhance its excellence in cattle and horses. Others left but carried with them the values and the teachings of the *Kineños*. No other ranch in this nation has produced a four-star general and a Cabinet secretary—my brother Richard and I, respectively.

My father was Lauro F. Cavazos and my mother, Tomasa Álvarez Quintanilla. Like my sister Sarita and my brothers Richard, Robert, and Joseph, I was born at home on the King Ranch. No one back then saw any reason for Mother to go to a hospital; she was not sick, just giving birth to a child. The local country doctor attended her. Also there were several members of Mother's family. My maternal grandmother (Mama

Grande Rita) and aunts helped out. They lived in the *barrio* in Kingsville, three miles away, and as was the custom, they came to the ranch to help Mother and Dad on the day I was born.

I have the letter Dad wrote on January 4, 1927, to my uncle and aunt, Mr. and Mrs. Edward C. Raymond, of Raymondville, Texas. Mrs. Raymond was my Aunt Leonor, my father's oldest sister. Dad wrote (and I quote exactly as he wrote), "We had a boy to call on us today he claimes his name is Lauro Fred and he wants work, ar at 7:40 p.m. Lauro and Tomey." The letter was postmarked in Kingsville, Texas, the next morning, and required a two-cent stamp. I treasure it because it connects me with my parents from the day I was born. And as my father sensed, to this day I continue to work, and to want to work.

Growing, learning, and working characterized my early days on the King Ranch. Neighbors were few, and all of our friends and many of our relatives lived on the ranch. We were, for the most part, self-sufficient. We had a school, and the commissary and the ranch garage met most of our needs. Reasons to travel the three miles to Kingsville were few. For the most part we were isolated, but Mother did frequently drive us to Kingsville to see our grandmother and some of our aunts, uncles, and cousins. Sometimes, but not on a regular basis, we attended mass at San Martín's Catholic Church. If mother needed something special for her cooking not available at the commissary, we went to Martinez's Grocery Store on East Richard Street at the corner of East Fifth Street, in the Hispanic commercial district. This neighborhood was a vibrant part of Kingsville, with many stores and businesses.

About the middle of the block, on the same side of the street as Martinez's, was a bakery. Handing us a quarter, Mama Grande Rita sent us to buy *pan dulce* at the bakery. We children readily volunteered to go after Mexican sweet breads. If we bought six or eight pieces, the baker gave us a *pilón*, a free cookie. Generally, the *pilón* was a *marranito*, a gingerbread pig. Two other grocery stores, a barbershop, a beauty shop, and a tailor shop completed the Hispanic business district. Around the corner stood a building with a bar on the first floor and outside stairs leading to the second-floor dance hall where Oscar Cabrera and his band played on Saturday nights. Salazar's Dry Goods Store was at the corner of Sixth and East Richard Streets. Everyone knew each other, and news and information spread rapidly through the commercial district.

Every Saturday morning, we children begged Mother to take us to the movie. We tried to convince her it was a great movie and we should go because we had been good all week. Mother often said she would like to take us to the show, but there was no money to spare.

One of her best initiatives for earning additional money was to send us to catch four or five chickens and gather all the eggs we could find. Mother would then take us to Martinez's Grocery Store; he bought each chicken for twenty-five cents and the eggs at ten cents a dozen. At Martinez's Grocery Store there was a coop on the sidewalk to house chickens. When customers wanted a chicken, they pointed out which one they wanted and one of the helpers pulled the chicken out of the coop. With our chicken and egg money we could then go to the movies.

On Saturdays there was always a Western film, with actors such as Buck Jones, Hopalong Cassidy, Tom Mix, Gene Autry, and Roy Rogers. They were our heroes, and we considered them the best actors in the world. A movie with the dog Rin-Tin-Tin was a "must see."

Serial adventure films ran for twelve Saturdays. Each Saturday, the serial film ended with the hero or heroine about to be killed by a train, or pushed over a cliff, or trapped in a burning building. The next Saturday the serial film started with how they escaped from certain death. We never went to the movies twelve Saturdays in a row, so we often missed the rescue or escape.

Dad came to work as a cowboy for Mrs. Henrietta King on the King Ranch in July 1912, when he was eighteen years old. Capt. Richard King, founder of the ranch, had married Henrietta Chamberlain in 1854. After Captain King died in 1885, she asked Robert Justus Kleberg Sr. to take over as manager of the King Ranch properties. In 1886, he married Alice Gertrudis King, the daughter of Captain and Mrs. King. Kleberg was the ranch manager, but it was really Mrs. King who ran it, almost until the day of her death in 1925. Dad worked for Mrs. King, Robert J.

Kleberg Sr., Robert J. Kleberg Jr., Richard M. Kleberg Sr., and Richard M. Kleberg Jr.—the leaders who truly shaped and built the King Ranch in the twentieth century.

On the Santa Gertrudis Division of the King Ranch, Dad's work was typical for young cowboys: riding fences, breaking horses, and herding and working cattle. In 1913, Caesar Kleberg, the foreman of the Norias Division of the ranch, had Dad transferred from the Santa Gertrudis to the Norias Division. There, he worked as a member of the *corrida*, or cow camp. Dad brought his many skills as a cowman to Norias. Many believed that when Dad rode a horse, he and it were as one. Dad and Robert J. Kleberg Jr., the manager of the ranch, were considered two of the best horsemen in Texas.

In 1939 Dad won the National Cutting Horse Contest riding a mare named Catarina. The event took place at the Fort Worth Stock Show. When he brought home the cup signifying first place, I asked him about the contest. He told me he had trained Catarina from the time she was a filly. She was out of the great line of King Ranch quarter horses. Dad told me that at the cutting horse contest one of the judges, a retired army cavalryman, asked to ride Catarina. Dad warned him she was quick on the turns following a calf. The judge mounted Catarina, started to herd a calf, and barely managed to stay in the saddle when the mare made a quick turn to follow the calf. Still, Dad was awarded first prize.

Dad was a man of considerable personal bravery. In France during World War I he had fought in three major campaigns. Time and time again, when his courage was tested working on the King Ranch, he remained calm, focused, and determined. Still, his coolness under fire and his ability to deal with life-threatening adversity was probably best demonstrated at Norias. Dad's bravery and discipline have always been an inspiration to me, especially after he told me about a gunfight at Norias in 1915. From the story he told, I learned a lesson about fighting for what is right and having a commitment to justice.

Dad said that from 1914 to 1917, when bandit raids had increased the tension and turmoil along the Texas-Mexico border, ranchers had to be vigilant. From Brownsville to El Paso, rustlers were striking hard, driving cattle and horses across the border into Mexico. To make matters worse, Germany was financing the Mexican border raiders in order to keep the United States distracted and out of the war in Europe. The King Ranch was not immune from the violence of the Mexican bandits.

In early August 1915 Caesar Kleberg learned that a large band of Mexican raiders was heading north to Norias from the Sauz Ranch, which was then part of the King Ranch. (Norias is about sixty miles south of Kingsville and seventy miles north of Brownsville.) In addition to its ranching activity, Norias was a place where Missouri-Pacific Railroad trains running between Kingsville and Brownsville stopped to take on water for their steam boilers. A small railroad section house stood along the tracks. Caesar Kleberg's two-story frame headquarters house was near the railroad tracks. While he was in Kingsville for the weekend, he learned that the bandits might hit Norias. By telephone, Kleberg notified the Fort Brown commandant in Brownsville of the movement of the raiders toward Norias and asked for assistance. The commandant assured Kleberg of his help.

On the afternoon of August 7, 1915, a Sunday, the commandant at Fort Brown sent a special train to Norias. It carried seven troopers and their commander, Cpl. Watson Adams, several Texas Rangers, and a group of peace officers. When they arrived at Norias, horses were penned and ready for saddles. Tom Tate, a King Ranch foreman, headed up a group of men, and they rode out toward the Sauz pastures, looking for the raiders. The eight troopers stayed behind and joined the eight ranch people. The ranch people included two cowboys (Dad and Frank Martin), a cook and his wife, a ranch carpenter and his wife, and two Mexican servant women.

After the departure of the special train and the men led by Tom Tate, the regular afternoon northbound train from Brownsville arrived at Norias at 5:30 P.M. to take on water. Three customs inspectors and a deputy sheriff of Cameron County, each carrying a rifle and a pistol, were aboard.

In Norias, the customs inspectors and the deputy sheriff got off.

They watched the train as it took on water and then pulled out, going north to Kingsville. The four men walked to Caesar Kleberg's house near the tracks and joined the troopers and the ranch people.

Late in the afternoon after dinner, the cowhands, soldiers, the customs inspectors, and the deputy sheriff sat on the porch or stood in the yard. Dad told me that Marcus Hinds, one of the customs inspectors, pointed to the east and said the rangers were returning to Norias. Then they heard the whine of bullets over their heads. Into view came thirty horsemen flying the red flag of their revolutionary band and firing Mauser rifles.

The men on the porch realized the bandits had circled behind the rangers and the peace officers hunting them and now were attacking Norias. The men on the porch jumped to their feet, grabbed their rifles and pistols, and ran for cover behind the railroad embankment. When the bandits were about 250 yards away they again opened fire with their rifles. The defenders returned fire, and they soon figured out the attack was coming not only frontally but also from the side. About fifteen bandits slipping to within 90 yards east of the defenders were also firing at them. Attacks were thus coming from the east and the south from forty-five raiders.

From horseback the Mexican bandits fired a steady stream of bullets at the men. In the exchange of fire, two of the troopers and Frank Martin, the other King Ranch cowboy, were wounded. The others returned continuous fire at the raiders. Dad killed the bandit leader's horse, stopping the advance. At this point, the bandits dismounted, regrouped, and continued firing. The defenders, still firing, managed to carry their wounded into the house as bullets raked its thin walls. Inside the house, George Forbes, a King Ranch carpenter, was shot in the lung.

Dad told me he quickly recognized that they would be killed if they continued fighting from the house. The walls were thin, and the defenders needed to draw fire from the women and wounded. They covered the women and the wounded with mattresses, and seeing that they had done all they could Dad urged the others to move outside and take cover behind the rolls of fencing wire and a steel trough in the yard. The men agreed. It was time to get out of the house.

One of the men pushed the door open, and with bullets kicking up dust around them and whizzing over their heads, they ran for safety as they fired. Once behind the barriers, they kept firing a steady stream of bullets at the bandits.

The bandits firing from the south dismounted and took cover in the nearby section house along the railroad tracks, another small building nearby, and from behind a stack of cross ties. The bandits fired continuously, but the Norias defenders were hesitant to shoot toward the section house, knowing that some of the railroad hands and their families were inside the small building.

On a sidetrack was a boxcar. In it huddled a Saint Louis, Brownsville, and Mexico Railway foreman, his wife, and their two-year-old baby. The foreman had seen the raiders galloping across the prairie toward them. Unarmed and apprehensive, he climbed into the boxcar, joined his family, and closed the door. Bullets punctuated the air, some pinging into the metal wheels of the car or splintering the wooden door. To the good fortune of the rail foreman and his family, the raiders thought the boxcar was empty so they concentrated their fire on the ranch house headquarters.

The cook, a black man named Albert Edmonds, crawled to the telephone on the outside wall of the house, reached it, and managed to get Caesar Kleberg on the line. Asking for help, he told him of the raid by the bandits.

Kleberg assured him that a train with armed men, supplies, and medical people was ready and would be on its way as soon as they found someone who knew how to operate it. That train from Kingsville did not arrive until long after the gunfight at Norias was over.

Knowing they needed more ammunition, Dad moved out from behind the wire rolls and ran for the house. Once there, he checked on the women and the wounded. He told them to keep down on the floor and remain covered with mattresses. He located the ammunition and again dashed across the yard. Dad jumped behind the bales of wire where the Norias defenders were firing rapidly at the bandits. He passed out the desperately needed ammunition.

The besieged men fired steadily at the bandits, killing several. As darkness approached, the bandits, urged on by their leader, charged the house and yard in the face of heavy fire from the defenders. During the charge, one of the customs inspectors, Joe Taylor, shot and killed the bandit leader. As a result the bandits became disorganized and lost their will to fight. They had come within forty yards of their goal of reaching the defenders, but accurate and steady shooting turned them back. By then, it was dark. They tied most of their wounded to their saddles and galloped away into the surrounding brush.

When the firing ceased, ten bandits were dead or dying. The defenders of Norias learned that the bandits had killed one of the women hiding in the section house—Manuela Flores, the wife of a railroad laborer.

The family in the boxcar survived without injury. While four of the defenders were wounded on the initial charge of the bandits, none of the men firing from behind barriers in the yard was killed or wounded. Dad estimated that the siege had lasted about two and one-half hours.

An hour after the bandits rode away, Dad and the others saw horsemen approaching. They thought it was the bandits returning, and the men became edgy and prepared to start firing again. Then, Dad recognized Tom Tate's voice calling out, and he shouted to the defenders not to shoot. It was the rangers riding back from their search for the bandits, unaware the bandits had struck Norias.

Greatly relieved, they welcomed Tate, the rangers, and the other peace officers. Although the fighting was over for the time being, they knew the bandits might strike again. Now, with additional men, they were confident they could hold off further attack.

The next morning, the job of burying ten bandits fell to Dad and one of the other ranch hands. Dad told me that digging ten graves did not appeal to them. The ranch hand proposed how to get the job done quickly. He suggested Dad slip a rope over the bandit's boots; the other ranch hand would stay on his horse and drag the bandit out to the sand dunes. There, they would kick sand over the body.

Dad agreed to the plan because it was too hot to dig graves. The two young cowboys started their grisly task.

Meanwhile, trains bringing relief for the beleaguered people at Norias finally departed Kingsville and Brownsville. On board were a doctor, several soldiers, and armed ranch hands. There were also press people eager to cover the story of the gunfight at Norias.

Dad and his partner were burying the bandits as one of the relief trains pulled in. It came to a stop; a photographer leaned out the open window and shot a photo of a man on horseback as he was wrapping a rope around the pommel of his saddle. In the photo, it was apparent there was a body on the ground with a rope slipped over the man's boots. Dad told me it did not take a genius to figure out they were dragging bandits out to be buried. He was not in the photograph because he was below the level of the train window.

Dad told me that when the picture was published, all hell broke loose. He said the people "up east" thought they were disrespectful and terrible in the way they treated the bodies of the bandits. According to Dad, some people did not understand the bandits had tried to kill them only a few hours before. Mexican officials were also angry, and Dad told me it was years after the border war with the bandits before he had enough nerve to cross the river into Mexico.

Dad said that in the end they got the best of the bandits. Five of the wounded, who had been tied to their horses by the raiders as they fled, died during the night. They were buried in the sand. Ranch hands later found their graves in the brush. About a dozen of those who raided Norias were killed by the rangers and soldiers at Los Cavazos, a small crossing on the Rio Grande, before they could make it to Mexico. A few got away, but not many.

As a result of the gunfight at Norias, there was a price on Dad's head. He explained that one afternoon he and another man were riding through a brushy pasture, looking for stray cattle. Seeing tracks, they checked them and decided it was someone leading a horse. It was obvious to them the person did not want to be seen. They followed the tracks and found a man asleep under a mesquite tree. He was sitting up with a rifle across his lap. Dad and his partner pulled out their pistols and hollered in Spanish for him to get up. Immediately, he awakened, jumped up, and, seeing the two cowboys with pistols, dropped his rifle, raising his hands.

He was told to pull out his pistol and drop it, as well as the big knife he had in his belt. The man did as he was ordered, saying nothing, but his anger was obvious. He was short and thin, wore a big hat, and was dusty and unshaven. It was apparent he had been traveling a long way.

Dad and his partner went through the man's saddlebags and found cartridges for the rifle and pistol, beef jerky, a few hard tortillas, and grounds for coffee. When Dad searched the man he found a pock-etknife, tobacco and cigarette paper, some Mexican coins and paper money, some U.S. dollars, and chewing tobacco. He also had a folded piece of paper in the pocket of his brush jacket. Dad pulled it out of the man's pocket, opened it, and was surprised by what he saw. It had the names of several of the men who had taken part in the Norias gunfight. Also on the list were the names of Bob Kleberg Sr. and Caesar Kleberg. There was a reward for the killing of each man on the list. The man they had captured was a bounty hunter who had crossed the river, planning to collect some reward money.

Dad explained to me that seeing his name on the list did not concern him, but it bothered him that the reward for Mr. Bob and Mr. Caesar was one hundred dollars each, and his was for only twenty-five.

Dad did not finish the story of the bounty hunter. I never learned what happened to him, and I knew it was not polite to ask.

The Quintanillas, my mother's family, came to Texas in an event now known to history as *la entrada*. It happened in 1854, when Capt. Richard King went to Mexico to buy cattle.

The original King Ranch acreage was once part of the Santa Gertrudis Spanish land grant, which was south of present-day Corpus Christi, Texas. In 1854, Capt. Richard King was stocking his Santa Gertrudis Ranch with cattle. He bought cattle in the towns of Camargo and Mier in Mexico and sent them across the Rio Grande to his ranch. On one of his cattle-buying trips, Captain King went to a drought-stricken village, Cruillas, in the hills of Tamaulipas, Mexico. He looked the cattle over and bought the entire herd.

The next morning Captain King noted that the villagers were sub-dued and somewhat unhappy. He inquired why they were dejected and was told that, with the cattle gone, the villagers had little left to sustain them. Their goats, pigs, and sheep were few in number, they worried about their families and how to sustain them, and they had been in a terrible drought for more than a year.

Knowing how difficult life was in northern Mexico, Captain King proposed a way to solve the villagers' problems and one of his own. He asked for help driving the cattle to the Santa Gertrudis and offered work on his ranch. Captain King promised to pay the villagers fair wages and to build them homes and a school for their children. He hoped that one day their children would work on the Santa Gertrudis.

Although he had no way of knowing it at the time, there on the remote desert in Tamaulipas Captain King struck a contract with the people of Cruillas lasting for generations. The villagers of Cruillas talked among themselves. It was difficult to leave their homes, but with the drought and harsh conditions of the land it was worth the gamble, especially with steady wages offered.

The village leader told Captain King he had discussed the move with the elders and families, and they had made a decision to go north with him to the Santa Gertrudis. A few of the old and sick decided to stay, but most were willing to go. Each family took their few possessions.

Captain King told the crowd gathered around him he was grateful for their help and support. He assured them that if they worked together, a great ranch would be built. Captain King said they would be as a family and help and provide for each other as best they could. He ordered that barrels be filled with as much water as they could hold because he knew that once they left the river and the valley on the other side, the long journey across the Wild Horse Desert (known to the Mexicans as *el desierto de los muertos*) to the Santa Gertrudis would be a hot and dry one.

More than a hundred men, women, and children—most of the people of the village of Cruillas—piled their meager possessions on *carretas* (high-wheeled wagons). Dogs, goats, sheep, and pack burros joined the exodus, and the villagers left Tamaulipas, never to return.

Immigration laws were not a problem in the 1850s. The villagers knew where the river was low and could be forded. Driving the cattle north and moving with their wagons and burros, they crossed the Rio Grande. Then, they traveled north through the Wild Horse Desert to the Santa Gertrudis Ranch. From those who participated in this journey—*la entrada*—came a special group of people dedicated to building a great ranch in a difficult and sometimes harsh land. They became known as *los Kineños*, King's people. They were the *vaqueros* and the men and women who laid the foundation for the King Ranch. My mother's family, the Quintanillas, participants in *la entrada*, became *Kineños*.

AN ANGEL AND TWO LANGUAGES

My mother, Tomasa Quintanilla, was also an Álvarez on her mother's side of the family. Mother was probably a descendant of Francisca (sometimes spelled Francita) Alavez, known in Texas history as the "Angel of Goliad." Her surname is variously given as Alavez, Álvarez, or Alevesco. She was the companion of Telesforo Alavez, a captain in the Mexican army who was married to Maria Augustina de Pozo, a bride chosen by his parents. Captain Alavez left his wife in 1834 but could not get Church approval for an annulment. Francisca, his beloved, simply went with him when the army sent him to the frontier. They traveled by ship from Matamoros to what is now known as Copano Bay, Texas. From Copano Bay, she and Alavez continued on to Goliad by land. The Texas war for independence from Mexico had started, and there were many Texas prisoners from the battles around Copano Bay and Coleto Creek being held at Goliad. Col. James W. Fannin Jr. was the commander of the captured men. Soon after Francisca and Alavez arrived in Goliad, they learned that Santa Anna, the Mexican general and president, had ordered the execution of all prisoners held there. He considered them rebels, not prisoners of war.

Francisca persuaded the officer in charge at Goliad not to execute some eighty Tennessee volunteers captured at Copano and brought to Goliad. Colonel Fannin's 342 soldiers, however, as well as Fannin himself, were executed on Palm Sunday, March 27, 1836, at Goliad. He was the last to die at the Goliad massacre.

Only twenty-eight of Fannin's men escaped the firing squads, and twenty-five more were spared to serve as physicians, interpreters, mechanics, or orderlies largely because of the intervention of Francisca. The Texas prisoners called her the "Angel of Goliad." After General Santa Anna's defeat by Gen. Sam Houston on April 21, 1836, at San Jacinto, the Mexicans retreated to Mexico. Francisca and Captain Alavez traveled to Matamoros, and she aided the Texans held prisoner there.

Some accounts of Francisca's life report that Alavez took her from Matamoros to Mexico City and subsequently abandoned her. She returned to Matamoros penniless but was helped by Texans who knew of her humanitarian work on behalf of Goliad prisoners.

Although tradition holds that Francisca died in poverty in Matamoros, there is an intriguing tale suggesting that she lived and died on the King Ranch. This story is happier, and one I tend to believe.

In 1902–1903, Mrs. Elena Zamora O'Shea was a teacher in the school on the Santa Gertrudis Division of the King Ranch. In 1936, she wrote an account now in the Texas State Archives about an incident that happened in 1902. (I have given my photocopy of her letter to the Southwest Collection, the archives of Texas Tech University.) According to O'Shea, during her years as a teacher she would often read to the retired ranch hands. Reading materials included Spanish-language newspapers and stories from her students' textbooks, which she would translate. Among those who listened to her stories was Matías Álvarez. When she read them the story of the massacre at Goliad, he asked why there was no mention of the person who saved so many soldiers.

Matías Álvarez related another side of the history of the "Angel of Goliad." After the Texas Revolution, Telesforo Alavez, by this time a colonel, and Francisca settled in Matamoros, Mexico. Two sons, Matías and Guadalupe, were born to them. After Colonel Alavez died, Matías and members of his family worked on the ranches and farms north of the border.

Captain King had known Colonel Alavez and was aware of the merciful work of Señora Alavez at Goliad. In 1884, he offered Don Matías work on the Santa Gertrudis, telling him to bring his family and mother to the King Ranch.

So Matías, his wife and family, and his mother moved to the King

Ranch. Among the eleven children of Matías were Gerardo and Rita. According to Elena Zamora O'Shea, Francisca lived into her late nineties. When the "Angel of Goliad" died, to prevent her gravesite from being disturbed Mrs. King ordered Francisca buried on the King Ranch in an unmarked grave.

By the time of Francisca's death, "Alavez" was spelled "Álvarez." Matías's son Gerardo eventually became foreman of the Santa Gertrudis. After his death, my father became foreman in 1926.

Rita Álvarez, a sister of Gerardo, married Francisco Quintanilla, a *vaquero* and *caporal* on the King Ranch who ran the Rancho Santa Cruz. Rita and Francisco Quintanilla, my grandparents, had a daughter, Tomasa Álvarez Quintanilla, my mother. In 1923, she married Dad. I believe through Mother's side of the family, I am a fifth-generation descendant of the "Angel of Goliad."

Still, because there were conflicting reports on the life of Francisca, I had some doubt about my relation to her. I needed confirmation that Matías was my great-grandfather. Seeking it, in 2003 I telephoned my cousin, Lupe Camacho, in Kingsville. Despite being in her late eighties, she clearly remembered growing up in Kingsville and visiting Rancho Santa Cruz, where my mother's family lived. Lupe is the daughter of Rita Quintanilla Rodriguez, my mother's oldest sister.

I asked Lupe if she knew the name of Mama Grande Rita's father, our great-grandfather. Lupe told me to let her think about my question. There was a brief pause, and then she said, without further hesitation, that his name was Matías. I thanked Lupe and told her that confirmation of our great-grandfather's name was important to me.

With Lupe Camacho's response, I was quite certain that Doña Francisca Álvarez, the "Angel of Goliad," was my great-great-grandmother.

The arrival of the Quintanillas in 1854 with *la entrada*, of the "Angel of Goliad" and her son Matías and his family in 1884, and of my father, after he crossed the Wild Horse Desert to work for Mrs. King and Mr. Kleberg Sr. in 1912, brought three families together. As a result of those three shifts, the Quintanilla, Álvarez, and Cavazos roots became intertwined with those of the King Ranch.

The King Ranch has been a special part of my life, and I continue to identify with it to this day, although I left many years ago. It was my birthplace, and as it had been for my parents, the ranch was my teacher and nurturer. I greatly value my education there and the positive impact it had on me for the rest of my life.

On the ranch I grew up speaking two languages, English and Spanish. I also learned the language of the ranch. A nod of the head or a handshake on a deal meant an unbreakable contract. A wave of a hat or an arm pointing was communication between cowboys as they worked a herd of cattle in noise and choking dust. When we said, "the ranch" in conversation, we knew it meant the King Ranch. When referring to "the river," it was always the Rio Grande, and "the Church" meant the Catholic Church.

My parents were remarkable people. They had great love for their children and worked to ensure that we would be nurtured and educated. They taught us ethics and values, not from a book, but by their example of day-to-day living. Their formal education was limited. Mother's education was perhaps limited to the second-grade level, so she was functionally illiterate. Dad attended high school. Still, they were very intelligent people who knew the value of education and the difference it could make in the lives of their children.

Our roots were Hispanic, and we were raised in the Hispanic traditions and language but taught always to have deep loyalty to the United States. Dad and Mother spoke Spanish to each other. However, from the time we were very young there was a rule that we children speak English to Dad and Spanish to Mother. And so we followed their directions, all of their lives. We children usually spoke English to each other, but the working language of the ranch was Spanish. When out in the cow camps or moving or riding about the ranch, or visiting with my grandmother, aunts and uncles, and cousins in Kingsville, I spoke Spanish. If, in speaking, I mixed Spanish and English, Dad reminded me to speak one language or the other and not to mix them. He considered each language beautiful and insisted I speak one or the other.

I still speak both languages. Most important, when I started to school on the ranch I was one of the few in my class who spoke English. Still, on the school playground we spoke Spanish.

The first bilingual press conference held by a Cabinet officer occurred because I spoke two languages. At my first press interview after I became secretary of education, most of the questions were in English, but the Latino networks were there and asked their questions in Spanish. I responded in Spanish and translated for the rest of the press corps.

One of the journalists from the Hispanic media asked what message I might have for Hispanics. I replied, "Niños, por favor, no dejen la escuela" (Children, please stay in school).

A few days later, Mary Futrell, then president of the National Education Association, quoted me and wrote of the eloquence, importance, and sensibility of my words. The NEA often was at odds with President Reagan's administration and especially with the previous secretary of education, William Bennett. I considered Futrell's article in the *Washington Post* a positive sign of her willingness to work with me. Subsequently, I invited her to my office, and we developed a working relationship and friendship.

At our first meeting, I suggested to Futrell that I had the same objective as she did. Both of us sought improvement of education and the professional lives of teachers; we wanted the best for children *and* for teachers. I told her that most of the time we would agree on the issues but that sometimes we would disagree. I asked that before we criticized each other in the media, we discuss our differences and resolve them face to face.

During my tenure as secretary of education, the NEA invited me to speak at their national convention. My talk was well received by the members. I felt I had opened a working relationship that would benefit my efforts to improve education. While in Washington, I enjoyed an excellent dialogue and good relations with Futrell and the NEA. As a consequence, when Keith Geiger followed her as president of the association, we continued a productive working relationship.

I also worked with the head of the American Federation of Teachers, the union ably led by Al Shanker. He and I had many discussions on how to improve the quality of elementary and secondary education. I soon counted Shanker as a friend and advisor.

These relationships with the NEA and the American Federation of Teachers were important to me, much to the dismay of the *Washington Times* and the Heritage Foundation, as well as some of the education conservatives in the Republican Party.

A few weeks after Peggy and I arrived in Washington, I told her I wondered how long it was going to take people to realize I did not have an educational ideology to the right, left, or center. I sought ideas and activities to improve education. My conservative friends did not acknowledge in public that I had met with Phyllis Schlafly, then president of the conservative Eagle Forum.

My first major press conference was held in the Horace Mann Auditorium in Washington in mid-October 1988. Afterward, I told Peggy I believed the press conference had gone well and that I had answered the questions in a sensible and articulate manner. I was pleased there were some questions in Spanish and that I could respond to them in Spanish. Many of the reporters groaned when I spoke in Spanish, but they must have been relieved when I translated my remarks for them. Peggy told me it was grand that I answered in Spanish, and that I should thank my parents for insisting I learn both languages.

One evening a couple of weeks after the press conference, I arrived at our apartment and told Peggy not everyone had appreciated my first bilingual press conference. The White House had sent me a copy of a letter President Reagan received, which protested my use of Spanish at the press conference. The writer thought it was disgraceful that a Cabinet officer had spoken in a foreign language at a press meeting.

The attitude and expressions of the letter writer did not disturb me, and I resolved to continue to respond in Spanish, when appropriate. I was determined not to be distracted by some peoples' attitudes about language, and I wanted to keep my focus on improving education for all people.

President Reagan never mentioned the letter to me.

While in Washington, I thought of simpler days on the ranch and my parents' insistence I use both English and Spanish in my daily life. As secretary of education, I was repeatedly asked my thoughts and attitudes about bilingual education. I should have known bilingual education would be a hot topic in Washington. I cannot think of many educational issues that ignite so much debate and passion. Bilingual education was introduced into the school systems in 1968 as the result of Title VII of the Elementary and Secondary Education Act passed by Congress. If a student could not speak English on the first day of school, he or she underwent immersion in English. Today, some people, espousing a political viewpoint, maintain that English immersion is far better than years of bilingual education. I was troubled by this attitude because it meant we had forgotten the purpose of bilingual education. To me, bilingual education is a method used to teach children English and it has nothing to do with race, politics, or political dogma.

I am a supporter of bilingual education and an opponent of the "English-only" movement flourishing in the 1980s and 1990s.

I do not believe there is one English-learning style for all children. Some may learn English faster with the immersion system, while others advance rapidly with transitional or developmental bilingual programs. Teachers must analyze and determine the best English-learning method for each child. Then they need to communicate with parents about the child's needs in bilingual education and the learning style the teacher recommends. Bringing parents into the decision about their child's bilingual education is important.

Regardless of the bilingual learning technique utilized, a child must move into English proficiency as quickly as possible. To me, it is important for students to retain competency in their native language. I tell students in bilingual classes to learn their culture, to treasure it, and, in time, to make it a part of the American culture. After all, this nation is an amalgam of the best from many cultures and races.

I made these points about foreign language retention and culture to a bilingual class for Latinos while on a school visit in California. The students seemed amazed and pleased when, after being introduced as the secretary of education and making some opening remarks in English, I spoke to them in Spanish. Afterward, one of the teachers observing my visit to the bilingual class remarked that I did more there in the classroom in fifteen minutes to advance bilingual education than Bill Bennett did in almost four years. Although his remark was not accurate and I did not accept his observation, the statement demonstrated the intense emotions bilingual education can generate.

One of the most striking aspects of teaching in the twenty-first century is the diversity of students in America's classrooms. Minorities are now the majority in more than 50 percent of public schools in a dozen states. This situation results in some special challenges and problems for teachers and teacher education. Many of these minority students speak a language other than English at home. Teachers need to be aware of these social and cultural differences among their students. Encouraging feedback from students with learning difficulties, communicating effectively with parents, and closing the gaps in student preparation enhance learning for non-English-speaking children.

I believe that teacher education must begin to emphasize language proficiency and an awareness of different cultures. Only 10 percent of baccalaureate degree recipients are proficient in a language other than English. I believe colleges of education should make proficiency in a second language mandatory for all students. The effort involved in learning another language and culture would help teachers not only communicate effectively with students who share specific languages but also help them empathize with any student who has had to adopt a new language and culture in order to flourish.

Although bilingual education can be taught in many different languages, I would like to address the language education of Hispanics. I am concerned about the quality of education all students receive, but as a Hispanic, I am dismayed by the lack of educational achievements of so many Hispanics. Part of this problem, I maintain, is rooted in inadequate development of English-language proficiency in the early childhood years. Without English skills, children will struggle to reach their full educational potential. We must help poor, undereducated Hispanic children whose language facility lags far behind that of their peers to learn English as soon as possible. This goal has to be a priority in our schools with diverse populations.

GRANDPARENTS

My father, Lauro F. Cavazos, a fifth-generation Texan, was born on February 15, 1894, in Cameron County (in an area later split off to create Willacy County) at the Laurel Ranch near San Perlita. This is a small ranching and farming community about forty miles north of Brownsville. The Laurel Ranch had been part of the original Spanish land grant to the Cavazos family. Dad was a descendant of Capt. Juan Cavazos, the first Cavazos in northern Mexico and what is now Texas. Captain Cavazos came to the New World in the service of his country from the village of Santa Maria, from the province of Old Castile in Spain. As a young adult, he entered New Spain (now Mexico) in 1628 during the conquest of *el nuevo reino de León* (New Lion Kingdom) or what is now known as the state of Nuevo León. There he married Doña Elena de la Garza in 1630.

For more than a century after the Spanish explorers landed in the New World, the Indians kept them on the south side of the Rio Grande. If the Spaniards moved across it, they faced fierce warriors who would not give up their lands to the invaders from the south. In the 1700s, Spain decided to divide the land north of the Rio Grande into large royal land grants and give them to settlers, expecting them to move there to farm and ranch. There was no risk to the Spanish Crown, but it was certainly a highly hazardous proposition for the ranchers and farmers north of the Rio Grande.

In 1781, José Narciso Cavazos, an ancestor of my father, received a land grant from the Spanish Crown. According to Tom Lea, in his book *The King Ranch* (1957), "José Narciso Cavazos was granted the largest single tract in the region, the vast acreage known as the San Juan de Carricitos." During the years that followed, the Cavazos family lived under the flags of Spain, Mexico, the Republic of Texas, the United States, the Confederacy, and again the United States. José Narciso Cavazos may have received the largest tract in the region, but it was situated in the most arid parts of the valley. The San Juan de Carricitos grant was more than half a million acres and included most of what is now Willacy and parts of Hidalgo and Kenedy Counties in South Texas.

Over the years, the San Juan de Carricitos grant was divided many times. The Cavazos family was large, and with each generation the number of inherited parcels further whittled away at the original grant. Some parcels of land were traded off, and other parts were sold. Land was cheap, but money was short. Between 1873 and 1889, most of the San Juan de Carricitos grant was sold to the King Ranch. It eventually formed much of the Norias Division of the ranch.

Dad's parents were Nicolas and Francisca García Cavazos. They spent most of their married life at the Laurel Ranch but maintained a home on East Jefferson Street in Brownsville, Texas. They had ten children. Their oldest son, Nicolas Cavazos Jr. (Uncle Nick), never married and lived with them. Dad went to school in Brownsville. I recall many visits to Laurel to see our grandparents, Papa Nick and Grandma Panchita.

Once when I was nine years old I watched Mother packing and sensed she was getting things together for a trip. I did not want to be left behind, so I stayed close to her. When I asked where we were going, she told me we were going to Laurel to see Papa Nick and Grandma Panchita. I was delighted because I always enjoyed visiting with them. Mother told me to get out of her way while she finished packing and go out in the yard and play. She told me Dad would be back soon from checking on the men working at the Rancho Plomo, and he wanted to leave as early as possible.

The trip to Laurel was a long one that would take most of the rest of the day. Upon departing our house, we drove to Raymondville and then went south to Lyford. From there, Dad turned east toward Laurel. The roads were unpaved, and after a rain cars frequently became mired in the mud. If this happened, there was usually a friendly farmer with a tractor to pull the car out of the mud.

Our trip took us across several small farms and ranches, so there were a number of gates to open and close before we reached Laurel. My younger brother Dick and I took turns with the gates. At one, however, I remember there was a boy who operated a small business. He sat on the gatepost. As a car pulled up, he jumped down and opened the gate. When the car went through, the driver usually gave him a nickel, or a few pennies.

Reaching Laurel, we pulled into the gravel drive, and several dogs of mixed breeds announced our arrival by barking enthusiastically. My grandparents' home was a wood-frame, one-story house with a shingled roof. A pipe ran from one corner of the roof to carry rainwater into a cistern. Water was always a problem at Laurel and the small ranches and farms in the vicinity.

As soon as she saw our car pull into the drive, Grandma Panchita hurried out of the house, quieting the dogs and calling for Papa Nick to come out of the house and see their grandchildren, Dad, and Mother.

My grandmother always hugged each of us as we stepped out of the car. We greeted one another, and she asked each of us about our health. Papa Nick stood by, nodding his head in approval of his son's children. Hugs were not part of his greeting; his was a handshake. The compliments and the conversation followed were always in Spanish. I never said a word of English to my grandparents, and they, in turn, spoke only Spanish to me. I asked Dad if they knew English because I had never heard them speak it.

He said they could understand English, but they just preferred Spanish. He reminded me they had grown up speaking Spanish and that I must respect their preference to speak Spanish. I told Dad I understood and would speak to my grandparents in Spanish. And so it was, always.

A trip to Laurel meant Grandma Panchita would have a great meal for us. She must have cooked all day in expectation of our arrival. Usually, the meal was enormous, with *carne asada* (grilled steak) and *cabrito* (kid goat). In addition to the meats, Grandma Panchita had *arroz con pollo* (rice with chicken). Pinto beans were also standard at every meal, and my grandmother's flour tortillas were truly grand.

Papa Nick was tall and thin, with a head full of white hair. His skin was leathered by years of exposure to the sun. I remember the wonderful big white mustache, curled upward at the ends. He was a handsome man, but after a lifetime of hard work on a farm and ranch he appeared tired and a bit frail. Papa Nick was soft-spoken, a kindly man whom I never heard raise his voice. I remember him as patient and understanding. Many ranchers regarded him as the finest horseman in South Texas, with skills that he had passed on to my father.

Grandma Panchita was the dominant one in the marriage of my grandparents. She was thin, not tall, with white hair pulled back in a bun, piercing blue eyes, and a wrinkled but white complexion. She wore silver wire-frame glasses. As a young woman, she must have been beautiful, and she retained her beauty and grace as she aged. She was extremely bright, determined, tough-minded, rather impatient, and outspoken. We always knew where she stood on an issue. If she were not pleased with the conduct or actions of one of her children, or grandchildren, she let them know without hesitation.

In Brownsville, my grandparents' home faced East Jefferson Street. It was a busy street, and, when not doing chores, they sat in the front room and looked out the window. At least once a day, usually after breakfast, they sat in rocking chairs on the front porch of their home watching friends and neighbors pass by. Greetings were exchanged and news related. Everyone seemed to know everyone's business, as well as his or her coming and goings. There were few secrets on East Jefferson Street.

On our visits to my grandparents' home in Brownsville, I usually sat quietly and listened to them recount neighborhood news to my parents. I was amazed at the considerable amount of information my grandparents gathered while sitting in the front room or on the porch of their house.

As the matriarch of the Cavazos family, Grandma Panchita was a primary source of advice for her sons and daughters. She suggested solutions to their problems or a course of action they should follow. In turn, she expected to be informed about how the problem or the matter was resolved or turned out.

If one of our cousins planned to marry, someone always asked if the intended had met Grandma Panchita. We knew Grandma Panchita's blessing was vital if a person expected to marry into the Cavazos family. In 1954, soon after Peggy agreed to marry me, I took her to Brownsville to meet Grandma Panchita. Papa Nick and my Uncle Nick had died by this time, and my grandmother lived by herself in the small house on East Jefferson Street. I told Peggy she did not speak English, but she could understand it.

Peggy told me not to worry. The two of them would get along fine because although she could not speak Spanish, Peggy understood a little. My bride-to-be was certain she and Grandma Panchita would manage to communicate.

On a Sunday afternoon, Mother and Dad traveled with Peggy and me to Brownsville. We gathered in the front room of the house on East Jefferson Street. After the usual sharing of news and inquiring about the health of the family, it was clear my grandmother wanted to know about this young woman with me. I told her I had known Peggy for almost six years and that we had met at Texas Tech as students. I explained that she had a degree in nursing and worked at a hospital in Lubbock. Grandmother asked several questions in Spanish, and I translated for Peggy and gave the reply in Spanish. This routine continued for what seemed like an interminable time to me, but it was probably no more than twenty minutes.

Grandmother looked at Peggy and then at me. Her eyes sparkled, and she told me she was so pleased I had found such a fine woman. Grandmother said she was sure Peggy would be an excellent and loving wife and that we would have many children, to whom she would be a wonderful mother. According to Grandmother, I was fortunate to have found Peggy. Then Grandmother gave us her blessings and wished us all happiness.

As usual, Grandma Panchita was right in her assessment and in her prediction.

Grandma Panchita was determined and ethical, set high standards for herself and her family, and stood by her convictions. And in the tradition of many Hispanic families, she and Papa Nick were raised Roman Catholic. Their home in Brownsville was three blocks from their parish church, Immaculate Conception. In the early 1900s, Grandma Panchita's mother died after a long illness. My great-grandmother lived on a small ranch near Laurel, but as her illness progressed my grandparents moved her to Brownsville to live with them. Soon after the move, she died in their home. My grandparents expected to bury her in the graveyard behind the nearby Immaculate Conception Church. Grandma Panchita went to the church to make arrangements for the funeral and burial services. She talked to a priest at the church about a funeral Mass and where she wanted her mother buried.

The priest slowly shook his head and refused Grandmother's request to bury her mother in the nearby church cemetery. He told her it was absolutely impossible. It was against the rules and could not be done. Grandmother bristled at his response and made it clear she was a longtime member of the parish and thus expected her mother to be buried at Immaculate Conception.

No doubt the priest felt my grandmother's cold blue eyes focused on him, and it was obvious he was dealing with a determined woman, but the priest was firm in his decision about the funeral. He offered to give grandmother the names of nearby funeral homes. Grandma Panchita insisted she would take this matter up with the pastor and, if need be, with the bishop.

When Grandma Panchita returned home, she told Papa Nick of the outcome of her visit to the church. Both were upset by the turn of events. They discussed their options and next steps.

Shortly afterward, the priest my grandmother had talked to at the church knocked on their door. They invited him in and offered a seat in the front room. No doubt they thought he had changed his mind about the burial. Dad, then a young boy of fourteen, was in the nearby bedroom and overheard the conversation between his parents and the priest. Years later he told of the discussion and the outcome.

According to Dad, the priest said he was sorry he could not bury Grandmother's mother from the church. Church rules had to be obeyed. Claiming he had my grandparents' best interests at heart, however, he informed them that if they gave him one hundred dollars, he was sure he could successfully plead their case.

My grandparents were appalled. Dad said Grandma Panchita stood up, drew herself to her full five feet, two inches of height, and told the priest to leave her home; she was not giving him a cent. She called him despicable and a disgrace to the Church. Somehow, my grandparents prevailed, and my great-grandmother was buried in Brownsville, at the Immaculate Conception Church's cemetery. I am sure Grandmother came down hard on the priests and gave them no peace until her desires were met. My grandparents did not pay any money. It turned out the priest seeking the money was a visiting priest. The regular priests at the parish church knew nothing about the request for money. Soon, the visiting priest left Brownsville.

Even though her mother had been buried in the nearby church cemetery, my grandmother remained angry and upset by the request for money. She had no tolerance for a corrupt priest and told Dad if there was one bad and dishonest priest at Immaculate Conception, there must be others.

Grandma Panchita left the Catholic Church because of the corrupt priest and became a Methodist. Some of her children stayed in the Catholic Church, but others became Methodists or Baptists. Dad, too, left the Church and became a Protestant.

Dad died in 1958, and we held the wake at a funeral home in Kingsville. The next day, a funeral Mass was to be said for him at San Martín Catholic Church, followed by burial at a cemetery along Santa Gertrudis Creek. The evening of the wake, the room was packed with relatives and friends. Grandma Panchita sat silently near Dad's coffin, slowly rocking back and forth.

I looked at her and thought of our conversation earlier at our home in Kingsville. It was early afternoon, and she had been driven from Brownsville for Dad's funeral. To me, she looked listless, sad, and tired. The two of us sat alone on the front porch of our house. She told me I could not know how distressed and sad she was that Dad was dead. Grandma Panchita recalled what a good and loving husband and wonderful father he had been. She said Dad's death was tearing her apart, and she had cried and cried; she had no more tears. Grandmother reminded me that many of her loved ones were gone. Papa Nick and several of her children had died, but she kept living, even though she was an old woman. Grandmother said she felt like an old tree, with limbs ripped from her; each of those limbs was one of her loved ones.

I put an arm around her shoulder and told her to cry no more. I said we all loved Dad; he had led a fine life and accomplished much, and we had to accept death when it came. I reminded her that the wake was at 7:00 P.M. and suggested she lie down for a while. I promised to wake her up in plenty of time to get ready.

At the wake, I sat close to Grandma Panchita, both of us near Dad's coffin. At Mother's request, the pastor of San Martín Catholic Church started the rosary for the repose of Dad's soul. We followed the priest's lead and gave the responses. I looked at Grandma Panchita. She sat in a chair, her shoulders slumped, eyes closed and brimming with tears.

Although she had left the Catholic Church for the Methodist Church more than fifty years before, I saw she clutched a rosary in her hand. Her lips moved silently in prayer.

"COW BOSS"

Dad had remained at Norias until May 1917, when he decided to enlist in the army. World War I had started, and he wanted to do his part in defense of his country. Dad left Norias and traveled to Brownsville, where he tried to enlist. He was told to come back later because they did not have enough guns and uniforms at that time. Dad was tall and slender and hoped to join the light artillery, but he was told he was "too light." In September 1917, Dad finally was accepted into the army, sent to Fort Sam Houston in San Antonio, and assigned to B Battery of the 345th Field Artillery, 90th Infantry Division. He stayed with this unit until after the end of World War I. After training his unit sailed for France, and by this time he was a first sergeant. Dad had never been on a ship, and he became dreadfully seasick. He told me he was below on his bunk when one of the men dashed in, shouting for him to get topside because they were under attack by a German submarine.

Terribly seasick, Dad moaned that he hoped the son of a bitch would sink them and put him out of his misery. Fortunately, they crossed the Atlantic safely, and after additional training in France his unit went to the front lines. Dad received three battle stars for three major campaigns in France.

The armistice was signed on November 11, 1918, ending World

War I. Dad became part of the Army of Occupation and remained in Germany for eight months before being sent back to the United States and given an honorable discharge in 1919. He was very proud of his honorable discharge paper, showing it to me and saying it was one of the finest pieces of paper he owned. Dad told me someday I might have to serve, and he was confident I would do my duty. I did serve in the army, and when I was discharged I, too, received an honorable discharge, which I treasure as much as Dad did his.

I was about ten years old when Dad showed me his honorable discharge, but I still remember the pride on his face as he held that document.

In January 1945, Dad and Mother drove me to Fort Sam Houston, where I was to report for duty in the army during World War II. As we drove onto the post, Dad pointed to the parade ground and said a haystack had stood there in 1917 when he arrived at Fort Sam. He soon learned why, when he and the other new soldiers had been ordered to take their mattress covers and fill them with hay. That was their bedding. He doubted that I would have to do the same chore he had done on his first day in the army.

Dad was proud that I had enlisted in the army and not waited to be drafted. He told me there were three things he expected me to do in life: one, serve my country; two, educate myself; and three, never disgrace the Cavazos name. Sound advice, and I hope I have lived up to it.

After he left the army in 1919, Dad returned to South Texas. He was twenty-three years old and, like many young men his age, uncertain about his future. Dad said he went to Norias and talked to his old boss, Caesar Kleberg, who had also served in the army during World War I. Dad told Kleberg he needed a job and was ready to settle down and stay in one place for the rest of his life. Kleberg invited Dad to come back to work at Norias.

He thanked Mr. Caesar for the job offer but said that before he made a decision he wanted to go to Santa Gertrudis and talk to Robert J. Kleberg Jr. He then traveled to Santa Gertrudis and stopped by the office in the commissary to talk to Mr. Bob. Dad told me of that discussion; it had a tremendous impact on his life.

Dad asked Mr. Bob about going to Arizona. He had heard there was money in sheep. Dad's real preference, though, was to stay at the Santa Gertrudis. Kleberg told Dad he could go to work for him the next day, or the next week, and to forget Arizona; it was too dry and isolated, and Dad did not know anything about sheep. Kleberg told Dad he was a cattleman and one of the best horsemen he had ever seen.

Kleberg said he wanted to develop a beef animal for the tough country the ranch was on, and he talked of his interest in quarter horses. He believed they were the best for working cattle on the King Ranch. Kleberg thought he could improve their herd and develop a breed of great cutting horses for the ranching industry. He asked for Dad's help with these projects.

For the second time in a few short days, Dad thanked a Kleberg for offering him a job. Intrigued by the prospect of developing new breeds, Dad left Santa Gertrudis that day and caught the train to Brownsville. He had not seen his parents since he enlisted in the army in 1917, but even as he left Santa Gertrudis he was anxious to return to the King Ranch and to work.

After Dad's visit to the Valley and Brownsville, he came back to Santa Gertrudis, ready to work. He became part of the *corrida* working cattle and horses. Dad told me he stayed busy, working every day of the week, but did not think he was being kept busy enough. He was tireless, disliking leisure time and preferring a definite, progressive work program to follow, day by day. He always looked ahead, but the work he was doing in those days did not satisfy him or give him a sense of direction.

Dad told me he started looking around and thinking about other jobs. He heard of an exciting job opportunity in South America from Maj. Tom Armstrong, who had commanded an army battalion during the war. He was from the nearby Armstrong Ranch, and Dad respected his judgment. Dad thought it over and decided to discuss his career options with Bob Kleberg Jr.

He told Kleberg that the job in South America sounded interesting, but his first choice was to stay on the ranch. He enjoyed his work and appreciated his job, but he did not think Kleberg was working him hard enough. Most of all, he could not see where this job at Santa Gertrudis was taking him. He told his boss he wanted more work or he was going to quit.

Dad told me that Kleberg believed he had done a great job since coming back, but he could tell Dad was getting restless and he had been thinking about what he could do to keep Dad on the ranch and busy. Kleberg told Dad he was beyond being just a regular cowhand; he was a natural leader with the ability to direct men. So Kleberg made Dad a proposition: if he stayed at the Santa Gertrudis, he could train for the job of "cow boss." Kleberg said it would take some time, perhaps several years, before Dad would be ready to be "cow boss," but he would work with him.

The idea of someday being the "cow boss" or general foreman of the Santa Gertrudis Division of the King Ranch appealed to Dad. He told me he thought about the idea for a minute, told Mr. Bob he greatly appreciated the offer, and asked him to lay out his training plan. Dad promised he would follow the plan and do his best; he was confident that with Kleberg's help and teaching he could become foreman. The two men shook hands.

Dad's "cow boss" training under Bob Kleberg Jr. began in 1920. Six years later, Dad became foreman of the Santa Gertrudis Division, a job he held until his death in 1958.

Dad's training as future foreman of the Santa Gertrudis began at a crucial and important time on the ranch. Until the late 1800s, the King Ranch was stocked with hardy and prolific but not especially productive longhorns or "Mexican cattle." They were not large cattle, were often inclined to wildness, and were not especially desirable beef animals.

At the turn of the twentieth century, the ranch brought in Hereford and Shorthorn cattle. These cattle were a step up from the longhorns but did not thrive in the severe environmental conditions on the ranch. The Klebergs decided to develop a breed of cattle capable of withstanding the harsh, dry summers and the disease and insects of South Texas. At the same time, the new breed had to be profitable; beef production per acre of grassland was important. In the early 1920s, the ranch started crossbreeding Brahman and Shorthorn cattle to produce calves with many of the desired characteristics.

The odds against breeding a new class of cattle having the characteristics the Klebergs sought were enormous. At that time a new breed had never been developed in the United States; specialized cattle raised in the United States at that time had all originated in eighteenth-century Europe. Eventually, through wise selection of cattle for inbreeding and crossbreeding, the Santa Gertrudis breed was developed and officially recognized as a distinct breed in 1940.

Each breed of cattle originates from a foundation sire, so the ranch sought to develop the desirable qualities and characteristics in one bull. The foundation sire would have exceptional transmitting qualities—color, confirmation, resistance to disease, and superior beef production. Calves of this sire would have all of the characteristics sought by the Klebergs. These calves, in turn, would produce offspring similar to those of the foundation bull.

The enormous amount of work that went into developing the new breed of beef cattle was undertaken without modern computers and massive databases that track efforts and results. The cattlemen on the King Ranch had only their knowledge of breeding line characteristics of cattle and common sense to help them decide which animals should remain in the breeding program. Most of them kept cattle breeding lines in their head and on small notebooks carried in a shirt pocket.

I remember watching Dad and Mr. Bob discussing a herd of cattle one time. It was during a roundup, and they were making decisions about which animals to keep for future breeding. They had to determine which heifers to keep and which bull calves to castrate. The final selection of animals to go into the breeding program was up to Mr. Bob.

On horseback, the two men looked over the cattle gathered into a holding area. Mr. Bob and Dad wore battered and stained Stetson hats pulled low. Each had a red bandanna around his neck. The cattle stirred huge clouds of dust, and the bandanna was an essential item. As the men worked the cattle, each adjusted his bandanna over his nose and mouth, hoping to block some of the dust and ease his breathing. From horseback, I saw Dad and Mr. Bob pull from their shirt pockets the small notebooks containing the breeding history of the cattle before them. The noise from the herd was deafening, and the air was filled with the loud voices and shouts of the cowboys as they worked the cattle.

Dad and his boss seemed oblivious to the dust, heat, and noise of cattle and men. Silently they studied the entries in their notebooks. Dad asked Mr. Bob what he wanted to do with three bull calves the men were holding.

Mr. Bob pointed to two bull calves and said that because they came from good cows and bulls, they had a good chance of being good breeding stock. He told Dad to castrate the other one, because he did not like its confirmation and thought the calf's bloodlines would not produce the cattle desired.

Mr. Bob and Dad used the information in their shirt-pocket notebooks to make solid judgments about the cattle. I doubt the experience, intelligence, and "cow sense" the two men developed over decades of working cattle could ever be recorded in a computer database.

In developing a hardy new breed of cattle, the King Ranch sought guidance from some of the best animal geneticists in the country. Dr. J. Lawrence Lush, a distinguished animal geneticist from Iowa State University, was one consultant who visited the ranch. Dad told me of Lush's reservations about the ranch developing a new breed of cattle.

Lush told them the odds were against establishing a breed of cattle with the hardiness to withstand the heat and insects of South Texas. He insisted the challenge was too great; it had never been done in this country, so how could the King Ranch expect to do it?

Dr. Lush believed it would be almost impossible not only to develop but also to identify the foundation sire bull.

Before the 1970s the King Ranch conducted two roundups a year, one in the summer, the other in the winter. Usually the summer roundup was in July and August and the winter one took place in January and February. Branding, castrating, vaccinating, and marking were done during the summer roundup, when it is hot and dry in South Texas and infection of cattle by insects is minimal. During those roundups, as many as six hundred head of cattle would be worked on one day. This pace produced enormous strain on the men and their horses.

During the summer roundup, *vaqueros* used four horses or more a day to maintain the pace required to work so many cattle. The day began at about 4:00 A.M. Each man knew his job and was expected to carry it out efficiently and quickly. The day ended at dusk. By this time, the men and horses were exhausted. After a quick dinner at the camp house, the men opened their bedrolls and quickly fell asleep.

Dad once told me about the summer roundup in 1921. He said they had been working hard, keeping up a fast pace to get them through the large herd. Late in the afternoon it was hot, the branding iron fires were adding to the heat, bugs were crawling on them, and the air was filled with choking dust. Mr. Bob Sr. and Bob Jr. worked alongside the men and stayed with the roundup until work finished for the day. Dad told me their shirts stuck to their backs with sweat, and dust covered them. Still, they kept pushing to get the cattle worked.

Mr. Bob Sr. usually made the decisions on which bull calves to keep and which ones to castrate. Dad dismounted and stood near the branding iron fire. His job was to castrate the bull calves after Bob Sr. made a decision.

Bob Sr., on horseback, pointed to a red bull calf and told him to castrate it. Dad nodded and told the men to throw the calf. He was stepping toward it when he heard Mr. Bob Jr. tell him not to cut the calf on the ground, saying to his father he knew its bloodline, from Vinotero, the Brahman bull. He insisted it would be the kind of breeder bull they wanted.

Dad told me that Mr. Bob Sr. again ordered him to cut the calf on the ground and to get on with it. He reminded the men they had a lot of work to do and there was no time for talking; they would not get through the herd if they didn't stay with it. Again, he urged them to move on and castrate the calf.

Mr. Bob Jr. repeated his belief in the breeding potential of the bull calf about to be castrated. Again, he insisted that the calf would be a good sire because he came from good bloodlines.

Both Kleberg men were wise, knew the cattle business, and were strong willed and determined. Eventually, they would build the greatest ranch in the world, but they were in the midst of a hot, dusty roundup, with many cattle to work and many decisions to make about the future of the cattle-breeding program.

Dad told me that Mr. Bob Sr. repeated his order for him to "cut that calf." Dad said he had his knife in his hand and was bending down to castrate the animal when he heard Bob Jr. tell him to stop. Then Mr. Bob Jr. told his father he would give him a hundred dollars for the calf on the ground. According to Dad, he saw just a twinkle in Bob Sr.'s eyes, a faint smile of approval, and a nod of his head. He heard him say to his son he had just bought himself a bull calf.

Dad told me that the calf he was about to castrate that day grew into a fine bull named "Monkey," eventually identified as the foundation sire for the Santa Gertrudis breed. In 1923, they bred him with selected cows, and Monkey was an active sire until he died in 1932.

With a shake of his head, Dad said they had almost lost years of cattle breeding that one summer day. He was certain if it had not been for Mr. Bob Jr. stopping him from castrating the calf, they might never have been successful in developing the Santa Gertrudis breed.

CHAPTER 2

⟨ೲ⟩

Life as a Kineño Kid

My mother, Tomasa Quintanilla Cavazos, was born in 1900 at Rancho Santa Cruz on the King Ranch. Her father, my grandfather Don Francisco, ran the Rancho Santa Cruz for the King Ranch. He was a *caporal* or leader of horsemen on the Santa Cruz until the day he died of pneumonia in 1929.

I do not remember my grandfather Francisco, since he died when I was only two. However, I do recall a photograph of him on a sorrel horse. In the photo a fence separates rider and horse from the photographer, and my grandfather wears a large white hat shading his handsome face. He appears to have been a determined man who expected his orders to be followed without question. He ran Santa Cruz with an iron hand, expecting the employees to do their jobs—as he ordered and to his high standards. Don Francisco's eyes were dark, and he had a large dark mustache. In the photograph, he wears leather chaps and a brush jacket.

For years, the photograph of my grandfather was on one wall of Mama Grande Rita's dining room. I ate many meals under the watchful eyes of Don Francisco. After grandmother died, the photograph of Don Francisco was moved to a wall in the "Big House" on the King Ranch, suggesting the high esteem the Klebergs had for him. The photograph has since been returned to one of the Quintanillas.

I remember Mama Grande Rita from my earliest childhood, until she died when I was seventeen. My grandparents had twelve children, including a set of twins. One twin died at birth, however, so eleven of their children reached adulthood. All of the children were born and raised at Santa Cruz. Mama Grande Rita kept them busy with chores. The girls learned to cook, clean and sew, and tend to matters of the home. The boys learned the skills of *vaqueros* and, most important, how to take care of themselves on a ranch.

The girls slept in the house with their parents, but the four boys had sleeping quarters in a small building near the main house. Mama Grande Rita saw to it her children bathed every night. They often used a large water trough behind the house. Other times, the children bathed in a washtub. A three-hole privy stood in the backyard. My grandmother insisted it be scrubbed with disinfectant every day.

My grandmother's house at Santa Cruz was painted white, and it had three bedrooms, a living room, and a kitchen. A porch ran the length of the front of the house. After supper, the Quintanillas and the other families living nearby would gather on the porch to tell stories, gossip, or just sit and rock. They watched the moon rise.

When the stars came out, Don Francisco told the children how to find the North Star. He said if they remembered his lesson, they would never be lost. However, Don Francisco also said that if they paid attention to where they were going while riding in the pastures or the brush, they would have no need for the North Star.

Don Francisco usually left the house at 4:30 A.M. to order and direct the ranch hands in their jobs for the day. Mother told me Mama Grande Rita awakened the children early and ordered them to get to work on their chores. There was no breakfast until their work was done and she had approved it.

The older daughters were pleased when they made cheese from the milk curds my grandmother saved all week. The daughters did not particularly like eating the cheese; they were happy because it could be sold and provide pocket money for them. Later in the week in Kingsville, the girls would go door-to-door in the barrio, selling the cheese. A ball of cheese sold for twenty-five cents, which was a lot of money; twenty-five cents bought each girl a small box of face powder, a lipstick, and rouge.

Mother told me how strict Grandmother was with all of her children, especially the girls. When they went to town, they had to be neat and clean, and once in Kingsville, she kept them in her sight or made sure they went in pairs. She said even though the girls used the cheese money to buy makeup, their parents would not let them wear it until they were fourteen years old.

In 1923, Mother and Dad were married at the house in Santa Cruz. They had met at Santa Gertrudis, where she worked as a chambermaid in the "Big House." Mother helped Mrs. Henrietta King, wife of Captain King.

Mother and Dad's marriage was a civil ceremony by a justice of the peace, although Don Francisco and Rita raised all of their children as Catholics. My grandparents approved Dad and Mother being married by a justice of the peace but with the condition that they marry in the Church soon afterward. A week later, after the wedding at Santa Cruz, the young couple traveled to Corpus Christi, where they married in the Catholic Church. Don Francisco, ever in charge, arranged for the couple to be married in the cathedral in Corpus Christi by the bishop.

My grandfather inherited three houses on East Lee Street in Kingsville from his father. On occasion, my grandparents would take their children to the houses in Kingsville to spend weekends or holidays. After Don Francisco died, Mama Grande Rita left the ranch and moved her children to the houses in Kingsville. She lived in the largest of the houses until her death in 1944. When her sons became adults, all of them went to work on the King Ranch.

Mother saw to it that we spent a lot of time at Mama Grande Rita's house because she wanted us to know her. Usually on Saturdays, Mother drove us to Kingsville so that we could pass the day at Grandmother's home. I enjoyed being there. The kitchen was a wonder. I watched her iron clothes with a flatiron heated on a wood stove in the kitchen. She was an outstanding cook. Grandmother's *arroz con pollo* was the best I ever ate, and she cooked delicious flour and corn tortillas. I sat in the kitchen watching as she prepared the noon meal.

In Grandmother's backyard was a small one-room house. My Uncle Manuel, whom we called "Tío Meme," lived there. He was my great-uncle, my grandmother's youngest brother, and he never married. Tío Meme was a quiet man, a gentleperson, tall and thin, with sparse gray hair, and he always looked like he needed a shave. Rarely did he speak to us children, but he patiently answered our questions. I never heard him raise his voice. Frequently, Tío Meme wore army cloth puttees, wrapped from knee to ankle, left over from his service in World War I. Some days he wore parts of his uniform as well, and he looked grand in his army tunic with polished brass buttons.

One day I asked Mother why Tío Meme acted so strange, and she told me he had been shell-shocked in France during the war. I am not sure as to this fact, but it was apparent to me, even as a young child, that Tío Meme was not well.

Tío Meme's room was sparsely furnished, having only a bed, a rocking chair, and a chest of drawers. On the top shelf of the chest was a small altar with plaster-of-Paris images of Jesus, the Virgin of Guadalupe, and other saints. Frequently, a votive candle burned, perhaps offered in fulfillment of a vow or in gratitude or devotion. Faded paper flowers completed the altar.

I remember Mother telling me to have great respect for Tío Meme, a brilliant man. After the war he studied for the priesthood, but then Tío Meme had a breakdown and left the seminary, never to return. Mother said he was a religious person with a deep faith in his church and God.

From time to time, Tío Meme disappeared from Grandmother's yard for several weeks. When I asked why he was gone, Mother usually told me the health people had come by and picked him up, to drive him to a hospital in San Antonio. I knew what she meant. Tío Meme was in the state mental health hospital in San Antonio. In those days, it was known as the "insane asylum."

My cousin, Lupe (Guadalupe) Camacho, daughter of my mother's oldest sister, *mi tía* Rita, told me a remarkable story about Tío Meme that attests to his religious fervor.

In 1935, Tío Meme left Kingsville on a pilgrimage to walk about eight hundred miles over poor and dangerous roads to pray at the Shrine of the Virgin of Guadalupe. This title is given to the Virgin Mary because of her appearance in 1531 before a fifty-five-year-old Mexican convert, Juan Diego, on Tepeyac Hill. The site is about three miles northeast of Mexico City. She asked that a church be built on the spot. As proof of her presence, she instructed Juan to pick the roses that were blooming miraculously in midwinter. He arranged them in his mantle. When he went before the bishop and opened his cloak, the roses spilled out and the image of a dark lady was imprinted on it. This miracle convinced the bishop of the appearance of the Virgin Mary. He built a great church at the site. The cloak is still preserved in the Shrine of Guadalupe. Pope Benedict XIV named Our Lady of Guadalupe the patroness of Mexico, and Pope John Paul II canonized Juan Diego as a saint in 2002.

Mama Grande Rita begged her brother not to undertake such a dangerous trip, but he told her he knew the Virgin wanted him to go to her shrine. He left the day he announced he was walking to Mexico.

Lupe told me that during the days Tío Meme was gone, Grandmother asked her to kneel with her and pray to the Jesús Niño de Atocha for her brother's safety, for him not to starve or die of thirst, and for him to return home. I asked Lupe why they prayed to the Jesús Niño de Atocha.

Lupe explained that in paintings of him, Jesus is holding a jar of water in one hand and food in the other. Mama Grande believed that if she prayed to Him, Jesus would share the food and water with Tío Meme and keep him safe.

Lupe told me Tío Meme arrived at the shrine and came back safely. He said people were kind to him, letting him stay in their little huts along the road and giving him food. Tío Meme worked to pay for his food by chopping wood, tending their herds of goats, or weeding their small gardens. Sometimes, according to Lupe, he caught a ride in the back of an old truck.

Lupe said Tío Meme was gone for more than a year, and then one day he came walking into the yard. She was there that day, and Tío Meme acted as if he had just been on a walk around the block. He had the most beautiful smile on his face as he greeted Lupe and hugged her. Then, he went to his little room in the backyard. Lupe was sure he had gone to pray and give thanks for his safe return. Lupe said later that he described his trip and how he prayed and lit candles for all of his family at the Shrine of the Virgin of Guadalupe. She said Mama Grande Rita was certain she had seen a miracle because Tío Meme had survived and returned safely. She knew their prayers were heard.

Mother was a beautiful woman, with black wavy hair, a light complexion, and dark brown eyes. She was not tall, about five feet, two inches, perhaps just a bit overweight, but she bore herself with grace and dignity. She was totally devoted to her husband and children. Mother told me Dad laid down the laws for the operation of the house and how the children were to behave, but she was the one who enforced the rules and made sure our father's ideas were followed. Mother was strong-willed and persistent. When she set her mind on a course, it was most difficult to convince her otherwise, and she was impatient as well. It was said of Mother that "patience" was not her middle name. These characteristics, however, were helpful in raising five children on a ranch in the 1930s.

With her children, she was a strict but loving person. Even though I was a young child, I remember telling Mother she favored Sarita, Bobby, and Joe. Dickie and I caught her wrath all of the time.

Mother, however, insisted she loved us all the same, but Dick and I were in constant trouble and mischief. She said when Dick and I were outside the house playing, there was no rest for her because of her constant worries about us. She was afraid we would be seriously hurt, which was easy to do on a ranch.

There was indeed plenty of opportunity for two young boys to get into trouble on the ranch. With only two years' difference in age between Dick and me, we were not only brothers but close friends. We were constantly together. Dick and I especially enjoyed sneaking off to the pasture and leaping into the horse trough for a quick swim. Neither of us could swim, but we pretended as we waded in the trough. When Mother reported our transgressions about the horse trough swim, Dad was always upset with us, explaining that horses and cattle would not drink from the trough if the water smelled of humans. The trough had to be drained and refilled. Dad's "talks" were such that Dick and I would have preferred a whipping for our sinful ways. Still, after a few weeks we forgot our "talk" from Dad and plunged into the horse trough again, taking the chance we would not be caught.

My earliest memory of growing up on the King Ranch dates to about 1932. I was five years old. Our house on the ranch was built on one of the highest hills on the Santa Gertrudis. As testimony to its sound building, it still stands today. The site is now known as "Lauro's Hill." Today, when buses take tourists by our home, the guides point out our home saying, "Born there were a former U.S. secretary of education and a four-star army general."

Our home was wooden, and it had two fireplaces for heat. Winters are mild in South Texas, so the house was built without any insulation at all. On any cold December morning when Dick and I awakened, we would wonder if Dad had built a fire before he left. One of us would throw back the covers and run for the dining room. If there was a fire in the fireplace, we ran to the dining room and dressed, almost pressed to the fire screen.

Our home had a living room, dining room, two bedrooms, the kitchen with a small dining area, and a room we called the "sleeping porch." Mother and Dad used one of the bedrooms, and Sarita, our sister, had the other one. The boys—Dick, Bobby, Joe, and I—shared the sleeping porch. It was a long room with four bunks, one closet for clothes, and another for boots and shoes. In one of the closets Dad also stored rifles, shotguns, and ammunition. A centrally located bathroom served the entire house.

The living room was special. Mother's best furniture was there. We had two sofas, a couple of easy chairs, a large bookcase, and a mahogany table draped with a wildcat skin, complete with snarling head. There was a fireplace in the living room with a deer head over the mantel. We children did not have casual use of the living room. It was for special occasions when we had visiting relatives, the priest, or special guests. It was also open to us on Thanksgiving and Christmas day.

We ate in the dining room only on Thanksgiving, Christmas, or when we had visitors. The rest of the time we ate in the dining nook off of the kitchen. The dining room was nicely furnished with a long table, chairs, a buffet, and a china cabinet. Over the fireplace mantel in this room was another deer head, this one with twelve points. On cold winter evenings, a fire was built and we would sit in front of the fireplace, cracking pecans or playing games. Sometimes, if Dad came home early, he sat with us and told stories of his childhood, his army days, or life on the ranch.

I have special memories of the dining room because it was there I made my First Holy Communion as a six-year-old Catholic. Once a year the priest came from Kingsville and visited our house to hold services. The word went out to the ranch people living near our home that there would be a mass and first communion at Don Lauro's house.

The priest baptized children born since his last visit, and he married couples sacramentally. Dad was the justice of the peace on the Santa Gertrudis Division of the ranch, so he performed civil marriage ceremonies, often in our living room. On his annual visit to the ranch the priest finished the work Dad began as justice of the peace.

Three or four times prior to my first communion, Mother drove us to Kingsville for instruction on the fundamentals of the Christian faith and first communion given by the nuns at San Martín's Parish. I must have learned my lessons well because I was allowed to make my first communion. The big concern on my mind, however, was my first confession.

Prior to the mass during which I would make my first communion, my sister's bedroom was converted into a confessional. All of us making our first communion waited nervously in line outside Sarita's room and took our turns kneeling before the priest in the bedroom to confess our many sins. I do not recall what terrible sins of disobedience to my parents or fights with my brothers and sister I whispered to the priest. Somehow I came up with a list of sins sounding real. I told the priest I was sorry for them. As my penance, I was to say three "Hail Mary's." I received absolution and the priest urged me to mend my sinful ways.

The dining room furniture, except for the buffet, which served as the altar, was moved out, and folding chairs brought in. The room was filled with ranch people, and we children stood in the back of the room. In those days, Catholics fasted and abstained from fluids after midnight until after communion. We young communicants were hungry and thirsty. To our delight, after the mass Mother and my aunts served us *pan dulce* and hot chocolate on tables placed in our sleeping porch.

I still recall the details of my first communion more than seventy-two years ago. The confession, the priest, and the many ranch people in our dining room preparing for mass are clear in my mind. Perhaps it was because of Mother's determination to save my sinful soul, or maybe it was because I sensed that the tenets of the Catholic Church were important in my life. Whatever the reason, I vividly remember my First Holy Communion day.

Mother struggled to maintain a front yard, and although there was no significant lawn, it did have grass but with lots of burs. There were only three trees in the front yard, two live oaks and a pecan. Hedges of purple sage or *cenizo* led from the front gate to our front door. We children usually did not go into the "front yard" but spent most of our time in the area behind the house and in the pastures surrounding our place on the ranch. The most unusual thing about our yard was the fishpond. Usually two or three goldfish swam about in it, and a few frogs called the pond home. It was built under Mother's direction and supervision by Vallejo.

Vallejo had come to work at our house in 1936. His real name was Maxcimiliano García, but to all of us on the ranch he was known as Vallejo. He had been assigned to assist us with chores in the yard, the pastures, and our home. Most of all, though, Vallejo was our friend, and he taught me many lessons about growing up on a ranch.

A windmill and a tall, white cistern adorned near its dome with the King Ranch brand, the "Running W," stood in one of the adjacent pastures. Both are still there today. The windmill and the cistern posed a challenge to Dick and me because we dared each other to climb the ladder up to the opening in the cistern and look in to see the water level.

Dick and I climbed the cistern and the windmill many times. The grand views made it worth the risk of being caught and punished by Mother or Dad. Across the pasture and on the other side of a clump of live oak trees we could see the home of the ranch veterinarian,

Dr. J. K. Northway. From our lofty perch we viewed the dairy barns, the workers' houses at the dairy farm, and the commissary and the main house or "Big House" at headquarters.

The washhouse was in the backyard. We called it "the washhouse" because it had an ancient washing machine, tubs, bars of soap, and scrub boards. We also kept chicken feed, sacks of oranges from our trees, sacks of pecans, and a trunk containing old clothes as well as Dad's World War I uniforms, gas mask, and helmet. Also in the trunk was Mother's old fur coat, adorned with a number of coyote tails. The washhouse also provided storage for saddles, bridles, and saddle blankets. If for some reason we had to pen our many dogs, we used the washhouse. Many litters of pups were born there. Vallejo carefully wrote the date of birth of each litter on a beam of the washhouse.

Mother used a large pot for boiling clothes. Vallejo chopped mesquite logs and built a fire under the pot. Once the water was boiling, soap would be added and the clothes stirred with a wooden paddle. There was always an ample pile of mesquite wood near the washhouse. This pile provided wood not only for the fire under the wash pot but also for our two fireplaces.

I look back and marvel at Mother's determination to raise her children in a safe environment. I'm sure Dick and I kept Mother and Vallejo on edge with our various antics.

When we were eight and ten years old, Dick and I found we could climb to the roof of the house using a large grapevine growing over several plum trees. We loved venturing up the grapevine, especially in the spring when it was in full leaf. Of course our adventures on the grapevine were inspired by Tarzan movies. In an attempt to emulate Tarzan, Dick and I built a somewhat unstable platform among the vines, using the plum trees as a base. We were never able to swing from tree to tree by swinging from a vine, although we tried. The vines, however, did not lend themselves to such Tarzan-like activities but gave us easy access to the roof of the main house. From there we saw pastures, a small stock tank, cattle, horses, and the top of the "Big House." Dick and I did not want Mother or Vallejo catching us on the roof, but we kept on climbing it because it was worth the risk to see our world from the peak of the house.

Three or four times a year, Mother drove us from the ranch to Raymondville, a small town in the Rio Grande Valley, to visit our uncles, aunts, and cousins who lived there. Today, it is about 72 miles from Kingsville to Raymondville on a major highway running through the Armstrong Ranch, the Norias Division of the King Ranch, and the Yturria Ranch. In the late 1930s, however, the trip to Raymondville was about 110 miles. In those days, there was no direct highway route from the ranch to the Valley. For years the state highway department had tried to build a highway linking the Valley directly with Kingsville, but the ranch resisted every move to build a highway across its pastures. As a consequence, the trip from Kingsville to Raymondville was a long one.

When Dad drove the family on the Raymondville trip, we cut through the ranch. The roads were unpaved, and if it had rained they were impassable. Rains were infrequent, so flooded roads were not a pressing problem. Dad followed the ranch roads, and when we crossed the Norias Division of the ranch he had keys to open each gate as we traveled from pasture to pasture. Although the trip was long and somewhat tedious because of so many gates to open and close, it cut many miles from the trip to Raymondville and back. I marveled at how he knew which key opened which lock on the gates. He must have had ten to fifteen keys on the ring, and he would select one, hand it to me, and tell me to open the gate. He always warned me to watch out for snakes.

After Dad drove through, I carefully closed and locked the gate. No gate was ever left unlocked or open on the ranch. It was a cardinal rule of ranch life we all knew and followed. If a gate were left open, livestock escaped from the pastures. If a gate was unlocked or left open, unwanted visitors had access to the pastures.

If Dad was not on the trip to Raymondville, Mother could not take his route across the ranch pastures. Instead, she drove onto the highway running west near our house and turned south on U.S. Highway 281. Then, after another seventy miles, she went east and traveled about twenty-five miles to Raymondville.

Dad took care helping Mother prepare for a trip with us children. After the bags were in the trunk and the lunches wrapped, he made sure we had plenty of drinking water. Then he checked the spare and all the tires, filled the radiator with water, checked the oil, and made sure the gas tank was full. As we were about to leave, Dad would hand Mother a pistol. He assured her it was loaded, telling her he did not think she needed it, but he felt better if she had a pistol for protection.

Mother nodded and placed the pistol under her car seat. Even as young children, we were disciplined enough to know we were not to touch the loaded pistol. Fortunately, in all of our trips to the Valley, Mother never had occasion to use the pistol or even threaten to use it. To us, it was natural to have a loaded pistol in a car with several children and one woman. The pistol under her seat, our determined mother, and a Saint Christopher medal above the rearview mirror ensured that no harm would come to us on our journey to Raymondville.

Before we got under way, Dad instructed us children to be good, no fighting or arguing, and to mind Mother. He warned us he did not want to hear any bad reports from Mother. After his little talk with us, he kissed her good-bye and we were on our way.

Mother was quite capable of using the pistol Dad gave her for her trips to the Valley. He had taught her how to shoot a rifle as well. This skill was standard for most women on the ranch. Often the ranch hands were gone all day and well into the night. During roundup time in the spring and fall, they might be gone for several days. So it fell upon the women of the ranch to be alert and know how to protect their children and their homes.

Our house was less than a quarter-mile from a highway. Often people driving through the ranch entered by the gate near our house, stopping to ask for directions, or food, or work. The economy was desperate. The depression was at its height, and jobs and money were scarce. Mother was quite willing to give directions or provide food for a needy person or family. She made it a rule to never turn anyone away who asked for food.

Mother told me that one morning, as she was cleaning the living room, she glanced out the window and saw a man approaching. She did not recognize him. His clothes were ragged and dirty, and he looked like a tramp. Mother was certain the stranger was up to no good, so she reached into the closet and got one of Dad's pistols. They were always loaded. She told us children to stay together in the main bedroom, to be quiet, and not to come out.

Mother held the pistol behind her back. When he knocked, she kept the screen door locked but opened the door. He looked at her, appeared somewhat startled, mumbled a few words Mother could not understand, backed off, turned around, and quickly went out the front gate. The last she saw of him, he was headed for the highway. Then she realized what had happened. There was a large mirror on the wall behind her. The man must have seen the reflection of the pistol in the mirror and he was scared off.

I asked Mother if she had been frightened. She said she was, but most of all she worried about her children and herself.

That was the only time I remember a threat of any kind in all of the years we lived on the ranch. Who knows? The man coming to our door may not have been a troublemaker. He may have been hungry and looking for a meal, but realizing he faced a woman holding a pistol behind her back and with a determined look on her face, he must have lost his appetite.

HEALTH CARE, BOOTS, AND DRIVING

There were two garages in the backyard. One was for Mother's ancient car and the other, for Dad's car. The ranch provided him with a new car every year, and every year he put considerable mileage and wear on that car. Often his work was on horseback, but on most occasions it involved driving from place to place on the ranch to see to it that work was progressing or problems were being solved. The seat covers in Dad's car were leather, the most durable seat covers possible. Each year when the new car arrived on the ranch, it went to the saddle shop and the seats were covered in leather from hides of cattle on the ranch. Occasionally, I found a Running W brand on the seat cover.

Also in the backyard were two wire lines on which to hang washing.

From time to time we also used the clotheslines to hang thin-sliced raw beef to dry in the sun for *carne seca* (beef jerky). Like most farmers and ranchers, we also had an extensive vegetable garden that kept us in fresh vegetables. We even had several beehives in the orange grove to provide honey.

The ranch also maintained a dairy farm, and the *lechero* (milkman), Don Lorenzo Salinas, delivered a gallon of milk every day. The milk was fresh and totally natural, complete with butterfat and lacking the vitamins or protein that producers began adding in later years. Each day, Mother skimmed the cream off the top of the milk and stored it in the very old refrigerator in the kitchen. By the weekend she had enough cream for churning into butter. Dick and I did the churning, a job we disliked.

Milk was delivered every day, and from time to time a truck with a couple of ranch hands would pull up to the house and unload beef. Cattle sales were slow during the depression. There was plenty of beef available, and the ranch would distribute it. Sometimes the trucks would leave a fifty-pound sack of pinto beans and a bag of rice. Beef, rice, and beans were staples on the ranch and deeply appreciated by those who worked there. Money was scarce and wages low, but by furnishing housing, beef, rice, and beans, the ranch paid its workers as best it could.

In addition to food and housing, the ranch provided its own form of health insurance. In the 1930s and 1940s there was no such mechanism as health insurance for ranching and agricultural employees. The ranch truly never thought of its workers as "employees." From the first days of *la entrada*, following Captain King's promise, they were family, to be cared for, nurtured, and sustained.

From time to time a ranch hand came to our door looking for Dad and wanting an *orden*. The *orden* was an informal document that entitled the ranch hand to take members of his family or himself to the general practitioner in Kingsville. Dad always expressed his hope that the man's child or wife or the ranch hand himself would soon be well. He asked to be kept informed. Then Dad pulled out a small book, wrote the orders with the needed information, tore out the page, and handed it to worker. There was never a charge to the ranch hand for the visit to the doctor's office. It was billed to the ranch. If hospitalization was required, the ranch paid all of the costs. If the ranch hand died, the ranch saw to it that he was buried at no cost to his family.

Hospitalization was rare for people on the ranch. If they were seriously ill or injured, they were cared for at home as much as possible. This practice was standard in the days before chemotherapy, radiation, tomography, emergency rooms, antibiotics, and intensive care units. If there was major disease or injury, the patient generally died.

I wonder how my parents managed to raise five children to adulthood. We grew up on the ranch at a time before antibiotics, and immunizations were few. We knew almost nothing about public health, and I am positive we were exposed to many different types of bacteria. We must have developed quite an immune system. I grew up on the ranch before there was a polio vaccine, and we knew little about how to treat the cancers afflicting children. Injury, a dog bite, rabies, or snakebite are constant possibilities on a ranch. Still, Mother and Dad kept us healthy, and when we were sick or hurt they soon nursed us back to health.

Dad was a handsome man. To all on the ranch he was "Don Lauro." He was tall, a little over six feet, lean, stood straight as an arrow, tough, and when necessary, he could be a very hard person. His face and hands were bronzed by the sun. Dad had a ready smile, and I rarely saw him frown. Life on a ranch was hard, with the men subject to physical injury or death, especially when working cattle. Dad was blue-eyed, but his left eye was clouded over because a mesquite limb with a thorn had struck him in the eye once when he was chasing cattle through the brush on horseback. Dad had been thrown from horses on occasion, and as a result his right shoulder bothered him from time to time.

Dad also had what is called the "mark of the roper." If a person roping cattle got a finger trapped in a loop of rope while the steer pulled in one direction and the horse set back on its haunches to counteract the steer, chances were the finger would be lost. Early in his work on the King Ranch, while roping a steer, Dad lost the distal part of the ring finger on his right hand.

As a small child, I remember asking Dad when his finger would grow back. Gently, Dad assured me the finger was gone forever. Then he explained that fingers, toes, arms, and legs did not grow back. I remember my sadness at his response, because I considered him the finest man I had ever known and he did not deserve to lose his finger. I kept hoping the finger would grow back. When it never happened, I recognized there were things in life even my great father could not overcome.

Dad worked on the ranch seven days a week, year after year. He took half of the day off on Thanksgiving and all of Christmas day. There was never a vacation for him or for Mother. Work and family consumed the entire calendar. Dad left the house about 4:30 A.M. every day. He was up early, bathed daily, and had coffee. He was gone before I even stirred in the morning and did not return until after dark. By then you could not see to work cattle, so it was home to dinner.

Dad's working clothes were khaki pants and shirt, boots, and white Stetson hats. On special occasions such as Christmas, Thanksgiving, a funeral, a wedding, or one of our commencements, Dad wore a Western-cut suit, white cuff-linked shirt, tie, and a spotless Stetson hat. Local tailors made his suits for him.

Dad always wore boots. I never saw him in a pair of shoes. He changed boots every day, just like most men change their shirt daily. Some pairs Dad wore only for daily work on the ranch, and others, his dress boots, were for special occasions. Dad's boots were not ordinary, off-the-shelf boots either. A bootmaker named Rios down in Raymondville made them for him. Rios was well known for high-quality boots, and he made many pairs for ranch notables throughout Texas, the Southwest, and Mexico. They were exquisite. Their tooling and stitching were magnificent, and Dad took pride in the comfort and quality of his boots. I have no idea how many pairs of boots he had in the boot closet, but there were enough for a change of boots every day of the week and twice on Sunday.

Dick and I had the job of saddle soaping and polishing Dad's boots every Saturday. The idea that he could work cattle in unpolished boots must never have occurred to him. So, for Dick and me, polishing boots was a Saturday ritual. On Saturday morning when Dick and I stepped out on the back porch, there were at least six pairs of Dad's boots lined up awaiting our attention. Mother did her part by remind-ing us we had to polish Dad's boots. There was to be no debate or dis-cussion, no escaping the job. Dad never offered to pay the two of us for polishing his many boots, nor did it occur to us to negotiate a fair price for boot polishing. We knew it was one of the jobs we were ex-pected to do.

Some evenings Dad came in from working cattle in stormy, raining weather, his boots muddy and soaking wet. Dad would ask Dick and me to take care of the muddy boots immediately. It was a job that could not wait till the next day. We scraped off as much of the mud as we could and took the boots to the washhouse, where Vallejo stored fifty-pound sacks of grain to feed our chickens. We filled each boot to the top with grain. When filled with grain, the boots would not shrink as they dried. The next day, if the boots were dry, the grain was emptied out of the boots and back into the feed sack. Nothing was wasted, and Dick and I had another pair of boots to polish.

During World War II, Dad volunteered as a second lieutenant in the local unit of the Texas State Guard. The guard stayed in Kingsville and drilled twice a month. Their major objective was to protect the home front, if the need arose. All of the guard members wore army-issue uniforms, but Dad wore his nonregulation boots to drill the troops. When I turned sixteen, I too joined the guard. I knew I was drilling and practicing to repel the enemy we expected to splash ashore at nearby Baffin Bay and invade Kingsville. Obviously, this invasion never happened, but we were prepared.

During those World War II years, Dad went to Fort Sam Houston in San Antonio annually for a few days of army training for officers in the Texas State Guard. On his first trip there, the army issued him the standard uniform, including shoes. Dad looked at the shoes and knew he was in trouble.

Dad told me that when they gave him a pair of shoes, he informed the supply sergeant he could not remember the last time he wore shoes and that he didn't even own a pair of shoes. The sergeant was not sym-pathetic to Dad's plight and told him he would soon adjust to shoes; everybody did.

Regardless of the supply sergeant's wise counsel, Dad could hardly walk in his army shoes. His feet blistered and pained him the more they drilled. Seeking relief from his foot problems, Dad went to his commanding officer, a captain. Dad explained that the army shoes were about to kill him because he had worn boots all of his life and could hardly walk in shoes. Dad asked the captain if he could wear boots while in uniform.

The captain was sympathetic to Dad's problem and to his delight gave him permission to wear boots while in uniform. The foot problem was solved, and during the rest of his time at Fort Sam Houston Dad was known as the "Cowboy Lieutenant."

We buried Dad in his finest pair of boots.

When I was eleven years old, I started pressuring Dad to teach me how to drive. He had promised that when I turned twelve he would give me driving lessons, and he held fast to his promise.

Finally, although I thought the day would never arrive, I turned twelve, and Dad said it was time for my first driving lesson. His car was a 1939 Ford sedan. It had a clutch and gearshift on the floor. For a twelve-year-old, gear shifting required synchronization and dexterity. Dad gave me my first driving lesson in one of the pastures on the ranch. The road was a single lane, somewhat rutted, and of course unpaved.

I was scared and nervous. I let out the clutch and stepped on the gas pedal, and the car lurched forward two or three times. The motor stalled and then stopped.

After a few more attempts, I moved the car ahead in a somewhat smooth manner. In the beginning, I drove at about 15 miles per hour, but as my confidence grew I drove faster. In fact, I drove a bit too fast as far as Dad was concerned.

Dad told me I was not driving a race car; I was to slow down, and most important, I was not to hit a cow, which to him was the worst thing I could do while driving. The second thing I might do by driving too fast was to kill us. I simply nodded my head in agreement. Still, the idea I would hit something as big as a cow bothered me, and I was sure he did not rank killing us below hitting a cow. At least, I don't think he did.

Today, I would not teach my twelve-year-old grandson or grand-daughter how to drive. Still, with the wisdom of age, I take comfort that my sons and daughters will send their sixteen-year-olds to a driver's education program operated by professionals. And I will never hint or whisper to them that their aged grandfather learned how to drive at the age of twelve.

LOST HUNTERS AND A NEW DEAL

There was a guard at the main gate near the highway running through the ranch. His job was to screen people who wanted to drive through the ranch. If they had legitimate business, such as visiting a relative or friend, he let them enter. Even as a youngster, I could see that security was not a major issue on the ranch. Our house stood near the highway that ran past the main entrance to the ranch. Near our home there were two gates, one on each of the fences bordering the highway. The north gate led to a small *colonia* where six or eight families lived. There were a number of children in this *colonia*, and we frequently played together. The south gate gave access to a road running in front of our home and to the ranch headquarters and the dairy farm. Both of these gates were usually open. Contrary to the rule on the ranch about open gates, these two gates were rarely closed and never locked. No guard was posted there.

Although the entire ranch was fenced to keep livestock in, people outside the ranch considered the fence a barrier intended to keep them off of the ranch. The real issue was hunting. The King Ranch had a conservation program to protect game animals such as deer, turkey, quail, javelinas, doves, and waterfowl. It had more stringent hunting laws and shorter hunting seasons than did the State of Texas. As a result, game was abundant on the ranch, and it was a temptation for some to climb the fence and poach game. State game wardens and *vaqueros* patrolled the fences, protecting the game and keeping an eye out for poachers.

Many poachers were caught and fined, but still others were never caught and probably managed to kill considerable game.

The disappearance of two hunters on November 18, 1936, only added fuel to the rumors that the ranch had a policy to shoot anyone caught poaching. Two men, a father and son, had left their place for a day of hunting. Their rural property was near the Sauz Ranch, at that time operated by the King Ranch, in Willacy County. The hunter's spouse reported that she heard two or three gunshots soon after her husband and son left their place but thought nothing of it. The hunters did not return during the day, and by evening she gave the alarm about the missing men. Search parties scoured the countryside looking for the missing hunters, but to no avail. Ugly rumors spread suggesting that the men had jumped the King Ranch fence and been killed by the *vaqueros* or the state game wardens assigned to the ranch.

Tensions already existed between the ranch and the people whose land bordered it. Some called it "the walled kingdom." Many were convinced that the King Ranch was responsible for the deaths of the two men. Local law enforcement people and the Texas Rangers searched the Sauz Ranch thoroughly but came up with nothing to suggest the men had died on the ranch. There was absolutely no evidence that the ranch was responsible for their disappearance. The two men were never located or heard from again, nor were their bodies ever found. To this day, their disappearance remains unsolved.

Although there was no evidence, the belief that the King Ranch *vaqueros* would shoot anyone who jumped the fence to hunt continued and grew. Those caught poaching feared for their lives. Dad told me of one encounter with a poacher. He was driving through a far pasture of the ranch when he spotted a man on foot and armed. Dad quickly drove to where the man was and got out of his car. Carrying his rifle, he walked up to him and ordered the man to stop and lower his rifle. Dad knew he had caught a poacher looking for deer.

Dad told me the man was so frightened and sure he was about to be shot that he threw his rifle at Dad's feet, fell to the ground on his knees, and begged Dad not to kill him.

False concepts about the "walled kingdom" and the fate of those who jumped its fences continued well into and after World War II. One evening when I was twelve years old Dad came home from work and told me he had an interview with a reporter from somewhere in the East. The reporter was working on a story about how the ranch was closed to everyone. He wanted to talk to the foreman about missing men and poachers. Someone had given him Dad's name as a person he should interview.

Dad said the reporter had a bunch of questions, most of which either did not make sense or were based on factual inaccuracies. Then, according to Dad, there was one question too many. The reporter asked Dad how many men he had killed.

I asked Dad what he told the reporter. He looked at me and shook his head. In a quiet voice he said he told him "only those needing it."

Dad was strict about what was right. He taught us always to obey the law. He believed in strong law enforcement. Sometimes, however, he enforced the law himself. For years, Dad operated a small ranch at Laurel, in Willacy County. It was the last piece of the San Juan de Carricitos land grant remaining in our family. At Laurel, Dad maintained a small herd of Santa Gertrudis cattle. He purchased a number of heifers from the King Ranch and was given permission to use ranch bulls as sires from time to time. These bulls he promptly returned. At first the ranch did not sell Santa Gertrudis bulls, but the policy was later altered and the ranch began selling Santa Gertrudis bulls to commercial ranchers in South Texas. Dad, through the use of a wise breeding program with fine bulls, soon had an excellent herd of Santa Gertrudis cattle at Laurel.

Adjacent to the Laurel was a small ranch with a number of mixed-breed cattle. The bulls were crossbred and rather ordinary. Dad received a report from his caretaker at Laurel about a neighbor's bull jumping the fence into one of our pastures and breeding a Santa Gertrudis cow. This incursion infuriated Dad, and he drove to the Laurel to see what could be done about the wayward bull.

After he returned, I asked Dad if he had worked out the problem of the bull jumping the fence and causing trouble. Dad assured me he had solved the problem. When he arrived at Laurel, the stray bull had jumped the fence again and was in the pasture with the Santa Gertrudis cows. Because of a bad shoulder, Dad could not throw a rope too well anymore, so he asked one of the hands to rope the bull. He did, and then Dad castrated it.

I was astonished that Dad would castrate the neighbor's bull, but when I asked why, he told me. The bull had been nothing but constant trouble, and Dad had talked to the owner a number of times about keeping his fences up and the bull out of his pasture. He did not pay attention to what Dad told him, so Dad decided he would have to take care of the matter himself, and he did.

I asked what happened to the bull. Dad replied that he didn't know, but the last time he saw it, the bull was bawling and running down the road. Dad guaranteed there would be no more problem with the bull.

When people were wrong, or did not respond to reason, Dad had a way of providing suitable and fair justice, as he saw it.

In 1933, Franklin D. Roosevelt was sworn in as the president of the United States. The nation was in the depths of the worst economic depression in its history. President Roosevelt's primary agenda was to bring an end to the depression by putting people back to work. He searched for ways to create jobs for the millions who were unemployed because of the economic conditions. The president proposed legislation focused on economic survival, and the Congress quickly passed it. The centerpiece of his first years in the White House was the Social Security Act and a series of programs to stimulate the economy—the New Deal.

Dad did not believe in Pres. Franklin D. Roosevelt's New Deal. Many of the federal programs under Roosevelt's economic plan were included in the Agricultural Adjustment Act and the National Industrial Recovery Act. The president's plan created the Civilian Conservation Corps (CCC) and the Works Progress Administration (later renamed Work Projects Administration or WPA), and the Public Works Administration (PWA). In addition, there were other, less focused programs that were essentially "make-work" efforts intended to mask welfare payments as wage income.

To Dad, the agricultural programs were especially disturbing. The idea that the federal government would pay a farmer not to raise cotton or would buy a rancher's cattle just to slaughter and bury them was unthinkable to him. Dad always relied upon his ability to make a living for his family, and he did not expect or want help from Washington or anyone else. Dad had no desire to let the federal government intrude on his ranching and farming practices.

The concept of "Social Security" was also difficult for Dad to accept. He told me that if I wanted to ensure that I would have income for my old age, I needed to start saving money. Dad could not understand why a person should give money to the government to save for them.

Dad was pleased that Social Security did not cover agricultural workers. He made it clear to us that he could look after his family and himself, and he could do it without help from "those folks" in D.C.

In the 1930s the depression was at its height. Money was always short around our house. Credit cards were nonexistent. Dad's approach to financing with credit was straightforward. Often I heard him say that if you couldn't pay cash, you didn't need it.

The economic stimulus package proposed by President Roosevelt was costly. Taxes were raised in an attempt to fund the New Deal programs. These taxes, however, did not generate sufficient funds for the many programs, and the federal government was forced to borrow money to operate. The national debt grew considerably, and the government could barely pay off the interest on the loans, much less the principal. This practice greatly upset Dad; it went against his ideas of prudent expenditure.

In the evening when he returned from work, and after dinner, Dad read the newspaper from front page to back. We did not own a radio, and this was long before television, but he read his newspaper almost daily. One evening, I passed by him as he sat in the dining room reading his newspaper. I was about eight years old.

Dad called me over to where he sat, held the newspaper in front of me, and tapped the page with the back of his hand, telling me to look at what was printed. I could barely read, but being obedient I looked. I saw a picture of President Roosevelt.

Dad told me the story was about how President Roosevelt spent money we didn't have to make work to do projects we didn't need. Dad went on saying day after day that the newspapers were full of stories about Roosevelt's New Deal programs and his strange ideas about giving people welfare. Dad considered the New Deal disgraceful.

He said Roosevelt was going to spend us into oblivion. Dad was certain the national debt would not be paid off in his lifetime and that I was going to have to pay off the debt Roosevelt was running up.

Dad was right that we did not pay off the national debt in his lifetime, but he was also wrong because we will not pay it off in my lifetime either. Dad should have said my grandchildren would still be paying on the national debt. I will never forget my early economic lesson on federal expenditure. Now, as I file our income taxes or make quarterly tax payments, I grumble and think back on Dad's vision of how the economy should operate. As usual, he made a lot of sense.

A CHRISTMAS STORY

The two-room schoolhouse was the base for the biggest and most important social event of the year: the Christmas barbecue dinner and dance. Ranch hands dug two or three large, deep pits about a week before Christmas Eve and built mesquite wood fires. Using mops, men liberally applied barbecue sauce to the quarters of beef cooking in the pits. By Christmas Eve, the meat was cooked perfectly. Potato salad, beans, rice, and salad filled tubs, and trimmings included pickles, onions, jalapeños, and chilies.

For us children, however, the main attraction was not the food or the dancing that followed the barbecue. The main attraction for us was in the commissary building of the ranch. On the first floor, one-half of the commissary was usually the general store where we purchased dry and canned goods. On Christmas Eve, however, a large decorated Christmas tree stood in the other half of the commissary. Several tables piled high with gifts for the children were nearby. A large wooden crate filled with brown paper sacks, each containing Christmas candy, nuts, an orange, and an apple, stood beside the tree.

In an orderly fashion, the workers on the ranch crowded into the room and took seats on benches brought in for the occasion. Children found a place to stand, and the younger ones sat on their parents' laps. It was traditional for Mr. Bob Kleberg Jr. to say a few words to the crowd. Since the depression had had a definite impact on the ranch and dollars were in short supply, the annual Christmas party was one way among many that the Klebergs acknowledged the fine work of its people. Dad called the assembly to order and introduced Bob Kleberg. He spoke, in Spanish, thanking all for their commitment to the ranch and their hard work. As Mr. Bob spoke, we all sat quietly. Everyone appeared to be listening to his every word. I, however, hoped for a short speech so that the festivities would start soon. To me, two-minute talks seemed long. Knowing I'd get a pinch from Mother, or one of her "could kill" looks if I appeared impatient and squirmed, I tried to sit still.

Finally, after Mr. Bob's speech, we lined up to receive our sacks of fruit and candy and a present. Usually, I eyed a pocketknife or a toy gun. With so many parents keeping a watchful eye, we children behaved ourselves and moved up the line to receive our present.

At home, preparing to go to the Christmas party, Sarita, Dick, and I had tried to convince Dad we should get the gift we wanted. Dick and I tried to convince Dad we desperately needed new knives. We pleaded for him to give each of us a knife at the party.

Knives were important to young boys on a ranch. We tried to sharpen them to such a fine edge that Vallejo could shave hair off of his arm. Dick and I did not have hair on our arms, so we asked Vallejo to check to see if our knives were sharp. I've never understood why we needed such sharp knives.

Dad listened to our requests for knives and always denied our appeal for special treatment. He told us we would get no favors from him at the ranch party.

Later, as we received our gift, each of us said "thank you" to Dad and smiled, suggesting we were immensely pleased to receive a gift. If I didn't get a knife, I was confident that I could trade my gift for a pocketknife the next day.

After the gifts were distributed, we moved to the schoolhouse yard, brightly illuminated by colored lights. The barbecue was ready to serve. Long wooden planks resting on sawhorses served as tables. They were placed about the yard and under a lone mesquite tree standing in the middle of the yard. After everyone had eaten, it was time for the dance; the schoolhouse became the dance hall. The two rooms were converted into a single large one by moving the dividing panel.

The adults sat against the walls, talking, gossiping, and watching young couples dance. Local talent provided the music. Evaristo Sáenz, known as "Maestro," was the conductor of the small band. His job was to run the ranch garage, but he was not only a fine mechanic and manager but also a musician. These dances were wonderful occasions, and people enjoyed themselves immensely. We children had the run of the schoolyard and left dancing to the "old people."

Dad ran the Christmas party at the Santa Gertrudis and also kept the peace. He made sure no one got out of line, had too much to drink, or misbehaved. I do not recall ever hearing an argument or seeing fighting at these Christmas gatherings. Such behavior was considered scandalous and would have been dealt with quickly. I remember watching Dad dress for the Christmas party. He always wore a fine suit and, of course, his best boots. I watched him as he straightened his tie and, satisfied with his appearance, reached for his pistol on the dresser. It was a .38-caliber pistol on a .45-caliber frame. It appeared enormous to me. Dad stuffed the large pistol into his belt, and it was concealed by his suit coat. Now he was ready for the Christmas party.

Dad was usually armed, keeping a pistol and several rifles in his car, which did not bother me. This practice was rather standard for ranch people in those days. There was something disturbing, though, in seeing him arm himself to go to the Christmas party. My worry as a child was that Dad would be hurt, or even killed.

As he dressed, I asked Dad if he had ever used the pistol at one of the Christmas parties. Dad said he had not, but one needed to be prepared. He advised that it was not possible to predict if something bad was going to happen. He told me that the previous year one of the town guests at the party got drunk and decided Dad had insulted him. The man pulled out a large knife from behind his coat and lunged at Dad.

Fortunately, it hit the pistol and bounced off without cutting Dad. He pulled out the pistol and hit the drunk in the head, knocking him unconscious.

When I asked what he did with the unconscious drunk, Dad said he had some of the men chain him to the mesquite tree in the back of the schoolyard. By morning he had sobered, and Dad turned him loose, telling him not to come back to the ranch. Dad made it clear that if he saw him on the ranch, there would be trouble.

Dad told me that chaining a man to a tree might seem hard, but with so many women and children at the party it was the best course. He said men who got out of line had to be dealt with quickly. Sometimes Dad spoke sternly to a drunken man and turned him over to his wife to take home. Dad chuckled, saying some men probably preferred being chained to a tree rather than listening to their wives fuss about their embarrassing behavior in front of the children and neighbors.

As a child, I had no concept of a "great national depression." Dad had a job, we had a home, and there was plenty of food. I was aware that money was tight, but everyone around us was in the same situation. I did see part of the migration from the farms of the Deep South and East Texas. In later years, when I read John Steinbeck's *The Grapes of Wrath*, I understood what I had observed on the highway near our house. I remember old cars and small trucks loaded with household goods, mattresses, and furniture. This procession was part of the great movement to the fields of California, as people without jobs, having lost their farms, and with no money, moved to find work. Many came to our back door and asked for food. Mother always fed them. They, in turn, offered to chop wood or do other chores, but Mother sent them on their way, often with extra food for the trip.

When I asked Mother where those people were going, she said they were probably on their way to California because there was field and orchard work there.

Even at an early age, I understood the economic needs of the people who drove by with all of their belongings on a small truck.

It was 1937, and I was ten years old. It was Christmas Eve, and we had just returned from the ranch party at Santa Gertrudis. The thought of presents under our tree the next morning excited me. Mother and I were in the kitchen when we heard the dogs barking. She looked out the screen door and saw two young boys at our back door. One knocked. I remember standing behind Mother when she answered the door. She called out for the dogs to be quiet, and they quit barking but kept a watchful eye.

One boy said politely that he hated to trouble Mother, but they were hungry. They asked for something to eat and offered to work chopping wood or anything else to pay her back for food. They said they had not eaten all day. They were Anglo youngsters, about fifteen or sixteen years old. Both carried a small bundle in one hand containing clothes and a rolled blanket; the other hand held a puppy, protecting it from our dogs.

Mother told them there was no need to work; we had plenty of food and we would be glad to share. She told them to come in and bring their pups with them. Mother said our dogs were not friendly to visiting dogs, no matter how small.

They declined coming into the house because they were dusty and dirty. They insisted they could eat on the porch. They asked for food for the puppies because they had not eaten in a while either. Mother said we would feed the dogs and directed the boys to a spigot to wash up. She told Dick and me to chase off our dogs and get some food for the pups and to give them plenty of water. Dick and I found some table scraps and a bowl of water for the puppies. They were hungry and ate hurriedly. Then they finished the bowls of water.

Dick and I sat with the boys on the porch while they ate. I asked where they were going. One said to California, where there was fruit to be picked and jobs—work for everyone. I said they had a long road to travel, and where did they plan to work in California? They were not sure, but they knew that if they went straight west they would get to California. Once there, they planned to find the orchards and go to work.

When they finished their food, one of the boys thanked Mother and told her how good it was and how kind she had been to them. The other said they had to be on their way because of the long road to California. Mother invited the boys to spend the night, reminding them it was Christmas Eve. They declined the invitation because they were anxious to continue their journey. One asked for a favor, though. They had been talking it over, and they wanted us to keep the puppies. They promised to be back soon to get them. They were certain they would be cared for and fit in with our dogs.

Mother nodded her head in agreement, and they handed Dick and me the little dogs. The two boys walked off into the night toward the highway. We never saw them again, and the puppies grew into fine dogs.

From time to time, I think about the two boys and the puppies, especially on a Christmas Eve. I wonder where the two young men were from and about their families. But most of all, I think about what happened to those boys. How did they grow into manhood during the depression? Did they educate themselves? I suppose they joined the military during the early days of World War II. If they did, did they survive the war? I am amazed I remember the night so vividly even though I was only ten years old. Even at ten years of age, I knew how fortunate I was on Christmas Eve. I at least had a home and parents and brothers and a sister who loved me and cared about me.

CHAPTER 3

⟨⟩

To School and the Barrio

In the early 1930s there were no kindergarten classes on the ranch. Therefore, by the time I was four years old Dad had tried to teach me the alphabet and how to count. I was not a scholar, and my preparation to start school "ready to learn" was minimal. When I turned six years old, however, it was off to school, where I joined my sister Sarita, a third grader. The school was about a mile from our home. Mother usually drove us to school, but sometimes we walked. The school building was wooden and was one room split into two classrooms by a portable divider. The schoolhouse had windows on three walls. To young people, the windows provided a major distraction because they gave us a grand view of activities around the ranch headquarters.

When I started to school, there were only a few buildings in the area. Across the road from the school was the ranch garage, which housed shops for maintenance and repair of ranch automobiles and trucks, farm equipment, and machinery. We purchased gas for Mother's car there, and at seventeen cents a gallon, it was expensive but necessary. Within the garage was a carpenter shop where cabinetwork, furniture, gates, and water troughs were made. The far end of the garage housed the blacksmith shop where the iron needs of the ranch were fashioned, including the branding irons.

Since 1869 the main brand of the King Ranch has been the Running W. To the *Kineños*, it was known as *la viborita*—the little snake.

Three large wooden barns filled with hay stood south of the garage. A corral surrounded each barn. Dick and I often went with Vallejo to the barn and sat on the corral watching the men gentle horses. We knew the cowboys and called encouragement as they skillfully worked to teach a horse to accept a bit, a blanket, or a saddle. They were all outstanding horsemen and had remarkable patience with the young horses.

The Big House, or Main House, or La Casa Grande—the home of the Kings and the Klebergs—stood on the south side of the headquarters area overlooking Santa Gertrudis Creek. This grand structure of Spanish-Moorish style was built between 1912 and 1915 to replace the Kings' home that was destroyed by fire in January 1912. It was built according to Henrietta M. King's specifications: "so men in boots and spurs will feel at home here."

The commissary or *tienda* stood at the bend of a road leading through the headquarters area. My Uncle Johnny (Juan H. Cavazos), Dad's younger brother, operated the commissary. He was rather thin, handsome, and tall. I remember my uncle; he always had a smile on his face and it was such a joy to visit with him at the commissary. He was married to my aunt Elida Hinojosa Cavazos. At the commissary one could buy staples such as beans and rice, canned goods, khaki pants and shirts, work shoes, and hats. In front of the commissary building stood a large mesquite tree, a great place for children to wait while their parents were in the store. It provided shade, and we children chewed the rather sweet mesquite beans.

Under this mesquite tree, I was introduced to politics. One day when I was about eight years old, Dad asked me to come help him run the polling place in front of the commissary. Seeing to the voting was one of his responsibilities as justice of the peace. A wagon with an open bed sat under the mesquite. The ballot box rested at the end of the wagon bed near the tailgate. Dad gave each adult a ballot and a pencil, and they sat at a nearby table to mark their ballots. My job was to put the ballots in the box. I do not recall what the election was about or who was running for office, but I was struck by the presence of a "sample ballot" posted near the wagon. The sample ballot was marked with suggestions as to how to vote. I asked Dad about this sample ballot, and he told me it was there only to help voters out because some of them could not read. With the sample ballot posted, they copied it to mark their own ballots. Dad said I needed to understand that his name was on the sample ballot. He added that he had been justice of the peace for the Santa Gertrudis for years, and he did not think anyone had ever voted against him.

Across the road from the *tienda* was, and still is, the old stable. Built of stone, it is distinguished by graceful arches. I remember a sculpture of a horse head and neck protruding from the Mission-style façade. The date 1853, the year the ranch was founded, appears across the front of the stable along with the inscription "Santa Gertrudis Ranch." The date 1909 (the year the stable was built) and Running W's are across the front of the stable. Today, the horse head is gone and its niche is empty. When I was growing up on the ranch, the stable was a favorite gathering place for men and boys. The stable master at the Santa Gertrudis headquarters was Don Jorge García, a jovial man, rather stocky, with a large flowing white mustache. He always wore khakis and a straw hat and usually had on his chaps. I believe he lived in a room in the stable.

There must have been seven or eight of us in the first grade. I remember my first teacher, Mrs. Erna Fisher. Also, my Aunt Dell (Adele Cavazos), was a substitute teacher. She was the wife of my Uncle Steve, my father's youngest brother. He served on the board of the Santa Gertrudis Division's independent school district for fifty years, but his main responsibility was to supervise brush clearing on the ranch. Brush was a constant battle on the ranch. Mesquite, huisache, and other harmful plants were a never-ending problem. They invaded open pastures and choked out precious grassland. I remember men clearing land on the ranch with axes and grubbing hoes. It was slow, back-breaking work. Brush was piled in large heaps, and after it dried, it was burned. When the ranch developed a tree-dozer, it was an important step in brush control.

Although the winters are mild in South Texas, the schoolhouse was cold and drafty. It was not insulated, and a small wood stove in the back of the room provided heat. At the noon hour we were dismissed to go home for lunch. There was not a blade of grass in the schoolyard, and only one large mesquite tree and a couple of live oak trees. Two privies, one for the boys and one for the girls, stood in back of the schoolyard. As we went out to recess, invariably the teacher would tell us to be careful and to watch where we stepped, because there were plenty of rattlesnakes out there. Our recess time was thirty minutes.

Recreational activities at the ranch school were minimal. There was a rather ancient merry-go-round and a couple of seesaws. Boys brought their baseballs, bats, and gloves to school, and there was usually a baseball game during our recess periods. For a week before Easter, our teacher asked us to bring eggshells to school. She said to tell our mothers when they cooked eggs to just crack the tip and then pour the contents out. Our teacher planned to show us how to make *cascarónes*. *Cascarón* means "eggshell" in Spanish, and *cascarónes* is a game children play. Brightly painted Easter eggs filled with confetti are hidden. When an egg is found, it is smashed over another child's head. After we gathered enough eggshells, our teacher had us paint them, fill them with confetti, and glue on a bit of tissue to keep the confetti in the shell.

During my time at the Santa Gertrudis School, I received a fundamental education. I learned how to read, write, and do basic mathematics, and I learned basic geography and history. Discipline was never a problem for the teachers, for we knew better than to misbehave. I went to school on the ranch for two years, and, although we continued to live on the ranch, my parents then moved me to a school in Kingsville.

I believe that the most important decision about my education was made when my parents decided that their children should be educated at the Flato Elementary School in Kingsville. Flato was about three miles from our home on the ranch. In the 1930s, and even until the late 1940s, there were four elementary schools in Kingsville. In the 1930s the population of the town was about seventy-five hundred. Of the four schools, one was for Hispanics, one for black Americans, and the other two, for the education of non-Hispanic whites. In Texas during those

times, this arrangement was standard. Segregation was deeply ingrained in the minds of the population and upheld by local ordinances
and the laws of the state.

In addition to being segregated in school (both elementary and high
school), black Americans in Kingsville could not eat in "white" restau-
rants, and they had to use separate drinking fountains. They lived in a
ghetto in the southwest part of town and had their own churches. There
were two theaters in town, and black Americans had to sit in the bal-
cony of the second-rate movie house. They were not allowed in the
other movie house. In the barrio was Jackson's Tent Theater, or *Teatro
Carpa*, which showed films in Spanish and featured Mexican movie en-
tertainers. At the railroad depot in the center of town were separate
waiting rooms and restrooms for black Americans. They even had their
own graveyard, the ultimate of the mindless acts of segregation.

Hispanics fared a little better than black Americans, but not by
much. The *colonia* or *barrio*, the Hispanic part of Kingsville, was on the
northeast side of town. Hispanic children went to Stephen F. Austin Elementary School. Hispanics lived east of the railroad tracks, which was
the line between the Anglo and Hispanic communities. In the 1930s and
early 1940s there was a sewage system in the Anglo parts of Kingsville
but not in the barrio. Homes in the barrio had outhouses or privies.
During Halloween, my grandmother placed a lighted lantern in her
privy for fear mischievous boys would overturn it. The lantern suggested that someone was using the outhouse and thus it would not be
wise to turn it over.

There was no electricity in the barrio, so kerosene lanterns lighted
most of the houses there. My grandmother cooked on a wood-burning
stove because natural gas had not yet come to the barrio either. Piled
outside on the back porch near the kitchen door were mesquite logs. In
addition to the lack of sewer lines and electricity, the streets of the barrio were unpaved. On occasion, the city sent a road grader to level the
holes in the dirt roads of the barrio. There were no paved sidewalks, just
dirt paths.

Mama Grande Rita's house was three blocks from San Martín

Catholic Church. Even here segregation persisted. San Martín was the church for Hispanics. Across town, outside of the barrio, was another Catholic church, Saint Gertrude's, for Anglos. Living on the ranch made regular attendance at Sunday mass difficult, however. When we spent the night at Mama Grande Rita's house, she or my aunts would take us to Sunday mass at San Martín. In the late 1930s and 1940s, men sat on the left side of the church. Women, with heads covered, sat on the right side of the church. Children sat in the first two or three rows, on both sides, up front. We children were expected to be reverent, quiet, and to pay attention. If we were not, adults seated behind us whispered an order to behave. They might even tap us on the shoulder or pull a pigtail, reminding us we were in church and expected to behave. Discipline of children was everyone's job at San Martín, and adults took it seriously.

Unlike black Americans, Hispanics could be buried in Chamberlain Burial Park, a cemetery maintained by Kingsville. It was named after Mrs. Henrietta King's father, the Reverend Hiram Chamberlain. As a child I went to the cemetery on El Día de Todos los Santos (All Saints Day) and on El Día de los Muertos (All Souls Day). My mother, grandmother, and aunts and uncles cleaned the plots where our relatives were buried.

I walked among the graves, those of my family and others, and realized all of the names were Hispanic. I did not see Anglos cleaning graves nearby. There were a few doing so in another part of the cemetery. Pointing to the graves beyond the dividing road, I asked Mother who was buried there. Mother said Anglos were buried on the other side of the cemetery. The road divided the cemetery.

I did not know the meaning of segregation, but I thought this situation strange. Looking back, it is still difficult for me to understand segregation in life, much less in death, but I remind myself that this practice was the norm in the South of the 1930s and 1940s.

In the early 1940s, before the beginning of World War II, there was a vacant block not far from Mama Grande Rita's house. There was nothing on the lot except weeds, trash, brush, and a couple of mesquite trees, but for a two-week period in the middle of the summer, in the early evening, the block was magically transformed into *la feria* (fair, carnival, or market). To children growing up in the barrio, *la feria* was a grand and exciting activity. Little entertainment existed for Hispanics in Kingsville.

It featured a few carnival rides, some game booths, and a number of cold drink and hamburger and taco stands. Hamburgers were five cents each, and a nickel would buy two tacos. Residents of the barrio constructed and operated the food stands. Small gas stoves cooked hamburgers, and washtubs filled with ice cooled the soft drinks. The economic depression was at its height and cash was scarce. *La feria* gave some people in the barrio a chance to make extra money. It was a great place to visit both for children and adults. Colored bulbs provided light, music blared from speakers, and a festive air prevailed. At *la feria*, neighbors had a chance to visit with each other, but they kept an eye on their children as they scampered about the grounds.

La feria was an annual social activity we all looked forward to, and it was important and meaningful to the Hispanics in the barrio. Often on a Saturday afternoon, Mother drove us in from the ranch to visit our grandmother. If *la feria* was in season, we pleaded with her to take us. More often than not, she gave in to our entreaty. Usually, two or three of our young cousins and one or two of our aunts and uncles went with us. It was a great family outing.

During one of our visits to *la feria* we saw at one booth a thick plank with a number of large nails partially driven into it. The object of the game, which cost five cents, was to hammer one of the nails into the plank in three strikes. If successful, the operator paid twenty-five cents, a grand prize in those days. We watched men try to drive nails in three hammer strikes. Most often, they bent the nail, it spun out, or did not drive it all of the way into the wood.

Dick and I saw a man we knew as "Towreno." I never learned his full name; we just knew him as Towreno. Towreno was short and stocky, had dark hair, and had strong and well-muscled arms. Because he worked all day in the sun, Towreno's skin was brown and leathery. He was about forty years old. Towreno was a carpenter, well known in the barrio for his fine work. In later years, he built our house in Kingsville when we moved in from the ranch.

Dick and I were standing in the front row watching what was going on. We heard Towreno ask for a hammer. He hefted it and lightly tapped the palm of his hand with it. He held the hammer over a nail, swung it rapidly three times, and drove the nail completely into the wood. The men around him cheered, and without much of a pause Towreno drove two more nails into the plank. Then the operator figured out Towreno was a carpenter and stopped him from driving any more nails.

Dick and I continued our walk among the different booths, and I spotted one that immediately got my attention: a shooting gallery. Dick and I went to the gallery. It was rather narrow and about twenty feet long. At the back of the booth were targets pinned to thick wooden planks. To the left of the targets was a door leading to a small back room. Dick and I watched as people tried their luck shooting the targets with .22-caliber rifles. None did well, and no one won a prize.

Dick and I considered ourselves good shots with either rifle or shotgun. When each of us was ten, Dad insisted we learn how to handle firearms, and in time we became crack shots. Dad told us we would be around guns for the rest of our lives, and we were not too young to learn how to use them safely and accurately. Dad instructed Dick and me on the use of rifles and shotguns. Before we fired our first shot, he drilled us on safety. Dad's rules were never to point a gun at a person and never bring a loaded rifle or shotgun into the house. We stored our rifles and shotguns, as well as ammunition, in the closet on our sleeping porch. I believe that because of Dad's constant emphasis on safety in the use of firearms, we never had a shooting accident in our home or while we were out hunting.

It was a treat for Dick and me when he would take us with him to hunt doves and quail. Time and time again as we aimed at a bird, Dad whispered to aim so that it appeared the bird was sitting on the front sight. He said to hold our breath, take up the slack in the trigger, and squeeze, don't pull.

During dove and quail season, Dick and I usually came back to the house with our limit of birds. As we unloaded, Dad ordered us to go pick and clean the birds we had shot. His instructions, time and time again, were that if we killed an animal, we had to eat it. Then he reminded us to clean our shotguns.

Dick and I sat on our back porch with two paper sacks and a pan, cleaning our birds. We tried to persuade Vallejo to help us pluck the birds, but he refused, reminding us of Don Lauro's rule about cleaning and eating game we shot. So Vallejo walked on, telling us to get to work picking the birds, unless we wanted to eat them with feathers.

At *la feria*, Mother gave in to our pleading for money for the shooting gallery. Dick and I hurried back, and Mother and one of our uncles followed. We paid our twenty-five cents, and each of us elected to shoot at a target consisting of a small red dot, about the size of a large nail head. The objective was to shoot away all of the red of the dot in three shots. If either Dick or I was successful in doing so, we won one dollar.

I told Dick to go first, and to give it his best. Dick was an excellent shot, and he quickly fired off three rounds, obliterated the red dot, and won a dollar.

I shot next and also won a dollar. The operator of the gallery looked at the target and shook his head. Mother and my Uncle Raúl Pérez were pleased and complimented Dick and me on our shooting ability.

Dick and I talked Mother into letting us shoot another round. We went back to the shooting gallery. Again, Dick shot out the red dot. When I fired my three rounds, I was sure I, too, had shot out the red dot.

The gallery operator looked pained. He took down the targets we had shot and told us he needed to check the targets in a better light. He said he had good lighting in the back room. Dick and I watched as the operator removed the targets, stepped in the back room, and closed the door behind him.

Soon the operator came back into the gallery and said he hated to tell us, but when he checked the targets in good light he saw some red on both of them. He declared that we were close but did not win a prize. He handed us the targets and told us to have a look at them.

Dick and I checked the targets. We were positive we had shot out the red, but there was a trace of red on each target. I shook my head, and Mom, Dick, and I walked away from the gallery.

Our Uncle Raúl came up and told us we had been cheated. He said he saw the targets and there was no red on them before the operator took them into the back room. Uncle Raúl said he probably had a red pencil in the back room and colored in the targets with just a touch of red.

The incident at the shooting gallery was significant to my education about life because it was the first time I had been cheated. On the ranch, we believed every person was honest. I do not recall dishonesty or cheating by any of the people living on the ranch. In all of the years we lived there, nothing was ever stolen from our home and rarely did we lock our doors. I never forgot the shooting gallery incident, nor did Dick. He reminded me of it a few months ago though it has been more than sixty-five years since the two of us shot out the red dots at *la feria*.

ACADEMIC CHOICE AND FLATO

My sister Sarita started to school on the ranch. When she was in the third grade, Dad and Mother decided that she, and her brothers, should go to the "best school possible," which was Flato Elementary School in Kingsville. To transfer from one school district while living in another is still difficult today, but it was almost impossible and unheard of in the 1930s. If a child were Hispanic, seeking transfer to an Anglo school would have been truly formidable.

When we were young, Dad and Mother had started thinking and planning on the best way for us to get an education. In order to improve our educational options, they purchased a lot in Kingsville on West Ella Street. Although we continued to live on the ranch, they expected to someday build a house on the lot. It was ideally situated in regards to education. The lot was within two blocks of a small college, Texas College of Arts and Industries, within two blocks of Flato Elementary School, and six blocks from the high school.

In the 1930s Hispanics in Kingsville did not build homes in the northwest or southeast parts of town, the area where most of the Anglos lived. My parents managed to buy a lot on West Ella, in the Anglo section of Kingsville.

After buying the lot, Dad went to work on transferring Sarita from Santa Gertrudis School to Flato Elementary School. He discussed the transfer with J. D. Bramelette, the superintendent of schools in Kingsville. Although sympathetic to Dad's request, the superintendent did not have the authority to act unilaterally on such an extraordinary request. Mr. Bramelette took the matter to the local school board for their consideration. The board refused the request for the transfer, but Dad did not give up. He went back with his request, pointing out to the board that he owned property and paid taxes in Kingsville. He asked to be treated as any other citizen. Dad was strong-willed and persistent. He was greatly respected in town for the excellent job he was doing as foreman of the Santa Gertrudis Division. He kept up pressure on the board, and they finally agreed that Sarita could transfer to a Kingsville school. The board insisted, however, that because she was "Mexican" she should attend Stephen F. Austin, the elementary school for Hispanics in the barrio.

Dad knew that the best school in town was Flato, and he continued pushing the board for a transfer of his daughter to Flato. He pointed out that Sarita was fluent in English, and a move to Austin Elementary would mean she would have to travel from the ranch and all the way across town to go to school. Dad's pressure on the board was supported by Bramelette. Finally, Dad and the superintendent succeeded in their effort to transfer Sarita to Flato and gained the approval of the board.

Recently, Sarita told me she remembered the day Bramelette came to our house on the ranch to talk to Dad and Mother. When he told them the school board had decided she could go to school at Flato, she was thrilled. Sarita told me that, at the time, she had not understood the significance or the implications of what her parents had done for her education, and she had been unaware of the discriminatory treatment she received at Flato.

In the fall, Sarita started to school at Flato Elementary. She came home from her first day of school in Kingsville all aglow, telling Mother and Dad that she had her very own table against the wall. She thought it was wonderful.

She later told me she was too young to comprehend that her "nice table" was a mechanism to segregate her from the rest of the class. Sarita said that as the weeks passed, she became accepted, made friends, and showed she could do the schoolwork. After a short time, Sarita said, they must have decided she didn't have lice or a disease, so she got a desk in the middle of the classroom and became part of the class.

After I completed the second grade at the Santa Gertrudis School, my parents transferred me to Flato. Sarita had paved the way, so now there was no resistance by the school administration to my going to Flato. Mother or Vallejo drove Sarita and me from the ranch to school each day and picked us up when school was over. There were no school buses.

The Flato School was an impressive building. In the 1930s, elementary or "grammar" schools generally had seven grades, and high school had four grades. Thus, I had an eleven-year elementary- and secondary-school education, in contrast to the twelve grades plus kindergarten most school districts offer today. Flato was opened in 1924 and closed in 1975. The building was stucco and had two wings and a central portion. The first, second, and third grades were in one wing, and grades four through seven were in the other wing. The one-room library and the principal's office connected the wings. The halls along the wings had balconies, and the floors were wooden and highly polished. The school-yard contained two large water fountains, bicycle racks, a slide, several seesaws, and two large mesquite trees.

The Flato School faced West Santa Gertrudis Street. A large ebony tree surrounded by a concrete bench dominated the front yard of the school. At one time, this tree had stood at the edge of a lake formed by a dam that Captain King built across Tranquitas Creek. In the late 1800s it was the only place between the Nueces River and the Rio Grande where you could water a thousand head of cattle at the same time. It is said that when Captain King worked cattle along the Tranquitas, Mrs. King brought lunch and they would share it under the ebony tree. As students, we played under the tree and told each other the story that this was the meeting place of the Kings.

I remember one of my young companions telling me as we climbed the branches of the ebony tree that this was where Captain King proposed to his future wife. I told him I doubted this was true, but the tree must be important because of the bench around it and the concrete patches on the tree trunk.

For as long as I can remember, the ebony tree stood in front of Flato, even after the school closed in 1975. On one of my trips to Kingsville in the 1980s, the tree was gone. It had died and been removed. I was pleased when, on a recent trip to Kingsville, I discovered that the town had planted another ebony tree where the old one had stood. The new one is not as grand as the remembered one that served as the Kings' meeting place, but give it time.

One school day after lunch I joined a group of fourth graders around the high flagpole that stood in the front of Flato School. We grasped the flag lanyard and swung high in the air, in a grand circle around the flagpole. Miss Ramsey, the fourth-grade math teacher, came out and told us to stop swinging on the rope. As soon as she was out of sight, we started swinging on the flagpole again. Soon, Miss Ramsey appeared and told us to follow her to the fourth-grade room. I knew we would be severely punished for our disobedience.

When we entered the room, Miss Ramsey ordered us to the blackboards. She said it appeared we were good at swinging on flagpoles, so she wanted to see how good we were at math. For the next twenty minutes she dictated math problems, and we stood at the blackboard and worked them. We certainly did not enjoy solving math problems, especially with Miss Ramsey standing over us, but none of us ever thought about swinging on the flagpole rope again.

When Sarita and I arrived at Flato, Miss Ruby Gustavson was the principal. She was the principal from 1935 until her retirement in 1970 and as a result knew thousands of students from Kingsville. Miss Gustavson was an attractive woman with light brown hair and blue eyes. I remember her as about six feet tall. An imposing figure, she had great poise. Her speech was rather soft, but precise. There was never any doubt in our minds what Miss Gustavson meant when she asked us to do something for her. Miss Gustavson was a wonderful teacher and administrator who knew every student in school. Applying a fundamental tenet of education—involving parents in the education of their children—she made it a point to visit the homes of her students. I remember seeing her come to our house in Kingsville and telling Mother how Sarita and I were doing in school. I knew I was doomed. A discussion of my educational progress (or lack thereof) at Flato was bound to be bleak, with perhaps a few bright spots.

Mother did not tell me how the talk with Miss Gustavson went or mention my academic achievements, but she praised me for my good behavior. Later, she would tell Dad of Miss Gustavson's visit.

Dad, without fail, discussed my academic progress with me and asked how I thought I was doing in school. I told him I believed I was doing well, and I especially liked reading. Invariably, Dad looked at me and acknowledged I did well in reading, but I needed to improve my math scores. Dad said he did not want another report like the one I had just received, and he expected me to bring my math scores up. I had no excuses, and I knew Dad would not accept one. I promised to do better in math.

Miss Gustavson was an educational constant in my life. All through elementary school, she watched and encouraged my education. Frequently, she told me I could do better in school or praised me when it was clear I understood the lesson. As a principal, she found time to be not only an administrator but also a teacher and friend to every child in Flato. After I left Flato for high school, I occasionally stopped by for a visit.

After I graduated from high school in 1944, I joined the army. When I was home on leave, I asked Mother about Miss Gustavson and she said she was fine and still principal. Miss Gustavson finally retired in 1970. For a time I lost track of her, but in 1981, when I was president of Texas Tech University, I gave a brief speech in Kingsville at the dedication of the Texas historical marker for the original Henrietta M. King High School building where I had gone to school. Miss Gustavson was there, and I was very pleased to see her. Although she had aged a bit and used a cane, she still stood straight and gracefully, and her speech, as always, was precise and proper. We had a brief visit.

She told me how proud she was when I was named president of Texas Tech and that all of my brothers and Sarita had been successful. The next time I saw Miss Gustavson was soon after my appointment as U.S. secretary of education. The first formal speech I gave after my appointment was in October 1988 on the campus of Texas College of Arts and Industries in Kingsville (now Texas A&M University–Kingsville). I do not recall the topic of my talk, but the highlight for me was seeing Miss Gustavson again. Prior to my speech we talked briefly about education, but she wanted to talk about me. I could not get her to talk about herself; it was always about her students.

Miss Gustavson told me how proud she was I was giving leadership to education in this country as secretary of education. She told me she had to admit she never dreamed I would be in the president's Cabinet. I told Miss Gustavson that she and my parents placed me on the path of learning. I owed her and them so much.

As I began my speech, I saw her on the left front row of the auditorium, where they had reserved a seat for her at my request. To the audience, I acknowledged her presence and told them of my debt to Miss Gustavson for the education she initiated in my life. I said that I asked but one thing from her: not to tell the press what a terrible student I was at Flato.

I remember her smile as she shook her head. I could sense her pride in having one of her students achieve national prominence in her field, education. For me, the event was one of the high-water marks in my term as secretary. While in Washington, I met presidents of this and other nations, educators, legislators and senators, Supreme Court justices, governors, and many other distinguished persons. Still, approval of my academic achievement by Ruby Gustavson ranks among the highlights of my career in Washington.

Miss Gustavson died on June 1, 2001. She was ninety-seven years old. Her obituary stated there were no immediate family survivors. I submit that there are many survivors, a very large family of her former students.

My parents continued to push our education, wanting us to have the best. Our opportunities were limited, but we learned the fundamentals at the ranch school and at the Flato School.

It was at Flato that I received my first dose of discrimination because I was Hispanic. This situation came as a surprise, because on the ranch there was no discrimination of any kind. At Flato, though, for a few weeks I was frequently in fights with bullies in the class or when a "big boy," a third or fourth grader, tried to beat me up. I fought as best I could, but those first weeks were not happy ones. In time, the fights and taunting subsided, and I became accepted. Some of my classmates stood up for me. One or two of them would jump into the fight to help me out.

One boy saved me from a beating once when I was waiting for Mother to pick me up. The classroom bully came up to me and he said he did not like Mexicans. Without further words, he attacked and pinned me to the ground. I tried to fight him but was no match. Then one of my classmates came toward us, riding his bicycle full speed. He skidded to a stop, dropped his bicycle, and jumped into the fight. He pulled off the boy who was beating on me and hit him a couple of times. The bully ran off.

It would not be the last discrimination I would face. I learned that racism against me as a child could extend into my adult life.

The boy who saved me from a beating was Dick Mosley, the son of the Kleberg County sheriff. Dick and I became friends. Our friendship lasted through high school. After I left for the army, I never saw Dick again.

I remember the night Dad came into the sleeping porch where I was in bed. I was nine years old. He walked up, saw I was awake, and said he was sorry to tell me, but Sheriff Mosley had been shot and killed as he sat drinking coffee in a café. This man walked up behind him and shot him. Dad said he knew that I and the sheriff's son, Dick, were good

friends. He added that Sheriff Mosley was a good man but in a dangerous job.

W. T. Mosley, Dick's father, had been sheriff of Kleberg County for
fourteen years, from 1922 until his death in 1936. I thought about Dick,
how he helped me out of a scrape, and his friendship. I also thought
about how I would feel if someone told me Dad had been killed. I said a
silent prayer.

CHAPTER 4

Vallejo

Next to my parents, the person most responsible for shaping my early childhood was Vallejo. I list him as one of my great teachers. It was in 1936 that I first met Vallejo. I was nine years old, and I will never forget the first time I saw him. He was a slightly stocky man, about five feet, eight inches tall or so, and in his early twenties. I watched as he pushed his bicycle into our backyard. His mixture of Spanish and Indian heritage came out strongly in his physical appearance. His skin was brown, his hair straight and black; a scraggly black mustache turned down as it followed the contour of his lip. He had piercing brown eyes, was broad-shouldered, and had rather short, but well-muscled arms. His hands were rough from a lifetime of work. Like most of the men on the ranch, he wore khakis. Unlike most of the men on the ranch, though, he was not wearing boots, but high-top work shoes. His hat, a rather worn and somewhat soiled white Stetson, was slightly pulled to one side. A black-and-white collie-shepherd mix followed him.

The first time I encountered Vallejo, he was a complete stranger to me. He greeted me in Spanish and asked who I was. I told him I was Laurie, the son of Don Lauro, and I asked his name.

When he told me his name was Maxcimilíano García but that everyone on the ranch called him Vallejo, I told him that was a strange name. I asked why people called him that, and he said it was because he came from an area in Mexico known as Vallejo.

Vallejo told me that the ranch bosses had sent him to work in our home, to do whatever my mother, *la madama*, told him to do.

Through decades of association, Vallejo and I never conversed in English, always in Spanish, even though Vallejo understood English and had some facility in the language. Still, I respected Vallejo's preference for Spanish. It was the primary language of most of those working on the ranch.

Over the years, a number of ranch hands had held the same job as Vallejo. Usually they worked outside in the yard or about the house. Mother would assign jobs each day. Most men stayed only a year or two and then transferred to other jobs on the ranch. I am sure many were glad to leave our place, because Mother was a tough taskmaster. She had high expectations regarding the quality of work she expected the men to do.

As I was getting acquainted with Vallejo, I pointed to his dog and asked what his name was. Vallejo replied, "Togoah." I thought the dog's name was even stranger than Vallejo's. When I asked what that meant, Vallejo said it was the Spanish word for "robed." I was still puzzled, so I asked why he had given the dog that name.

Vallejo told me to look at the dog and tell him what I saw. All I could see was a black-and-white dog. But Vallejo pointed out that the dog had a wide band of white around the neck and shoulders, and he thought it looked like the dog was wearing a robe or toga. So he named his dog Togoah.

Although I had no idea what a toga was, after Vallejo had explained why he called his dog Togoah, I understood. In time, Dick and I came to believe that Togoah was one of the finest hunting dogs we had ever seen. Soon we learned we had to speak to Togoah in Spanish because the dog did not understand commands given in English. Most of the time we had five or six fox terriers about the yard. Our terriers, unlike Togoah, were bilingual dogs. They were not as disciplined or trained as Togoah and were capable of ignoring or obeying our commands in either English or Spanish.

Vallejo was a survivor. He stayed with us as long as Dad and Mother lived. To us, he became part of our family, and we cared deeply about him. Although at times Mother would fuss at him about some issue or how a job was done, he appeared to listen, nod his head with a "*Sí, señora*," or "*Sí, madama*," smile, and quietly go on his way. Vallejo had a thick skin, and Mother's words rolled off his back. He never said an unkind word to her or tried to argue with her, nor did he ever raise his voice to her.

Chores and work around a ranch house are never-ending. Vallejo chopped wood, painted, did carpentry, hung wallpaper, did masonry work, ran errands, and helped out with the cooking. Most of all, Vallejo kept an eye on my brothers and me to be certain we were not in some kind of mischief or in danger of getting hurt. My sister Sarita was Mother's responsibility.

Vallejo did little actual cooking. His kitchen work was usually chopping meats and vegetables, and he had the daily job of starting the pinto beans to cook. This chore was the first one he did soon after he walked into the kitchen in the morning. Just before the meal, Mother arrived in the kitchen and put the meal together.

Vallejo was a patient man, especially with us children. He could be quite stern with us, especially if we did not do our assigned work on the ranch or did not do it well. I remember one day when he gave me a job to do and I did not follow his directions or do it well.

Quietly, Vallejo told me I would some day be a leader of men and women, but before I could lead and give orders, I had to learn how to take orders. After giving me that advice, Vallejo told me to go back and do the job again, and this time, do it right. It is telling that his words have stayed with me more than sixty-five years.

Vallejo was a legal immigrant from Mexico to the United States. In those days, if one entered legally into the United States, they were said to have *papeles*, that is, immigration papers. These papers proved legal entry into the United States, and Hispanics were often stopped on the highway or the street and asked for their *papeles*. Today, this practice would be considered racial profiling, but the government was not too concerned about such a thing in the 1930s, 1940s, or 1950s. In my childhood, I learned about the deportation of Mexican citizens without permits. They did not want to be known as "illegal aliens." Those who crossed the Rio Grande to seek better lives for themselves and their families did not believe they had committed a crime. They considered themselves undocumented workers.

Vallejo delighted in telling us the story about his free trip to Brownsville and the border courtesy of the U.S. government. He explained that before he came to work at our house, *la migra* picked him up. *La migra* was a slang term for the federal Immigration and Naturalization Service (INS). From time to time, the INS swept through the ranches in the area in search of "illegals," or "wetbacks," or "*mojados*," as they were called in those days. When the INS officers found an undocumented worker, the person was sent by bus to the interior of Mexico and released. The INS agents did not listen to Vallejo when he insisted he was legally in the country and tried to show them his *papeles*.

Vallejo told us that the next thing he knew he was on a bus to Brownsville, and he knew that from there he would be sent to the interior of Mexico. Vallejo kept telling them he had papers, but they still would not listen. *La migra* told him to sit down and be quiet, so he did. Finally, after the bus arrived in Brownsville and as the INS workers filled out forms to send him to Mexico, someone listened to him, checked his papers, and found them in order.

Once the INS discovered he was legal, Vallejo said, they had to pay his way back to Kingsville. Vallejo said he enjoyed the bus ride to Brownsville and the chance to visit with some nice people being sent back to Mexico. According to Vallejo, they were good men and women, many with children, looking for work. He told them to contact him when they returned to South Texas and the nearby ranches and farms. Vallejo was sure they would be back soon.

Vallejo's major vice was chewing tobacco. His favorite brand was *Pato Negro* or Black Duck. He paid a nickel a package for the dried black tobacco leaves, and I remember how terrible it looked and how strong it smelled. To Dick's and my credit, we never tried to talk Vallejo into sharing a plug of *Pato Negro* with us. I doubt he would have given us any. Dick and I contained our nicotine urges by smoking cedar bark off the fence posts around our house and the pasture.

One of Vallejo's major jobs was to teach us about horses, especially how to care for them and how to ride. We kept several horses in a pasture not far from the house. Almost every weekend Vallejo, Dick, Bobby, and I saddled up, called our pack of fox terrier dogs and Togoah, and went in search of armadillos, bobcats, rabbits, or raccoons.

The first time Vallejo took us riding, I mounted my horse and was ready to leave. Vallejo said to get off my horse. I just looked at him; I did not understand why he wanted me off the horse, but I dismounted.

Vallejo called all three of us boys to gather around and listen to what he had to say. Vallejo told us that when we mounted a horse, we must say, "*Con el favor de Dios.*" Riding a horse can be dangerous, he said. He reminded us that we could be injured in a moment. Those words were a prayer said by every person who mounted a horse on the ranch, asking for God's blessing and protection. Vallejo said we must do the same. We listened, understood, and nodded in the affirmative.

From then on, we said "*Con el favor de Dios*" as we mounted even the most gentle horse we had ridden many times. I am convinced that the prayer for the blessing or grace of God worked. None of us children was ever thrown or seriously injured while riding. Some horses bit me or attempted to kick me and others stepped on my foot or tried to lie down in the water as we crossed a creek, but they were just teaching me a lesson about crowding or riding them. Once a horse walked under a clothesline with me on its back, and I got a scrape on my face. Immediately afterward, I understood the lesson the horse was trying to teach me: "Pay attention."

Vallejo's insistence on a prayer as I mounted a horse has stayed with me all of these years. Although I rarely ride horses now, Vallejo's prayer crosses my mind as I board an airplane on one of my frequent trips. "*Con el favor de Dios*" has seen me through many journeys throughout the United States and the world.

Accidents on horseback reminded us of the dangers of life on a ranch. We tried to be careful and knew better than to take chances or do foolish things while on horseback. If we did, we could be hurt. One day Dick, Bobby, Vallejo, and I were riding across a pasture. A large rabbit bolted in front of Vallejo and his horse. He chased it and was rapidly gaining on the animal when his horse stuck a hoof into a hole. Vallejo flew out of his saddle and went over the horse's head, and the horse tumbled after him. When we galloped up to him, Vallejo was dusting himself off and his horse was standing near him. Blood was on Vallejo's shoulders and his shirt, which was almost ripped off him. I thought he must be seriously hurt.

Vallejo said not to worry, that he was a bit bruised but was sure he would recover. He said he was being punished for trying to catch such a small rabbit with such a big horse.

Soon after he came to work at our house, we caught an armadillo on one of our rides. Watching Vallejo clean and remove viscera from an armadillo provided me with one of my early lessons in anatomy. As Vallejo started to work on our first armadillo, he said if he cut the intestine and it leaked, the armadillo was poisonous and not edible.

Neither my brothers nor I had ever eaten armadillo. Vallejo assured us they were tasty and good for us. Vallejo skillfully removed the viscera from the armadillo without mishap.

We caught and brought home many armadillos. Almost every time we rode into the brush, our dogs jumped an armadillo or two, so we had an ample supply to cook. Vallejo was right about their value as food. Dick, Bobby, and I soon developed a taste for armadillo. Mother, on the other hand, abhorred the thought of an armadillo cooking in her kitchen. She told Vallejo he was not to cook armadillos in her kitchen, so Vallejo barbecued them outside if she was at home and cooked them in Mother's kitchen when she was away.

Mother's only acceptance of our armadillo activity was to use their shells as flower planters. Vallejo dried the shells in the sun, filled them with dirt, planted flowers, and suspended them with a wire from the tail to the front of the shell.

Vallejo also used the armadillo to teach me an important lesson on how to handle difficult situations. When we chased an armadillo, it headed for its hole. If we were fast, we grabbed its tail and pulled it out of the hole. Armadillos have long claws they use to grasp the roots and earth in their burrows and are capable of expanding their shells to make it very difficult to pull them out.

My lesson on dealing with adversity started with my trying, without success, to pull an armadillo out of its hole. Vallejo watched me struggle and said for me to use my head, not my strength. I looked at him, not understanding.

He grabbed and lifted the armadillo's tail, picked up a dried twig, and inserted it in the armadillo's anus. Vallejo gave the twig a twist, and the armadillo quickly let go. Out it came from its hole.

Heartless carnivores that we were, we never had a qualm about humiliating the armadillo in that fashion. And in later years, as I dealt with a variety of people in politics and academia, I found myself thinking at first fondly, and then guiltily, of Vallejo's down-to-earth wisdom. Fortunately, I was always able to keep a straight face and employ more traditional and humane methods of persuasion.

Looking back on our armadillo capers on the ranch, I wonder why we did not get Hansen's disease. Maybe it was because we had never heard of leprosy, or maybe it was our trust and faith in Vallejo's wisdom keeping us healthy. Perhaps it was because he never nicked the intestine of the armadillo when cleaning one. Who knows?

Another of Vallejo's favorite meals was roadrunner, and if we saw one, we shot it and took it home for Vallejo. He insisted they had a fine taste, like chicken, and he told me they had medicinal value. I asked how eating roadrunners would improve my health. He told me that eating roadrunners would make sores on my legs go away. I told Vallejo I didn't have sores on my leg, so I passed up the roadrunner treatment.

Today, driving through the Southwest, I often see roadrunners. When I do, I think fondly of Vallejo's prescription of roadrunner for sores or imagine how good they are to eat. I've still never tried one.

Although I did not eat a roadrunner, Vallejo insisted that we eat every bird we shot. With air rifles Dick and I shot meadowlarks, doves, or grackles and left them where they lay. We considered it sporting, but Vallejo said it was a waste of good food. Like he did with the armadillos, Vallejo waited until Mother was away from the house and cooked the birds for our lunch. They were not tasty, and Dick and I quit shooting birds around the house.

Vallejo also had a cure for dogs that had mange, a skin condition caused by itch mites. Several of our dogs had recurring mange, and we applied sulfur and other powders to try to control it, without much success.

One day when we were riding horses across a pasture, I learned Vallejo's cure for mange. It was direct, practical, and cost nothing. Our dogs ran besides us as we rode, and soon we came upon ten or fifteen head of cattle. Scattering, they left large piles of manure. It was then that Vallejo told he was going to teach us how to cure mange.

He dismounted, caught one of our mangy dogs by the collar, and covered him with hot cow manure. Vallejo proclaimed that manure was the best treatment for mange.

A few days later, after a couple more manure treatments, the dog was free of mange. Although I do not know if Vallejo's prescription cured the mange, I do remember that it made quite an impression on a young boy. Today, knowing some biology, I might speculate that cow manure is toxic to mites, but I have not run the experiment again. I have not applied cow manure to a dog with mange to this day, nor do I expect I ever will.

Vallejo seemed to have a cure for many maladies or minor injuries, not only for the dogs but for us children as well. He treated our illnesses using materials at hand. Once, while I was making an arrow from a shingle, the large knife slipped, cutting me deeply near the base of my left forefinger. It bled profusely. I wrapped a handkerchief around the cut and went looking for Vallejo.

When Vallejo saw my cut, he shook his head and then led me to the washhouse. He reached up to the roof beams, gathered some spider webs, and applied a liberal dose of them to my cut. They looked dirty, but I didn't say a word. Then he made me elevate my arm while he lightly squeezed my wrist.

After applying more cobwebs, Vallejo said he was going to pour monkey blood (iodine) on the cut and bandage it. He said I was fortunate my finger was not cut off because he wasn't very good at sewing them back on.

Looking back, I know I should have gone to the doctor and received several stitches to close the wound. That would have been followed by a tetanus shot and then an antiseptic and bandages. It is a miracle I did not have a severe infection from the dirty cobwebs. I suspect, though, there was some rationale for the use of cobwebs on the wound. They formed a structure upon which the blood could clot. By having me raise my arm to slow the bleeding, Vallejo was simply applying principles of physics and anatomy. The cut left quite a pronounced scar on my finger. On days when I notice it, I think of Vallejo and how he cared for us.

In his later years on the ranch, Vallejo had a reputation as a good *curandero*. In the late 1920s, 1930s, and early 1940s, many small communities and ranches had at least one *curandero* or *curandera*. These were men and women who worked with natural plant materials to cure the ills of people or to relieve pain. Vallejo had a remedy for almost any illness. He grew in his front yard many of the medicinal plants and herbs he used. From the pastures or brush he gathered other vegetation he could use to treat various ills. When we rode together, he picked plants and weeds and carefully placed them in his saddlebags. Some, he said, were good for a toothache, and others were used to make tea to soothe a stomachache.

We had faith in Vallejo, and in later years many of the ranch hands stopped by his place to talk to him about their ills and take his advice as to which herb or plant to use to cure the problem.

Vallejo had his hands full trying to contain Dick and me and seeing to it we were not injured in our escapades. One morning, Dick and I, then about nine and eleven years old, decided to clear out some snakes. Behind the storehouse, situated among a row of mulberry trees, were a number of long boards left over from a small construction job.

Snakes were common on the ranch, and we often saw them about the yard of our house. Rattlesnakes and coral snakes were of special concern because they were so poisonous. Mother and Vallejo repeatedly warned us to watch out for snakes. If we spotted a snake, we called Vallejo, who quickly killed it. None of us was bitten by a snake, but when our dogs went after snakes and were bitten the dog's face or leg would swell. They usually recovered, though. I suspect the dogs survived because they had developed some kind of immunity to snake venom. The dogs never learned, and although snakes often bit them, the dogs continued to attack the reptiles.

For our snake hunt we armed ourselves with hoes, and when one of us flipped over a board, the other stood ready to decapitate a snake if it was there. Under the next board Dick turned over, we saw a large rattlesnake. Both of us repeatedly hacked the snake with our hoe and cut its head off. Our reward was a set of rattlers.

As I started cutting off the rattlers with my pocketknife, Vallejo came around the corner of the storehouse, saw the dead snake, and two young boys obviously doing something they should not have been doing. He lectured us on the dangers of snake hunting, but Dick and I explained we were trying to kill snakes before they got into the house. We thought we were defending our home.

Patiently, Vallejo explained that snakes struck only to defend themselves. He told us we had invaded the den of the snake and that we were the trespassers, not the snake. Both Dick and I nodded. For a moment we felt badly about killing the snake, but soon the hurt passed and we forgot Vallejo's words. For us, snake hunting was recreation, and woe to any snake coming near Dick and me.

On the ranch, one often saw snakes hanging over the fences. As a child, I thought they were there because someone wanted to show they had killed a snake and how big it was. One day while on horseback, Vallejo, Dick, and I followed a fence line along a pasture. Vallejo quickly dismounted, telling us to stay on our horses and hold them tight. He said there was a big rattler in front of us on the path, and the horses would be spooked if we did not rein them tightly.

Vallejo carried a club when we were out on horseback. He quickly killed the snake with the club. After he had cut off the rattlers, he picked up the snake and hung it over the wire fence. When I asked him why he hung the snake on the fence, he told me if you did, it would rain in a week. In the dry Southwest a rain was always welcomed, so I decided if hanging the snake made it rain, it was worth taking time to toss a dead snake on a fence.

I don't remember if it rained in the next few days, but if Vallejo said it would, I'm sure it did.

Vallejo introduced Dick, Bobby, and me to what we considered a lucrative business. We sold the hides of coyotes, raccoons, and javelinas (wild peccary) we hunted and trapped. Vallejo taught us how to skin animals, taking care not to nick the hide. We nailed the hides, fur down, to the garage wall and let the sun do the rest. It was a sight to see so many hides nailed to a garage wall. After they dried, Vallejo rubbed salt into each hide to preserve it further.

When we had collected quite a few, Vallejo took the stack of hides to town and sold them for twenty-five cents a piece. Upon his return with the money, he called Dick, Bobby, and me together. There followed a precise accounting of how much he had received for each hide and how much in total. Then he divided the money three ways, giving each of us one-third. We always insisted Vallejo deserved some money, so the final split was four ways.

One day as we rode through one of the pastures, our dogs jumped a wildcat. We yelled at the dogs to make them stop fighting, but they paid no attention to us. They were focused on the wildcat. To our surprise, it did not turn and run but stood its ground. Soon the wildcat was dead. We dismounted to get a closer look. It was a sad sight to see such a beautiful animal killed.

Then we saw the reason why the wildcat had not run from the dogs. We spied a small den with four baby wildcats, their eyes barely open, under a large pile of mesquite brush. Vallejo collared the dogs with a rope and held them off. They were eager to get at the little wildcats.

We held the dogs, and Vallejo decided to take the wildcats home. All four kittens were soon in a sack. Vallejo was sure Dad would not like our bringing home four wildcats. When Dad came home, we ran out to tell him about the wildcat the dogs had killed. Dad told us he was glad we were able to get rid of some wildcats. He said they caused a lot of damage on a ranch, so he had no use for them. They were nothing but trouble.

Dad was astonished when we told him we had four little wildcats in a cage in the washhouse and that we wanted to raise them. He said it was out of the question, that wildcats couldn't be tamed and that they would not survive in a cage.

Dad went off to find Vallejo. He found him, and we saw them talking quietly, Vallejo nodding his head. The next morning the wildcats were gone, and we never found out what happened to them.

Vallejo was a source of common sense and guidance for me for many years. As we grew up on the ranch, he was with us almost daily. From the time I was nine, his knowledge and wisdom influenced me. Even as secretary of education, I sometimes thought back to Vallejo's lessons when I was pushing an educational program. Vallejo was always a part of our life, both at the ranch and in town.

All of us appreciated Vallejo, his fine work, and his attitude. As children, we developed affection for him and counted him as a close friend. We knew we could always go to him if we were in trouble or needed advice. Vallejo would calmly tell us what to do or how to solve the problem. He never got excited.

In 1940, Mother and Dad built a house in Kingsville so we could go to a better school. Dad continued to live on the ranch but was at our house in town almost every day. We, in turn, spent considerable time on the ranch, especially on weekends. When we moved to town, Vallejo continued working for Mother, cooking, helping about the house, and gardening. At the same time, he worked at our place on the ranch.

In later years, after I had gone to the army, completed college, married, and lived in the East, I expected to see Vallejo on trips to visit with Mother and Dad. If he were away when we arrived in Kingsville, I always asked about him.

Mother told me Vallejo still came by her place almost every day and was usually there all day, and she assured me he would be by because he was eager to see me, Peggy, and our children.

And so he would. Before the end of the first day of our visit to

Mother's house in town, Vallejo would show up. He would ask Peggy how she was and say how well she looked. Vallejo said he was certain I helped with our family because on the ranch I had worked hard and almost always did everything he asked me to do. He said our children were beautiful, and he knew they would bring the two of us happiness in the years ahead.

Vallejo usually told me that I, too, looked well, and Mother had told him of my work in the medical school. He reminded me of how he struggled some days to teach me the simplest thing, believing I didn't want to be taught, but he persisted. Vallejo said he thanked the Lord he had given him time to see me grow into manhood. Vallejo said I would go far in life, especially if I remembered what he tried to teach me as a small boy on the ranch.

After Dad's death in 1958, we had the painful job of closing the house on the ranch. Mother directed us. It was difficult and painful for me to empty the house because for thirty-two years I had considered it home. Although we had a house in Kingsville and later I lived in Richmond, Virginia, the house on the ranch was home. It was a reference point from which my life evolved, and I constantly looked back to it with great joy and some sorrow. To this day, the house on the ranch is still my home as much as my homes in Port Aransas, Texas, or Concord, Massachusetts, are now.

After Mother died in 1986, when Peggy and I were in Kingsville we usually stopped by the cemetery where Mother and Dad were buried. On one of our visits to my parents' graves, Peggy and I noticed a new gravesite adjacent to that of my parents. I walked over to the grave and read the tombstone. It was Julieta, Vallejo's wife, who was buried there. Then we noticed the stone next to her grave had Vallejo's name and date of birth. He's saved this grave for himself, I thought. I wondered about Vallejo and how he was doing, hoping his health was holding up.

Over the years, Peggy and I returned to Kingsville as much as our schedule allowed, which was not very often. For me, visiting Kingsville was a memory trip. As long as my Uncle Steve was alive and lived on the ranch, we visited with him and Aunt Putt, whom he had married after some years as a widower. When I told the guard at the gate that I was going to see my Uncle Steve and that I was a son of Don Lauro, they told me I was always welcome and to go ahead.

After Uncle Steve died, I found it much more difficult to go onto the ranch. A visitors' center was built, a fee was required, and the only way to go on the ranch was to take a tour. I was troubled that I had to pay to visit my home. Peggy and I settled on driving down the highway past our home. We could see it from the highway.

Over the years, all but a few of my relatives who lived in and around Kingsville had died. My academic career and my days in Washington had taken me far away. In the meantime, raising our family kept Peggy and me busy. Trips to Kingsville became infrequent, and as a consequence, I lost track of Vallejo.

Kingsville changed considerably over the years, especially the streets. Some were closed and others added. Eventually, two major highways bypassed the town. On one of our visits, in 1998, I missed a turn and became lost. Peggy and I continued on the road and it led to the east side of town. It was still the Hispanic area and still part of a barrio. As I drove, fussing to myself about being lost in my own town, I saw a man pass me on a three-wheeled cycle going in the opposite direction from us.

I was almost positive the cyclist was Vallejo. I turned the car around and overtook the man. Peggy and I got out and walked up to him. "Laurie!" he said.

We embraced. I saw tears in Vallejo's eyes. One eye was clear and brown, the other dimmed by a cataract. He was thin, his hair and his mustache gray, his face wrinkled, and he was slightly stooped. A large smile broke out on his face, not unlike the ones I remembered when he worked for us on the ranch. He was overjoyed to see us, and we, him.

Vallejo told me he had prayed to God that he would see me one more time before he died. He was almost ninety and running out of time.

We stood along the edge of the dusty road in the hot sun. Both of us knew there was much to say but little time to say it. He asked about Dickie, Bobby, Sarita, and Joe, and I told him of my siblings' lives and how my own family was doing. He said that he had lost Julieta four years earlier and that two of his sons were also dead. We lamented that the old-timers from the ranch were gone and that it had seen so many changes. Vallejo admitted that his health was failing, but he said he didn't let it worry him.

Vallejo seemed tranquil. He was prepared to accept what he knew would soon come. Peggy and I hugged him, and we parted. I did not ask Vallejo for his address nor did he ask for mine. Both of us sensed what the future would soon bring and we knew part of our life was rapidly closing. I did not see Vallejo again.

Later, on one of our visits to my parents' graves, Peggy and I saw that Vallejo had been buried next to his wife. I couldn't believe Vallejo was gone. I told Peggy I was disappointed that no one had informed me of Vallejo's death.

Vallejo's and Julieta's graves were adjacent to and at the foot of my parents' graves. All four had spent a lifetime together, and now they would be near each other in eternity. I said to Peggy that if we had known Vallejo had died, we would have traveled from anywhere in the country to be at his funeral. Vallejo was part of our family.

I thought that with his death, all connections to Vallejo and our friendship had come to a close, but I was wrong. There is one more story to write about Vallejo.

While gathering material for this memoir, I had called our good friend Stephen "Tio" Kleberg to arrange a visit to the ranch. I told him that I wanted to see Santa Cruz, where my grandfather was *caporal* and Mother was born, and to ride across the ranch and recall my days there. Unfortunately, Tio had to be out of town during our scheduled visit, but his wife Janell said she would be delighted to drive us around the ranch.

A few days later, Janell Kleberg called to say that she was looking forward to seeing us and that she had arranged for Beto Maldonado and his sister Alicia to be there the day of our visit. Beto would drive us around.

I was delighted. Beto and Alicia were the children of Librado Maldonado, whom I well remember. Librado was in charge of the dairy operation and the herd for many years, and he was considered one of the best showmen of dairy cattle in Texas. He also looked after some of the top American Quarter Horse stallions on the ranch. After a lifetime spent working on the ranch, in his last years he was responsible for showing Santa Gertrudis bulls and cows throughout the United States and in many foreign countries. He was a master at showing cattle and had great control of the animals as they moved into the show ring.

I thanked Janell and told her how much we looked forward to seeing her. We expected to arrive around nine in the morning, so I asked her to be sure and call the front gate and let the guard know we were coming to visit her.

At the entrance to the ranch is a guardhouse where security guards screen and direct visitors to the ranch. The morning of our visit to Janell Kleberg's home, Peggy and I drove up to the guardhouse a little before 9:00 A.M. A fine-looking young man stepped out. With great courtesy he greeted us and inquired as to our destination. I told him my name was Cavazos and that we had come to visit Janell Kleberg.

The young man asked if I knew my way around. I told him I did, and when I gave my full name, he was amazed and said his grandmother Julie had worked for my mother.

If Julieta was his grandmother, then his grandfather was Vallejo.

I told the guard that I had known his grandfather from the time I was a small boy and that he had taught me a great deal. I asked his name.

The guard introduced himself as Gilbert García and said that it was an honor to meet me. His grandparents had told him of their days at our home and about the Cavazos family. Gilbert said his grandfather thought the world of me and our family, and he was so proud when he read about me in the newspaper or saw me on television.

I told Gilbert it was amazing for us to meet in this manner and that I had great respect and affection for his grandfather.

After good-byes, Peggy and I drove on to our appointment with Janell Kleberg. I told Peggy that when Gilbert said he was Vallejo's grandson I almost got out of the car and hugged him.

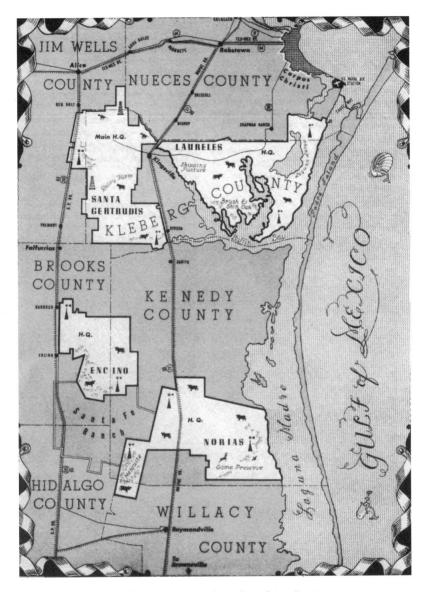

Map of the King Ranch and its four divisions:
the Encino, the Laureles, the Norias, and the Santa Gertrudis.

Reprinted with permission from *King Ranch: 100 Years of Ranching*,
copyright 2005 by the Caller-Times Publishing Company.
All rights reserved.

A baby picture of me on the King Ranch, 1929.

Left to right: My father with Jake Forrester and
Fausto Yturria at Punta del Monte Ranch, Texas, 1915.

My mother, Tomasa Quintanilla Cavazos, with my sister Sarita, me,
and my brother Richard (on Mother's lap), 1931.

My father, Lauro F. Cavazos Sr., in the U.S. Army, 1917.

King Ranch cow camp, early 1930s. *Left to right:* Lauro F. Cavazos Sr., E. E. D. White of Queensland, Australia, and Robert J. Kleberg Jr.

Photograph courtesy King Ranch Archives, King Ranch, Inc.

My father, Lauro F. Cavazos Sr., when he was foreman of
the Santa Gertrudis Division, early 1940s.

Photograph by Toni Frissell. Courtesy King Ranch, Inc.

My maternal grandfather, Francisco Quintanilla,
at Rancho Santa Cruz, King Ranch, about 1927.
Courtesy Cynthia Quintanilla.

My U.S. Army induction photo, 1944.

Maxcimilíano (Vallejo) García, 1956.

The two-room schoolhouse at the King Ranch,
where I attended from 1933 to 1935.

Photograph by Toni Frissell. Courtesy King Ranch, Inc.

CHAPTER 5

⌒ⅢⅢ⌒

The Road from Kingsville

Shortly after graduating from high school in 1944 I enlisted in the army, and I reported for duty as soon as I turned eighteen. In September 1946 I was put on terminal leave and honorably discharged at Fort Lewis, Washington. I was given one hundred dollars as discharge pay, a train ticket on a chair car to San Antonio, and a bus ticket to Kingsville. The second hundred-dollar increment of my discharge pay was to be sent within thirty days. Feeling rich, I boarded the train in Tacoma, Washington, and two days later I was in San Antonio. From there, I caught the bus to Alice, Texas.

As promised, Dad was waiting for me at the bus station. We shook hands; he welcomed me and told me how good it was to have me home again. He expressed his appreciation for my service to our country.

We drove the twenty-eight miles from Alice to Kingsville. As we entered the town and went past the Texas College of Arts and Industries (Texas A&I College, now Texas A&M University–Kingsville), Dad wanted to know my plans for the future. I replied that I had been giving my future a lot of thought. Reminding Dad that I was an ardent fishing enthusiast, I told him of my plan to seek work as a commercial fisherman on a boat out of Corpus Christi.

Dad glanced at me, turned his head back to the road, and said he wanted me to go to Texas A&I and enroll. He said new classes were starting the next week, and he went on to say that what I studied was up to me, but I was going to go to college.

I expected Dad's response. When we were children growing up on the ranch, I remember Dad saying time and time again that all of his children were going to go to college. We were in the depths of the depression, and as a family we had little money. Even as a youngster, I thought college attendance was not possible for me. I knew it required money we did not have, and I was not sure I qualified academically. Still, my parents continued to raise our expectations that we would go to college. My childhood on the ranch was before television, so we did not have that as a distraction. We could not afford a radio, but we did have books. Whenever Dad traveled to stock shows in Fort Worth or San Antonio, he returned with a box full of used books he had purchased. At least a couple of times a month Mother drove us to the library and we came home with an armload of books. Eventually, as Dad predicted, all five of his children went to college, and all of us received at least one degree.

So, having heard Dad's plans for our higher education for many years, his current insistence that I go to college and give up my fishing career did not surprise me. As far as he was concerned the discussion was ended. I had learned years before that when Dad made a decision, there was no use debating the issue. I replied, "Yes, sir," and so ended my fishing career. But as that dream ended, my academic career began.

TEXAS A&I COLLEGE

I enrolled at Texas A&I College and planned to major in journalism. For two years I had worked on the high school newspaper, the last year as editor. I thought I could write, so perhaps a job on a newspaper was a possibility. In addition, I wanted to write the great American novel. I was not sure what its topic would be, but I was convinced that I had at least one good book in me.

Having declared journalism as my major, I was told that for a bachelor of arts degree I needed a two-semester science course in biology, chemistry, or physics. I told the registrar that I would take biology to fulfill my science requirement. I didn't know it then, but it was one of the most important academic decisions I ever made.

As the first semester progressed, I enjoyed my journalism, English, and history courses, but the biology course was far better than I expected. It was one of the best courses of study I had every undertaken, and the professor, Dr. James C. Cross, was outstanding. Although a demanding teacher, he truly made the subject interesting. I did well in the course, and the following semester I signed up for another biology course under Dr. Cross. I read far beyond the course requirements, and if I had difficulty understanding some aspect of biology, I soon learned that I could go to Dr. Cross for an explanation. His office door was always open to students, and I took advantage of his generosity. He became my mentor.

One of my best friends from high school also enrolled at Texas A&I as a journalism major. D. Ashton Crossley, nicknamed "Dac" for his initials, was in many of my classes in high school, and both of us had worked on the school newspaper. He, too, selected biology to satisfy his science requirement, and we were laboratory partners and often studied together. Dac also found Dr. Cross to be an exceptional professor in the way he explained biology in his lectures and laboratories.

As the second semester came to a close, Dac and I discussed our interest in biology, and both of us decided we wanted to change our college major from journalism to biology. We went to talk to Dr. Cross about switching our majors. He was pleased we wanted to make a change but warned us we would never make much money, and a career in biology required graduate study. At age nineteen, neither Dac nor I considered making money a priority in our lives, and the thought of graduate school did not deter us. We were thrilled by the subject matter of biology and committed to excelling in it. For both of us, it was a change in major we never regretted.

TEXAS TECH AND IOWA STATE

The second year at Texas A&I continued to excite Dac and me as we took more advanced biology courses, and those courses affirmed our decision to major in biology. Late in the spring of our second year in college, Dr. Cross said he had accepted the chair of the Department of Biology at Texas Technological College in Lubbock. Dac and I were disappointed that Dr. Cross was going to leave Kingsville because we considered him one of the best teachers we had ever had. In addition, he was our advisor, and our friendship had grown over the last two years.

Dac and I talked the matter over and realized that Texas Tech might be as good for us as for Dr. Cross. We knew our grades were good enough to transfer.

We told Dr. Cross we planned to transfer to Texas Tech. He was flattered and pleased we elected to follow him to Lubbock. Dac and I visited the Texas Tech campus during the summer. It was impressive, and the Department of Biology had many more options for study than were available at Texas A&I. We went ahead and applied to transfer to Texas Tech. In addition to Dac and I, two other students majoring in biology, Matt García and Judson Marsters, also chose to transfer to Tech, giving further evidence of Dr. Cross's teaching ability.

I still had to tell Mother about my transfer to Texas Tech, knowing she would not be happy I was leaving home. I knew Dad would support my decision, though. After I had been accepted to Texas Tech, I told Mother. We were standing in the front yard of our house in Kingsville. Mother looked at me, clutched her hand to her chest, and with a pained expression said I had been gone for two years in the army now I was going away again. She asked if going to school there was worth being six hundred miles away from home. When I told her I believed it would truly help my education, she accepted my decision.

In the fall Dac and I enrolled at Texas Tech. For several years he was my roommate in one of the dormitories, and we took many classes together. After he finished two degrees at Tech, Dac went to the University of Kansas for further graduate study and received a Ph.D. degree. Dac became an academic and had a brilliant career as a university teacher and researcher. To this day, we remain in contact and our friendship grows.

I received my bachelor of arts degree in zoology from Texas Tech late in the summer of 1949 and started working on my master's degree in zoology. I received a graduate assistantship, so in addition to studying and doing research I taught a number of laboratory sections of biology. Just before the Christmas break in December 1950, I completed the work for the degree and received it *in absentia* in January 1951. Earlier that month, I had left Kingsville via train for Ames, Iowa, to start working on my doctoral degree.

I arrived in Ames on a bright, sunny day, but there was snow on the ground. I caught a bus to campus and asked the driver to drop me off near the Zoology Building.

My contact at Iowa State was John Porter, a graduate student who had been in the biology graduate program with me at Texas Tech. He had finished his master's degree a year before I did, and now he was on a research fellowship working for Dr. Robert M. Melampy, a distinguished physiologist nationally known for his research on reproduction and endocrinology. At Iowa State Porter finished his Ph.D. on the biochemistry of reproduction, and he eventually became a full professor and an outstanding researcher in the Department of Physiology at Southwestern Medical School in Dallas.

A few months before my arrival in Ames, Porter had visited Texas Tech and I had shown him some of my research slides. He was impressed with their quality. Porter told me that Melampy was looking for someone who could prepare excellent slides and knew histology. He was starting a new initiative on the male reproductive tract and had a couple of large grants for the projects. Melampy wanted someone to do the histochemical studies while Porter did the biochemical work. Porter asked if he could show my slides to Melampy. If he liked them, maybe he would offer me a place in his lab; if so, perhaps I could work on my Ph.D. with him.

On returning to Ames, Porter showed my slides to Melampy and also gave me a strong recommendation, telling the professor how knowledgeable I was in the histology of the male reproductive tract and how skillful I was at preparing microscopic slides. Melampy offered me a fellowship. I was delighted and accepted it by return mail. As a research fellow I would receive one hundred dollars per month, tuition waived. I knew I could live on the stipend. Since I was a veteran, the G.I.

Bill had paid me sixty-five dollars a month while I completed my baccalaureate degree. At Tech, I supplemented that money with a job in the
stock room of the biology department that paid twenty dollars per
month. The fellowship stipend provided enough funds for me to pay
room and board and expenses. I considered that stipend of a hundred
dollars from Iowa State a princely sum.

After the bus dropped me off in front of the Zoology Building, I entered and, with my one bag in hand, walked up to the fifth floor. I spotted a door labeled "Room 501" at the head of the stairs. Timidly, I
knocked, heard someone invite me in, and opened the door into a laboratory. To my relief, John Porter met me at the entrance. He had a big
smile on his face and extended his hand.

He welcomed me to Iowa State, inquired as to the quality of my
trip, and led me to a small office to introduce me to Dr. Melampy. We entered and I saw him sitting at a large rolltop desk piled with paper. The
desktop was not even visible. I was nervous and shy, because I knew
Melampy's reputation as one of the leading physiologists in the nation.
I hoped I had the academic background, intellect, and skill to be successful in his laboratory.

Porter told him who I was, and Melampy rose from his chair with
a smile on his face and welcomed me. He told me how pleased he was
I had decided to work in his laboratory. He recounted how outstanding my microscopic slides had been and told me I was just the person
he needed to make high-quality slides. Porter had told him I was a
hard worker, which pleased him, and he said he knew I would fit in fine
in his lab.

Melampy was about five feet, eight inches tall, and broad-
shouldered. A bit on the stocky side, he had piercing blue eyes and a
ruddy complexion, and his rather sparse dark hair was combed straight
back. His warm and friendly manner helped my unease, and I soon felt
comfortable.

Melampy asked me to take a seat so we could talk about the laboratory. He offered to have a desk for me by morning and said the next day
we needed to have discussions about a research program he had in
mind. Melampy then told me that there was a biological seminar in

thirty minutes and that I should attend. Porter was going, so he could show me where the seminar room was located. I responded that I, too, would attend the seminar.

Then Porter stepped into the discussion and told Melampy that I had just arrived after a long trip, my bag was in the lab, and I did not even have a place to sleep that night. Porter suggested that some living arrangements had to be made for me, and he asked Melampy if he really thought it was necessary for me to go to a seminar an hour after my arrival on campus.

Melampy thought about what Porter had said and told him he was right; no need to go to the seminar. Melampy said he was just trying to start my education as soon as possible. He agreed we needed to find me a room for the night.

Porter reminded Melampy it was getting late and said finding a room that afternoon would be difficult. He said he was going to invite me to stay in his room for the night; I could curl up on his small sofa. The next morning we would come to work, and in the afternoon we would find a place for me to stay.

So began my graduate career at Iowa State and my friendship with Melampy. The pace Melampy set the first day I arrived in Ames continued unabated for the three and one-half years we worked together. Melampy understood my education goals, appreciated my technical skills in the laboratory, and was patient with me when research plans did not work out.

I spent almost every waking hour in Dr. Melampy's laboratory. I devoted countless hours to studying slides I prepared from tissues of the animals in our experiments. Each day Melampy and I reviewed my findings, analyzed the results, and worked on writing scientific papers for publication.

Rarely was there a day off from laboratory work and study. I was in the laboratory seven days a week, usually arriving by 7:30 A.M. Frequently I left about midnight. The only exception to the schedule was Sunday, when I attended mass at the Catholic student center across the street from the university. Melampy kept much the same work schedule I did. If he left before midnight, often his parting words to me were to leave something for the hereafter. By the time I graduated, I had eight scientific publications on the biology of reproduction.

As a graduate student, I never ceased to be amazed at the commitment Melampy had to research. He was demanding of himself and had high expectations of my abilities and of me. Almost each day, after we reviewed our research results, we planned the next series of experiments. Once we came to closure on the protocol for the next experiment, Melampy turned the effort over to me. He expected me to order animals, do the surgical interventions required, carry out the hormone therapy as needed, sacrifice the animals, prepare the slides for microscopic study, and interpret the results.

Melampy taught a number of graduate physiology courses at Iowa State. I enrolled in his courses, and subsequently he asked me to do all of the animal preparations for his graduate courses because I had a fair knowledge of anatomy and had far more surgical ability than he did; my hands were much steadier than his. With a smile he assured me that when I was as old as he was, I, too, would lose some of my steadiness of hand.

Melampy was constantly thinking about my education. He arranged for me to take canine anatomy at the Iowa State University School of Veterinary Medicine. One day he told me he thought I should go to the University of Michigan Medical School and take their summer course in human gross anatomy. Taken by surprise, I asked why I needed a course in human anatomy at the medical school level.

Melampy told me he believed that in order to be a successful physiologist one had to have a thorough knowledge of human anatomy. He found it troubling that so many graduate students in physiology, although well versed in biochemistry, did not know anatomy. As a result, they sometimes had trouble understanding some physiological phenomena. Michigan taught a summer anatomy course for medical students from throughout the county who had failed anatomy in their first year. If they took the Michigan course and passed it, then they could continue in medical school. Melampy believed he could have me admitted into the anatomy course even though I was not a medical student.

I told Melampy I would take the anatomy course if he thought that would be good for me. I knew it would be difficult because I would be in a class with medical students who had already had the course once, and I had not had a rigorous course in human anatomy.

Melampy assured me I would do fine, so we agreed I would spend the summer in Ann Arbor taking human gross anatomy. In retrospect, Melampy's advice to take the course eventually changed the discipline I would teach for the rest of my academic career. I became enthralled with all of the disciplines of anatomy, so when I finished graduate school I did not look for a job teaching physiology but applied only to medical schools to teach anatomy.

After I had completed the human anatomy course, Melampy had even higher expectations. He wanted me to do the surgery on the animals in our experiments. Melampy and I developed the experimental hypotheses and planned the experiments, and then it was up to me to move the study along.

At the beginning of my third year of graduate study at Iowa State, there was an incident that gave me further insight into Melampy's commitment to research. The two of us kept up our busy work schedule of seven days a week in the laboratory. One day, however, he came into the laboratory and told me he had to go to the hospital in Ames for some workups because he had not been feeling well. He would not be back in the laboratory until after his hospital checkup, and he did not know how long that would be. Melampy assured me that he had every confidence I would keep the work going in the lab.

A couple of days later, I got a call from Dr. Melampy's wife, Carolyn, telling me he was going to have surgery the next day. She had seen him in the morning, and he wanted me to come by the hospital late in the afternoon or the evening. I was to bring pen and paper.

I ate dinner at the student union on campus, caught a bus, and got off in downtown Ames, not far from the hospital. I found Melampy's room, knocked, and went in. I could tell he was under sedation in preparation for surgery the next morning, but he was pleased I could stop by and asked me to pull up a chair. Melampy told me we needed to talk about a new set of experiments he had been thinking about during his time in the hospital. He wanted me to start on the study while he was out of the lab, and if I did, then there would not be too much lost time when he returned.

I tried to persuade Melampy to quit thinking about experiments and the laboratory, and I assured him I would keep the work going. I emphasized that the most important matter was for him to get well, but I knew he was not paying attention to me; he was thinking about experiments.

As we spoke, the sedation was really starting to take effect. Melampy was becoming groggy, and his words were somewhat slurred. He told me he was fine, we had to keep the work going, not to worry about him, and he would be back soon. Then Melampy told me to pay attention because he was going to tell me about a new experiment I was to start as soon as possible.

The two of us must have been quite a sight. On the eve of my professor's surgery, we were planning an experiment. We debated how many rats we would need and what surgical interventions we needed to do. As was usually the case when experiments were the topic, Melampy soon dominated the conversation, and I became the note-taker. He dictated the research protocol, or the process and procedure for the experiment. I wrote as fast as I could. I kept interrupting him, asking for clarifications and suggesting other approaches to the experiment, and he would nod or shake his head. Finally, he said I knew what to do and that he knew I would do it well. He thanked me for coming by, but he said he was having trouble keeping awake. He promised to call me after he came out of surgery.

I walked out of the hospital and stood by the bus stop. I thought to myself that I had just seen the epitome of dedication to research by one individual. Here this man was going into surgery in the morning and he was thinking about the next experiment. My bus came; I boarded and returned to the campus and the laboratory. It was late, and I was alone. I kept thinking about Melampy and his commitment to research. I worked for several more hours into the night as I refined Melampy's research protocol.

Melampy did well after his surgery. Within three weeks after he left the hospital, he was back in the laboratory, though only part-time. Not long after that, he was again working his extended schedule as if he had never been in the hospital. He never told me why he had to have surgery, and I never asked. I knew that if he wanted to discuss it with me, he would.

One day Melampy told me that I needed a break from my research efforts. He insisted that I had been working too long and hard and suggested I take three days off. I told Melampy I was fine, that I didn't know what I would do with three days off. My schedule was full of microscopic slide preparation, analysis, and writing.

Melampy persisted, saying that he knew better than I when I needed a break. He suggested that I take the train to Chicago and then go to a show, the opera, or a play and visit some of the great museums. He wanted me to relax and get my mind off of work.

Finally, I agreed. I had never been to Chicago nor had I ever seen an opera. I looked forward to the museum visits. Then I found out Melampy's true reason for ordering me to go to Chicago. He told me that inasmuch as I would be in Chicago, there were several people with whom I should visit. Melampy told me to take some of my slides and spend some time discussing my research with Professors Carl Moore and Dorothy Price, eminent scientists in the Department of Zoology at the University of Chicago. Then he suggested that I also go to Northwestern University's medical school and show Dr. Harold Davenport my slides, which I had made using a staining method he had developed. Almost as a concession he reminded me to be sure to go to the museums and a show or two.

My trip to Chicago was a success. I stayed in a cheap hotel on the Chicago Loop and found time between academic assignments to see a show and go to the matinee of the first opera I had ever attended. Melampy never ceased in his efforts to educate me.

The graduation ceremony at Iowa State is a formal occasion with considerable pomp. Each person receiving a doctoral degree walks across the stage accompanied by his or her major professor and is given a diploma and then hooded by the university president and the graduate's major professor.

A few weeks before my graduation from Iowa State in 1954, Melampy told me he had a schedule conflict and was not going to be able to be with me at graduation.

I told Melampy I was disappointed. Then he said that he had asked a good friend, J. Lawrence Lush, to take his place and hood me at graduation.

Some thirty years earlier Dr. Lush had been one of the scientists that the King Ranch had consulted about developing a new breed of cattle suited to South Texas conditions, and he had been skeptical of the project. By the early 1950s, Lush, still on the faculty at Iowa State, had gained a reputation as one of the leading animal geneticists in the world. He received many honors for his fine scientific work and was elected to the prestigious National Academy of Science. In 1954, in recognition of his work in bovine genetics, Pres. Dwight D. Eisenhower presented him with the President's Medal of Science.

I had met Lush during my time at Iowa State, and he had spoken highly of Dad, saying how much he had enjoyed working with him on the cattle-breeding program at the King Ranch. Melampy knew my parents were coming for graduation, so his asking Lush to represent him would also provide an opportunity for Dad and Lush to get together after many years.

I told Melampy that if he could not be at graduation, then the next best thing was for Lush to walk across the stage with me. I was certain that he and Dad would have a grand visit and spend a lot of time talking about cattle.

After reviewing the graduation details, Melampy asked me to maintain the experiments in the lab until I left Ames. I assured him that I would keep up with the lab work while he was gone and see to it that the rats were injected each day.

On ranches, there is also work to be done each day, so the idea of a two-week vacation never entered a rancher's mind. Dad, however, made time to attend special events in the lives of his children, and he and Mother never missed a high school or college graduation. On one of my visits to Kingsville, I gave Dad and Mother the date of my graduation.

Dad was very pleased about my upcoming graduation and assured me that he and Mother would attend. They also planned to bring my youngest brother, Joe, with them. Dad was driving to Ames because getting Mother on an airplane was impossible.

I told Dad it was a long drive from South Texas to Ames, and although I greatly appreciated their wanting to come up, it wasn't necessary. I explained to Dad that the whole graduation process took only a few seconds, but he assured me that those were important seconds to Mother and him. He said he had waited a lifetime for those seconds, so there was no need to argue. They would be at my graduation.

When I learned that Mother and Dad would be at graduation, I invited Peggy Ann Murdock, a close friend of mine for many years. She agreed to come to Ames, and I suggested she ride up with my family. Peggy was able to get only a few days off from the hospital in Lubbock where she was working, so she decided to fly.

Peggy and I had known each other since 1948, when I enrolled at Texas Tech. When I met her, she was a first-year student and I was classified as a third-year student. From the first meeting, Peggy and I became close friends and saw a lot of each other. She was a convert to the Catholic Church, and we attended mass at nearby Saint Elizabeth's Church. The year before my graduation from Iowa State, she had earned a bachelor of science degree in nursing from Incarnate Word College.

Before my family and Peggy arrived, I stopped by to see Lush. I told him I was honored that he would participate in my graduation and he assured me that he was pleased to help out. He also reminded me of his great respect for Dad and his fine work on the King Ranch. Knowing Mother and Dad were coming up for graduation, Lush asked for two favors from me. First, he wanted me to find out if Dad was willing to talk to his advanced animal genetics class. Lush said he had fifteen graduate students who could learn a lot by listening to Dad talk about cattle breeding. If Dad agreed, he could talk to the students the morning of graduation day. Then Lush told me that he would also like Dad to go out to one of the research farms with him to see the cattle and give his opinion on the work Lush was carrying out. He also invited me, my family, and my guest to join Mrs. Lush and him for lunch on graduation day. I told Lush I was certain Dad would be pleased to talk to his students, and I accepted the lunch invitation.

Two days before my graduation Dad, Mother, and Joe arrived in Ames. I had booked rooms for them at a nearby motel. The next day I borrowed Dad's car and drove to the Des Moines airport to pick up Peggy. When we returned we spent the day touring the beautiful Iowa State campus and I showed them where my laboratory was located.

The evening before my graduation, my family, Peggy, and I had dinner downtown. After dinner, I drove them to their motel, and I asked Peggy to go on campus with me and help me inject some rats I had in an experiment. I told her that as a nurse, she should be an expert with needles and injections. Peggy laughed and assured me she had never had a rat for a patient, but she agreed to help out.

We drove to the campus, and I parked near Curtis Hall. The year before, Melampy had moved his lab from the Zoology Building to Curtis Hall. The move gave us much more space than our old quarters. Peggy and I arrived at the laboratory and had it all to ourselves; no other students were working late. I explained to Peggy that each rat was to be injected with testosterone, the male sex hormone. I filled the first syringe to the exact amount of hormone, handed it to her, and then reached into the cage and grasped a large white rat. I held it and told her where to inject the animal. She followed my instructions, and quickly we finished with all of the animals. After we cleaned up, I invited Peggy to see the beautiful campanile on the Central Green.

We left the laboratory and walked to the campanile. It is a magnificent structure dominating the central campus at Iowa State. We sat on the bench under the campanile and talked about many things, including our hopes and expectations. I told Peggy there was something I had to ask. I said we had known each other for about six years, and lately I had been thinking about the future. I asked her to marry me; I wanted our futures to be the same.

Peggy's sharp intake of breath told me I had taken her totally by surprise. Peggy said a proposal was the last thing she expected from me,

but she did not have to give my proposal much thought on the spot because she had already given the idea a lot of thought long before I asked.
Her answer was "Yes."

I told Peggy I would always love her and that we would work together to raise a fine family. I promised I'd work hard and be a good husband and father. Peggy said she knew I would be a great husband and
she would always love me too. Then she said she wanted to be up front
with me from the start. Peggy told me she wanted ten children and then
added that she hoped I wouldn't take back my proposal. I told Peggy ten
children sounded grand, and then I told her I was interested in a job in
the Department of Anatomy at the Medical College of Virginia
(MCV). It was an excellent department and one in which I thought I
could grow professionally. I told Peggy the chairman had said he would
hire me to start in the fall if I took the neuroanatomy course at the University of Michigan medical school the coming summer. He wanted me
to be able to teach any of the anatomy courses they offered. I told Peggy
I could teach them all, except neuroanatomy, which I had never taken.

Peggy encouraged me to go to Ann Arbor and learn neuroanatomy.
My real reason for mentioning the course at that moment, though,
wasn't about the future but about my current financial situation. I had
estimated that tuition and living expenses for the summer would be
about four hundred dollars, which I had managed to save. What I didn't
have was the money to buy her an engagement ring. I told Peggy I was
sorry I did not have a ring to put on her finger. She told me to quit worrying about engagement rings, that it was more important I go to Michigan. She said she was certain she would get the engagement ring later.

But Peggy never got her engagement ring. For years we talked about
one, but as our family grew to ten children, there were other priorities.
Later I learned to facet gemstones, and I gave Peggy many rings. I called
them "homemade," but Peggy insisted she preferred them to rings purchased in a jewelry store. Finally, forty-eight years after our marriage,
Peggy and I gave each other "store-bought" rings to celebrate the anniversary, but they were not engagement rings.

In 2004, I was asked to give the summer commencement address at
Iowa State University. The morning before the graduation, Peggy and I

delighted in walking about the beautiful Iowa State campus. Naturally, we went to the campanile and were pleased to see that the bench where we sat when I proposed to Peggy was still there. I told her I had just thought of my opening remarks to the graduating class.

When I stood before the graduates I told them the story of my proposal under the campanile. I didn't mention injecting the rats. I told the graduates that almost fifty years before, when I proposed to Peggy, I had promised I would give her an engagement ring as soon as I could afford one. Then I said that fifty years later, Peggy still had not received her ring but that she still expected to receive one, and I still expected to give her one. I told the graduates they too should lead lives of great expectations.

The day of my own graduation in 1954, Dad talked to Lush's animal genetics graduate class. Because of his international reputation as a scientist, Lush had students from many countries in addition to those from the United States. Dad described the work they had done on the King Ranch and their efforts to develop the first recognized pure strain of cattle in the United States. He emphasized their successes and discussed their failures and mistakes. Dad described the crossbreeding program that produced the sire bull, Monkey, and the eventual development of the Santa Gertrudis breed. Dad responded to the students' many questions, and he thoroughly enjoyed his two hours in front of the class.

Afterward Dad told me how bright the students were; they had asked tough questions and had some good ideas and comments. Dad said he was just an old cowboy, with barely a high school education and no college, teaching graduate students from all over the world. It had been a treat for him to teach the students.

I told Dad I was sure the students learned a lot because he was a natural teacher, and the students would remember his discussion in the years ahead, applying some of the principles of animal breeding he described. I then asked Dad about the cattle Lush had wanted him to see. Lush had shown him a small herd of Angus bull calves because he was working on ways to identify cattle carrying the dwarf gene. Dwarfism in Angus cattle could be a major problem if it gets into a herd, resulting in diminished beef production. Dad said it was a tough problem to solve, but Lush was going after it in a way that surprised him. He x-rayed the calves and took numerous measurements using a variety of calipers. Lush and his group performed many calculations and sought consistency in predicting which animals carried the dwarf gene. Lush's group thought they had identified some of the dwarf gene cattle. They asked Dad what he thought of their work.

Dad told them they were doing important work and that he hoped some day their results would cut down on the dwarf problem. He told me he looked over the herd and pointed to one bull calf and told them he would bet that it carried the dwarf trait. Dad added that he identified two other calves in the pens he was pretty sure were dwarf carriers. Lush and the students were amazed by his comments because their studies with x-rays and measurements indicated that the animals he had pointed to were indeed dwarf gene carriers. Confirmation of their studies had to await calf production. Lush wanted to know what Dad had seen in the bull calves to suggest that they were dwarf gene carriers; he made it clear that it was incredible Dad could walk up to a set of pens and simply point to the same calves it had taken so much measuring and calculating for them to identify.

Dad told them that years of judging lots of cattle gave you a good eye. He looked at the confirmation of the calf, including the slope of the rump, the head, and the rise of the shoulders. Dad insisted it was tough to explain how he knew which animals were dwarf gene carriers; what he was describing did not make sense to a scientist.

My graduation took place on a beautiful spring evening in Ames. The campus sparkled with lights. After it was over I saw the pride in my parents' eyes. To them, it was wondrous their son was receiving a doctorate from one of the leading universities in the nation. Of course, I was happy I had finished my Ph.D., and I felt prepared to begin my professional career as a scientist and teacher. But most of all, I was thrilled Peggy had accepted my proposal of marriage.

Just as I found my family and Peggy after the graduation ceremony ended, a grand thunderstorm rolled across the campus, and we ran for cover as the rain started. I thought about the summer evening I had re-

ceived my baccalaureate degree from Tech. The commencement ceremony was supposed to be outdoors, but just as it was about to start, a
West Texas thunderstorm broke over the campus and we were ordered
to run to the gym. After we reorganized, the ceremonies started. I don't
remember the commencement speaker's message. I do remember the
opening remarks. He said that when one plants seeds, one always hopes
there is plentiful rain to water the new crop. Then he said that with all
the rain falling, he knew this was going to be a fine crop of people they
were graduating.

I'm convinced the rains at my Tech and Iowa State commencements
were a blessing.

CHAPTER 6

꒰ᴍᴍ꒱

A Companion for the Road

In late June 1954, a week after graduation, I left Ames for Ann Arbor to enroll in the neuroanatomy course at the University of Michigan Medical School. The course was of the highest quality, and by the end of the summer I felt confident I was qualified to teach all of the disciplines of anatomy.

I accepted a job at the Medical College of Virginia and arrived in Richmond in late August 1954. Starting at the bottom of the academic ladder as an instructor, I promised myself some day I would reach the pinnacle and be a full professor. I focused on excelling in teaching and research. The faculty and staff in the Department of Anatomy welcomed me and assisted in my transition from graduate student to faculty member. I felt fortunate I had joined the faculty there.

The Medical College of Virginia prided itself in having been the only medical school in the Confederate South to stay open during the entire Civil War. The building housing the Department of Anatomy was named McGuire Hall after the Confederate surgeon who amputated Gen. Thomas J. (Stonewall) Jackson's arm after he was wounded at the battle of Chancellorsville. Directly across the street from McGuire Hall stood the "White House of the Confederacy," the home of Pres. Jefferson Davis.

The chair of the department, Dr. Erling S. Hegre, became my friend and mentor. Day after day we worked together, and some days we spent hours discussing fine points of human gross anatomy or embryology. He provided laboratory space, and I quickly obtained funding from the National Institutes of Health for my research program.

In December 1954, as the first semester ended at the Medical College of Virginia, I left Richmond for Kingsville and then drove with Mother and Dad to Lubbock. Peggy and I were married at Saint Elizabeth's Catholic Church on December 28. It was a beautiful wedding, although it snowed six inches the night before the ceremony and was still snowing the next morning.

I was pleased to see that Peggy's mother, Gertrude Hunsucker, and Peggy's three sisters were there for the wedding. Peggy's father, Jesse L. Murdock, had divorced her mother when the children were in grade school or high school. Since the divorce, Peggy's father had remarried twice, and both of those marriages ended in divorce. After our marriage, Peggy and her mother stayed in touch but only briefly visited each other. As the years went by I thought how unfortunate it was that Gertrude Hunsucker barely knew the grandchildren we had given her.

My brother Dick was my best man at the wedding. Upon graduation from Texas Tech, Dick had accepted a regular army commission as a second lieutenant. When he completed basic training, he went on to finish Ranger School and qualify as a paratrooper. Soon he was on the front lines as an infantry officer in Korea. Dick, recently returned from the war in Korea, had been highly decorated, earning the Distinguished Service Cross, the second highest military medal for bravery in action, and a Purple Heart, for wounds received in combat. Years later he received a second Distinguished Service Cross in Viet Nam. Dick had decided to make the army his career and was now a captain. At the wedding rehearsal, the priest who would marry Peggy and me emphasized to Dick that it was important he close the door to the vestry as we entered the sanctuary for the nuptials.

At the beginning of the ceremony, when the priest motioned from the altar for Dick and me to enter the sanctuary, Dick turned to me and said that when paratroopers jumped from a plane, the jumpmaster would tell them to stand up, hook up, and shuffle to the door. Then he would shout for the last man out to close the door. Dick looked at me and said that this was it: time to stand up, hook up, and shuffle, and then he would close the door. He wished me luck.

The traditional wedding march began, and all of us turned to see Peggy walking down the aisle. I thought to myself that she was the most beautiful bride I had ever seen. Afterward, I told Peggy what I had been thinking as she walked down the aisle, but she never believed me. To this day, I continue to insist she was the most beautiful bride I have ever seen, and to this day she still doesn't believe me.

My one major disappointment was that Peggy's father was not there to give her away. Peggy had told me about her father's reaction to our marriage plans; he was strongly opposed and could not believe she was going to marry a "Mexican." Her father told her she was making a big mistake and predicted the marriage was not going to last. (Peggy and I recently celebrated our fiftieth wedding anniversary.) Peggy's father believed I would be a terrible husband and had absolutely no future.

Peggy told her father that she did not see me as a "Mexican" but as the man she loved. In reply he told her that if she married me, he would disown her. Disregarding her father's reaction and the possibility of being cast out of the Murdock family, Peggy talked to her only brother about giving her away on her wedding day, but it was to no avail. Her father had already persuaded her brother, Jesse L. Murdock Jr., not to participate in the wedding.

When Peggy told me about her father's reaction to our marriage, I told her not to worry about it, to forget it. I knew what he thought about "Mexicans." Having put up with racism most of my life, I was certain his deep-seated prejudices toward and dislike of Hispanics were not going to change. I felt sorry for him that he would let his bias stand in the way of being at his daughter's wedding. I promised Peggy we were going to be happy and have a fine family. A good friend of ours, Lubbock businessman N. K. Parrish, offered to walk down the aisle with Peggy to give her away.

We never reconciled with her father, and he never accepted our marriage. Peggy's father did attend my inauguration as president of Texas Tech University, but he hardly spoke a word to me and did not congratulate me on my appointment. Jesse Murdock could not admit he had been wrong in his opposition to my marriage to Peggy.

Soon after his third divorce, he moved to a small farm in New Mexico and his son, Jesse Jr., went with him. On one occasion, soon after I became president of Texas Tech, we had a brief visit with Peggy's father and brother. Their mobile home was cluttered and falling into disrepair. The visit was painful, and Peggy and I were relieved when we left the farm, never to return for a visit.

Jesse L. Murdock never showed any interest in his ten grandchildren and did not know them. He lived to be ninety-nine years old, and when we attended his funeral in a country cemetery in East Texas, I could not help but think how much happiness he missed by not knowing our children, his grandchildren, all because of an unyielding prejudice toward "Mexicans."

I think back on the day Peggy's father told her of his opposition to our marriage because of my Hispanic heritage. Her decision to go ahead and marry me despite objections from her father was a sign of her love and commitment to me. The wedding was beautiful, with much joy and happiness. After a brief reception, Peggy and I left in a snowstorm and headed for Richmond to start our life together. The storm continued, and with the snowing piling up I could hardly see the road.

I said to Peggy I had promised to take her away from Lubbock on our wedding day, but I suggested we stop at a motel. We were barely out of the city limits, but the storm was not letting up. In fact, it seemed to be getting worse. Peggy agreed.

The next morning, the sun shone brightly, and the new-fallen snow glistened on the West Texas landscape. As we got into the car I told Peggy we were finally on our way to Richmond. With a long road ahead I estimated it would take about four days to reach Richmond.

Peggy asked the route to Richmond. I told her our drive would be as straight as possible. From Lubbock, we would go to Dallas, on to Shreveport, across the Mississippi at Vicksburg, then on to Birmingham, Alabama. I estimated we would be in Atlanta on New Year's Day. From there, we would go up to Charlotte, North Carolina, and on into

Petersburg, Virginia, and finally, Richmond. I told her the roads weren't bad, and I only hoped the weather would hold.

In 1954, the interstate highway system had not been completed. Only a small part of our trip was on four-lane roads; the rest were two lanes and narrow, so our progress was slow. It took us five days to drive from West Texas to Richmond.

On New Year's Day, 1955, Peggy and I drove down Peachtree Street in Atlanta. This was long before there were bypass highways around cities. In those days, the major highway through Atlanta went right down Peachtree, the main street of downtown Atlanta.

Peggy suggested we eat lunch in Atlanta and asked me to find a place serving hog jowls and black-eyed peas. When I questioned the lunch selection, she told me she was surprised I didn't know that if you had them on New Year's Day, you would have good luck all year. Peggy spotted a cafeteria and asked me to pull in for lunch.

I agreed but doubted there would be hog jowls and black-eyed peas on the menu. I told Peggy I was not superstitious, but why take chances? Besides, we were starting our married life, and if the menu enhanced our good luck, I was all for it.

We walked in and Peggy was pleased that hog jowls and black-eyed peas were the featured special. She told me she would get some and suggested I do the same. I declined and told her I would have a steak, but I'd try two or three peas and a bite of hog jowl from her plate, just sufficient for me to have good luck all year.

Peggy's idea must have worked. We had a grand first year of marriage, and since then black-eyed peas and hog jowls have been on our menu every New Year's Day.

Our first home in Richmond was on the third floor of an apartment building. It did not have an elevator, but it had a grand view of Byrd Park. The rent of sixty-five dollars a month got us a bedroom, a living room, a dining-study area, a bathroom, and a kitchen. Each of those rooms was quite small.

Peggy thoroughly cleaned and decorated our apartment. When she finished, she announced it was time to look for a job as a nurse in one of the Richmond hospitals.

Two weeks later she was interviewed and offered a job as a nurse at Pine Camp, a tubercular hospital. My concern about Peggy working at Pine Camp was heightened in August 1955, when we learned she was pregnant. I was worried about her workplace exposure to x-rays and fluoroscopy. When Peggy had her initial obstetrical examination with Dr. Henry Bullock Jr., he told her to our relief that there was no problem with her working at Pine Camp. He said that the baby was due in late March.

In January 1956, with the due date for the baby approaching, Peggy and I decided to move to a two-bedroom house with a yard. We soon rented one and moved in, and Peggy told me she planned to quit working at Pine Camp Hospital about mid-March.

The day before our first child was born started as usual. I had to teach an early morning gross anatomy class for medical students, so I drove Peggy to the Pine Camp Hospital before 7:00 A.M. As she got out of the car, she said she would be through by 3:00 in the afternoon and would take the bus home. I told her I might be home a little late in the afternoon, about 6:00 P.M. I explained to Peggy that after dinner, I needed to go back to the medical school to teach the anatomy course for surgical residents. I taught them two evenings a month. In this class the residents dissected cadavers, and then I reviewed their dissections and we discussed the anatomical relationships important to the area.

When I arrived home from my work at MCV late that afternoon, I found Peggy cleaning house and baking a pecan pie. I asked what she thought she was doing, and she assured me that she felt fine and had felt only a few minor contractions. She did not consider them significant.

After dinner that evening, I returned to the medical school to teach the anatomy course to the surgical residents. I was delighted I had this opportunity to run the course because it added to my teaching credentials. In addition, I earned twenty dollars per session, which was a welcome supplement to the forty-eight hundred dollars I earned per year as an instructor in anatomy.

The anatomy class lasted until 10:00 P.M. and I hurried home. When I walked in, I found Peggy sitting in bed, and her face showed she was in pain. I asked if she was in labor, but she told me she wasn't sure.

Then, after a few more regular contractions Peggy asked me to call Dr. Bullock. I was relieved when I was able to reach the obstetrician by telephone at the Medical College of Virginia Hospital. I told him the labor pains were five minutes apart, and he said I'd best get Peggy into the emergency room right away. He would wait for us there.

It was about 11:30 P.M. as I bundled Peggy into our car. I pulled out of our drive in a hurry and was soon moving down Broad Street. I was exceeding the speed limit, and I kept hoping the police would stop us. If they did, perhaps I could talk them into leading me to the hospital with sirens blaring and lights blazing. As I moved along, I mentally reviewed what I would have to do if I had to deliver the baby in the car.

We arrived at the emergency entrance of the Medical College of Virginia Hospital, and Dr. Bullock was waiting for us. Less than an hour after we reached the hospital, our first son was born at 12:37 A.M., March 10, 1956. I told Peggy it was a handsome son and asked if she was doing all right.

She assured me she and the baby were fine. Peggy had decided on a name for our son. She said he would be named Lauro F. Cavazos III, after the two most favored men in her life—my father and I.

In late 1957, my sister Sarita telephoned to tell me that Dad was ill and in the hospital in Kingsville. For several years he had suffered from diabetes, but the hospitalization was because of liver problems and the diagnosis was cirrhosis of the liver. This condition is usually associated with alcohol abuse. Although Dad drank alcohol, I never saw him intoxicated or drinking too much. Cirrhosis can be caused by other factors, such as viruses, genetic diseases, or a nutritional deficit. For many years after we moved into town to be near the schools, Dad lived alone on the ranch. He stopped by the house almost daily but rarely had meals there. I suspect his diet left much to be desired. I never learned the cause of his cirrhosis, nor did I care. He was ill, and I was deeply concerned. It was a shock to Peggy and me. Dad had always seemed indestructible, and now he was hospitalized. I had always thought that if he were hospitalized it would have been for injuries related to working cattle from horseback. I knew him as a vigorous and disciplined man. We decided to leave the next day for Kingsville.

By the time we arrived in Kingsville just days before Christmas, Dad was out of the hospital. He was not at our home in Kingsville when we arrived, but Mother felt he was making some progress. She was so glad we were there. It gave her a chance to see our family, which now included two beautiful babies, but Mother was very worried about Dad. She hoped Peggy and I could reason with him because he was a terrible patient, so difficult to manage, and he would not stay in the hospital one minute more than he had to. Mother said he fussed at the doctors for not letting him out sooner and kept the nurses on the run. He hated the hospital food, and he even arranged for one of the cooks from the cow camp to bring him his meals.

Shortly after we arrived, Vallejo drove Dad from the ranch to the house in town. He was now spending the evenings in town, and Mother made sure he took his medications. When he walked in, I was shocked, but I did not let him know how I felt. Instead of the vigorous man I had known and left just a few months prior, there was now a very thin one. It saddened me to note that the twinkle in his good eye was gone. Dad was slightly jaundiced and I thought a bit disoriented. It broke my heart to see him in that condition.

When Dad saw us, he smiled and said how good it was of us to make the long trip from Richmond to Kingsville. He asked about the babies and was anxious to see them. He was delighted we were going to be there for Christmas. Mother told him my sister Sarita had called us about his being in the hospital, and he hoped we didn't worry about him. He said he would be fine, that the illness was just a little setback.

I assured Dad that Peggy and I and the children were doing fine. I also told him that, considering what he had been through, it appeared he was making progress in regaining his health. I added that getting over his illness and getting back on his feet would take time.

Dad told me he was doing everything the doctor ordered, but he wanted to get back to work full time. There was so much to do. Then he asked me to drive him to the feed mill in town because he had a crew of men unloading feed sacks from a couple of boxcars. So I did. At the feed mill I helped him out of the car, and together we walked to where the men were working. After an exchange of greetings, Dad gave them some rather confused orders. Then he told them they knew what to do and he was sure they would do it right. He promised to check back with them later in the day.

I saw the men look at each other. They too were sad to see Don Lauro in this physical and mental condition. They nodded and started back to work. I helped Dad back to the car. He was silent on the way home, and I could tell he was somewhat aware of his confusion and frustrated he was ill and couldn't work.

Peggy and I and our two children, Laurie and Sarita, returned to Richmond in early January. It was good to be back in our home on Park Lane. We frequently checked on Dad's condition and learned he was making progress and showing signs of recovery. Our third child, Ricardo, was born June 30, 1958. Mother had come to Richmond when Sarita was born and had stayed a week to help Peggy. She did not come after Rick was born because she did not want to be away from Kingsville with Dad so ill.

In early October 1958 Peggy and I received a letter from Dad informing us he was coming to Richmond for a visit. "I want to see you all," he wrote, "but especially my new grandson, Ricardo." Dad planned to fly into Washington National Airport. The letter was brief and had been typed for him, but I could tell Dad had signed it. His usually bold signature was now a bit shaky.

When we met him at the airport, it appeared he had made some progress toward regaining his health, but physically he still had not completely recovered. His confusion, though, was gone, and he was alert and talkative.

We had a wonderful week together. Dad especially enjoyed visiting with his grandchildren. I drove him around Richmond and showed him the medical school, and he had ample time to get to know his three grandchildren. The week went quickly and it was time for him to return to Texas. When Dad traveled, he dressed in his best suit, cuff-linked white shirt, and boots. His white Stetson hat and his bright tie caused those who saw him at the airport to turn and stare at this distinguished and handsome man.

In 1958, long before airport security and terrorism, one could walk out on the tarmac to a gate, to watch as a passenger boarded the airplane. Peggy carried Rick in one arm and with her other held Sarita. Laurie and I were hand in hand and walked beside Dad. When we arrived at the gate where they took his ticket, he turned to me and said I had a beautiful family. He was so pleased he saw his new grandson, Rick, and he said he knew I would take good care of Peggy and the children.

He hugged Peggy, kissed each of the children on the forehead, and turned to me. Dad and I had rarely displayed much emotion toward each other. Although it was obvious we loved each other, over the years a handshake was the limit of touching. This time, after the handshake, he gave me a hug, whispered "good-bye," turned, and walked toward his airplane. I wondered when we would see him again. Even though ill, Dad carried himself with great dignity, straight and tall. Before he boarded, he turned to us and waved. We waved back, the last time we saw Dad alive. He died a few weeks later on November 30, 1958.

Some weeks after Dad's funeral, we returned to Richmond. Both Peggy and I were deeply feeling the loss of Dad, and we thought about his visit to Richmond. I asked Peggy if she thought Dad knew he was dying, knew he didn't have much time left. I was certain he desperately wanted to see Rick, his last grandson, and Laurie and Sarita one more time. Peggy agreed.

Washington National Airport is now Washington Reagan National Airport. A new set of terminals is there now, but the original terminal, the one from which Dad walked out with his family for his airplane ride home, remains and is still in use. Quite frequently I fly in or out of Reagan National for meetings and conferences in Washington. When I see the old terminal, I always think of Dad. I see him walking out to his airplane, with great dignity, straight and tall.

CHAPTER 7

⟨ﾟﾟﾟ⟩

Moving to Concord

Peggy and I had ten children, five boys and five girls and only ten years between the oldest and the youngest. Eight of the children were born in Richmond. They were Lauro Fred III, Sarita Maria, Ricardo Esteban, Alicia Maria, Victoria Maria, Roberto Sebastian, Rachel Maria, and Veronica Maria. Tomas Martin and Daniel Nicolas were born in Concord, Massachusetts. Whenever I am asked why so many, I tell them it was because we wanted ten. I usually do not tell them Peggy and I had agreed on ten children when I proposed by the campanile at Iowa State.

We were able to accommodate Laurie, Sarita, and Rick, our first three children, in the little house on Park Lane in Richmond, but when Peggy became pregnant with our fourth child, Alicia (Lisa), we decided we needed to find a larger home. We bought a three-bedroom house in Henrico County, paying $18,500 for it. The attic was left unfinished, and eventually I built a bedroom there for Peggy and me. The basement opened at ground level and was also unfinished. I converted this basement into a playroom for the children and completed the unfinished bathroom. It was a tri-level home and quite modest, but Peggy and I considered it a palace.

We faced all of the trials of families with young children, and there were never enough hours in the day. Those were truly busy times. We were thankful all of our children were healthy, and other than the usual childhood illnesses they were well most of the time. We did have a lesson in communicable disease, however. Laurie, the oldest, came home from school one day and was not his usual frisky self. Peggy said she was concerned about him. She asked me to check him, and I saw spots on his belly and thigh. I told Peggy I believed he had chicken pox and by now the rest of our children had been exposed. In fourteen days, we had seven more cases of chicken pox. Obviously we were very busy looking after so many sick children.

Some had more severe cases than others, but they all soon recovered. Our pediatrician offered advice, but there was not much we could do except keep the children comfortable. Later, he told us we had driven the communicable disease statistics off the chart and created a major epidemic of chicken pox in Henrico County, Virginia—all in one family!

Our ten years in Richmond were happy ones. Our focus was on our eight children. Often on weekends we drove to Williamsburg or Jamestown. Peggy packed our lunch, and we would have a picnic on the way. It was a delightful time in our marriage. Seeing the children grow and start their education was rewarding. One day, as Peggy and I were talking, I said we had the best situation in Richmond that a young couple with a large family could want. We had a comfortable home, and my work at MCV was on the upswing.

One day Peggy remarked we had all good things going for us. We were busy and working hard, and Richmond was a great place to live and to raise children. She asked if I had been thinking about moving to another medical school, because she knew sometimes one's career could be advanced with the right move.

I told Peggy I hadn't been thinking about a move and that I believed it would take a major offer from another medical school to persuade me to leave Richmond. My academic career was advancing rapidly; I was doing well at MCV and I liked the faculty in the anatomy department. Although I had a considerable teaching load, my research program was flourishing and my grant funding had increased. Every year I had published several research papers, and I had a number of graduate students working with me.

Momentous happenings and their dates on the calendar are often fixed in one's mind, and we can describe exactly what we were doing or where we were when we heard the news. For example, I clearly remember where I was on December 7, 1941, the day Pearl Harbor was bombed. Also, April 12, 1945, stands out in my mind. I was a young soldier at an Infantry Replacement Training Center in Camp Hood, Texas. We had just come in from an exhausting march, and our tough first sergeant, with tears in his eyes, told us Pres. Franklin D. Roosevelt had died. September 11, 2001, and the destruction of the World Trade Center will forever be in my mind. On November 22, 1963, I had just completed a lecture to first-year medical students on the anatomy of the heart. I entered the departmental office and was told that Pres. John F. Kennedy had been shot in Dallas.

With others, I stood by the radio and listened to the sad news. Soon it was confirmed that the president was dead. I heard reports that at some schools in the South there was cheering when his death was announced. The struggles for civil rights were just starting. The South was still segregated, and the thought crossed my mind that perhaps it was time to leave the South and to raise our children in a more liberal environment.

I talked to Peggy about my feelings and disappointment with the reaction of some to President Kennedy's death. Both of us had voted for him even though we doubted he would carry Virginia. We had stayed up most of election night listening to the presidential election returns and hoping Kennedy would win the tight race. We were delighted when Kennedy won the election, and now his death from an assassin's bullet was a blow to us. Peggy and the older children spent most of the next two days in front of the television, watching first the news coverage on the assassination and then the president's funeral.

After the president's funeral, Peggy and I discussed our future. I pointed out that I was happy with my job at MCV and I was making a lot of progress on my research and teaching. I also told her I was pleased that she was happy in Richmond and liked our new home. But then I said that if the right job came along, we might think about moving. Peggy and I concluded that one of the major reasons for moving from

Richmond, in addition to advancing my career, was that we found troubling the racial problems of the South and the prejudice we saw almost every day. Both of us were certain there was going to be a lot of turmoil and trouble in the years ahead on the civil rights issue. We wanted to bring up our children in an environment where everyone was equal and schools were not segregated. Peggy and I decided I should keep my eyes open for a new academic opportunity, preferably out of the South.

In December 1963, Emory University in Atlanta invited me to consider a job as chair of the Department of Anatomy. I was not thrilled about staying in the South, but I thought I should look at the opportunity because it was at Emory, one of the finest universities in the nation. After a visit during which I presented a seminar on my research, I decided that although it was a grand opportunity for professional advancement, it was one for which I declined to compete. I withdrew my name from consideration. Early in 1964 I had another offer. The University of New Mexico was opening a medical school in Albuquerque, and I was asked to consider the job as chair of the anatomy department and assistant dean. Peggy and I had our roots in the Southwest, and New Mexico held many attractions for us. I went to Albuquerque and spent several days looking at the facilities and the overall situation.

The night I returned from New Mexico, Peggy told me that the dean's office at the Tufts University School of Medicine in Boston had called. I knew they were looking for someone to chair their anatomy department. Dr. Benjamin Spector had been chair at Tufts for a long time and retired the previous year, and an acting chair was now running the department. I had never been to Boston. I asked Peggy what she thought about the situation.

Peggy told me there was no harm in calling back, so I promised I would return the Tufts call first thing in the morning. Meanwhile, I started thinking about Tufts. Its reputation among universities was excellent, its medical school was respected, and Boston was one of the truly great academic centers in the nation; it would be an interesting place to live. Still, I could not believe they would be interested in me as chair of anatomy. They would certainly have no trouble attracting an outstanding anatomist to the job. Also, I was only thirty-eight years old and an associate professor, and I felt certain they would be looking for a senior person with a national or international reputation in anatomy.

The next morning I told Alton Brashear, professor of anatomy at MCV and a close colleague, about the call from Tufts. Brashear, like Erling Hegre, had been one of my mentors at MCV from the first days after my appointment. Under his direction, I started out teaching gross anatomy to dental students as well as teaching anatomy to medical students. Within three years, I was running the gross anatomy course for medical students. I asked Brashear what he thought about the call and told him I doubted I had much chance.

To my surprise, Brashear told me he had submitted my name for Tufts to consider as chair. He had called the dean of dentistry, a good friend of his, and suggested I was someone they should look at for the chair of anatomy. He told him I was highly qualified, that I was a great teacher of both medical and dental students, and that my research was well funded by the National Institutes of Health.

When I called Tufts later that day, the receptionist said she would get Dean Joseph Hayman on the line. A gruff voice greeted me, and after a few pleasantries about the weather, Dean Hayman said he wanted me to come to Boston for a campus visit. I told Hayman it was kind of him to invite me and I was interested in the possibility of moving, but I had to admit I knew nothing about the Tufts anatomy department.

In his blunt manner, the dean told me there was not a lot to know; there was not much research in the department. According to him, the anatomy department at Tufts needed a lot of work, and he urged me to come take a look at it.

Hayman gave me some possible dates for a visit. I still did not believe Tufts could be serious about my candidacy for the chair, but I figured I would at least have a nice visit to a city about which I had heard so much.

It was late February 1964 when I visited the Tufts University medical and dental schools in downtown Boston, close to the New England Medical Center. The rest of the university is in Medford, about eight miles away from the professional schools.

At that time, the garment industry surrounded the medical school. Building after building was filled with workers making clothes. Men pushed racks of suits and coats down the crowded sidewalk to waiting trucks double-parked on the street. The medical school stood on the edge of Chinatown. I watched women picking through piles of fabric remnants on the sidewalk. The streets were jammed with traffic, and the sound of blaring horns filled the air. Cars and trucks blocked intersections. There was absolutely no order I could detect, nor did anyone seem to care about moving traffic in an orderly fashion. A traffic police officer stood at the street crossing and ignored the chaos. Compared to Richmond, with its wide and clean streets and orderly traffic patterns, Boston was the opposite.

The streets were rutted with dirty snow and ice, and the sidewalks were barely passable because of the racks, the crowds of people, and the snow. I looked at the medical school building located at 136 Harrison Avenue. It looked like an old shirt factory, and I later learned it had indeed been exactly that. In 1949 the medical school purchased the building, converted it into classroom, administrative, and research space, and moved there the following year. In addition to the medical school, the building housed the dental school and its clinics.

I thought to myself, "What am I doing here?" The facilities were terrible; they didn't begin to compare with what was in Richmond. Still, I had committed to look at the job at Tufts, so I went into the medical school building and found the dean's office. I spent the next two days talking to faculty, students, and administration. Quickly, the quality and standards of the faculty were apparent to me. All of the basic science departments, including biochemistry, physiology, microbiology, and pharmacology, were of the highest quality. The research programs were active, well funded, and productive. There was considerable research funding in each of the basic science departments.

In contrast, however, the Department of Anatomy had little or no research activity under way, and the faculty had a significant teaching load, providing instruction in anatomy for all of the medical and dental students. It reminded me of an anatomy department in the early 1940s.

At Tufts, the anatomy department did traditional morphologic research, whereas my own research was physiological and histochemical, concerning itself with cell and membrane structures. Cell biology was now the concentration of the top-flight anatomy departments in the country, and gross anatomy had been markedly reduced as a percentage of the overall curriculum.

I knew I could bring positive changes to the anatomy program at Tufts in a brief period of time. The following day, I interviewed with faculty and talked to a number of students. Later, I spent considerable time with the dean. I had many questions to ask of Dean Hayman and he of me.

I returned to Richmond late in the evening, and Peggy greeted me and asked about my trip. I told her Tufts medical school had the worst physical plant I had ever seen: a couple of converted garment buildings. I explained that the whole place was a mess, but if they offered me the job of chair, I wanted to go. The faculty was excellent, really first rate, and the students, top flight. The research programs in the other basic sciences were thriving, and the administration was committed to building an anatomy department of the highest academic quality. I told Peggy the dean wanted the anatomy department to match the excellence of the other basic science departments at Tufts. I thought it was an exciting place and one with which I'd like to be associated.

Peggy asked about the other places I had visited looking at the job of department chair. I told her they were excellent and had fine facilities, but I believed Tufts and Boston would be the best place for us. If Tufts offered the job, I would take her to visit Boston before we made a decision. Moving would mean a major change for our family, and I didn't know the first thing about housing in Boston, but I told Peggy I thought we should seriously consider the job if it was offered.

A week later, the letter arrived. Dean Hayman offered me the job as professor and chair of the Department of Anatomy. The salary was twenty thousand dollars per year, and my academic appointment was a tenured (permanent) one. The salary was almost double what I was making at

MCV, where I did not have tenure. Although the promotion and salary were important, they were not what attracted me to Tufts. In addition to placing our family in a better economic situation, Tufts was not in the South, where racial tensions were increasing. Also, the job at Tufts gave me an opportunity to build a department from the ground up. As an enticement for me to take the job, the dean had committed to a total physical renovation of the department and several new academic positions.

After Peggy read the letter, she asked if I was going to take the job. I said it was a great opportunity for us, and I believed living in the Boston area would be attractive. I still could not believe that such a prestigious medical school had picked me for the job, and I told Peggy I suspected they had offered the job to more highly qualified anatomists who had refused it because there was not much of a department there. I wondered about my judgment.

Peggy said I was talking nonsense, that they had offered me the job because I was the best person for it and Tufts was lucky to get me. Peggy liked the idea of a move to Boston, saying it was time for a change and a good time to move. Only Laurie and Sarita were in school; the rest were too young.

I told Peggy I would accept the job after I had discussed my plans with Erling Hegre. I was sorry to leave the department at MCV because Hegre and the rest of the faculty and staff had been so helpful to me in my years there. The faculty in the department truly contributed to my growth as a teacher and as an investigator. I was fortunate MCV had been my first job out of graduate school. I could not have had better mentoring in academia than I had received in Richmond.

Over the next few weeks, Peggy and I did a lot of planning for the move. Our major concern was a place to live because we knew nothing about the Boston area. It was late winter, and I was committed to start the job in the spring. Peggy stayed with the children in Richmond and I visited them often. This schedule gave us a few months to find housing, sell our home in Richmond, and move. By the time we expected to move, the children would have finished school and be on summer vacation.

We decided to build. With a large family, we wanted to design a house that would accommodate us comfortably. We chose to build a modern house on Annursnac Hill Road in the woods of Concord, Massachusetts. Our acre and one-half of land ran down to a pond. Before we bought it, we looked at several other sites away from the pond because with eight children, Peggy was very concerned about the safety factor. We agreed that the lot we liked best was situated by the pond, but none of our children could swim. She told the sales agent of her worry, and he told her to buy the lot and teach the children how to swim. So we bought the land on the pond, built the house, and all of our children became excellent swimmers.

Once I went to work in Boston that spring, I took some extra time and drove to White Horse Beach, a rocky beach resort that was near Plymouth but still a long commute to Boston. I located a cottage that was reasonably priced and would accommodate our family. On August 6, 1964, we watched the movers in Richmond load the last of our furniture for storage until our house was finished in Concord. The date is memorable because we celebrated our daughter Veronica's first birthday that evening in a motel outside of Richmond. The next morning we got the children up early, packed, and started our drive to Massachusetts.

Although our home in Concord was not yet finished, we enrolled Laurie, Sarita, and Rick in elementary school and Lisa in kindergarten. The principal informed us of the start dates and times and the place to catch the bus on Annursnac Hill Road. Each morning at about 5:30 A.M., Peggy and I loaded all the children into our station wagon and drove them from White Horse Beach to Concord. Our builder let us use a house he had just finished as a sort of way station, so Peggy stayed there with the rest of the children during the day. After lunch Peggy and the children walked Lisa to the nearby bus stop, so she could attend kindergarten. Later in the day, Peggy and the children waited for the four others to return from school. When I arrived from Tufts in the late afternoon, we drove back to White Horse Beach. This routine went on for almost two weeks.

Earlier I had gone by the Concord Town House, our "city hall," to ask about our mailing address. I introduced myself, saying that I was building a house on Annursnac Hill Road. The clerk welcomed me and told me my mailing address would be Annursnac Hill Road. I said I knew the name of the street but needed to know our house number for mail delivery.

The clerk told me there were no house numbers in Concord. My address would be Cavazos, Annursnac Hill Road, Concord. Concord had never had house numbers, and she doubted they ever would. She explained that the police, fire, and mail people knew who lived in each house. They could find me, and I was not to worry; my mail would be delivered. Finally, after the urging of the police, fire, and mail people, in the 1970s the town agreed to have house numbers.

Our plan to commute from White Horse Beach to Concord worked much more smoothly than I had expected. The children took it all in stride, and Peggy had them convinced it was a grand experience. We were delighted when we finally moved into our new house in Concord. Although the move had been rather difficult, we were pleased with our new home.

Because our land ran down to the pond, we built a beach, and swimming, fishing, and picnics became a part of our lives. The pond quickly became the centerpiece of our landscape. It is about three acres in size and approximately twelve to fourteen feet deep. It is fed by a spring and a small amount of runoff water from the hill.

In 1965, the first summer after we moved in, I frequently took Laurie and Rick fishing on the Concord River. It was a delightful place to fish. From our launch site, we soon drifted under the historic North Bridge, where, as Emerson so memorably wrote, "once the embattled farmers stood; / And fired the shot heard 'round the world." I explained to the children how the Concord River is formed by two rivers, the Assabet and the Sudbury, where they join just north of a place called Egg Rock, not far from where we launched our boat. I told the boys someday we should follow the river in much the same way Henry David Thoreau and his brother did in 1839, when they spent a week on the

Concord and Merrimack rivers. Unfortunately, we never did make the trip down the Concord River.

ANATOMY AND EMERSON

In January 1965 our ninth child, Tomas, was born in Concord. The next year, our tenth child, Daniel, was born. Now our family was complete, with five boys and five girls. For Peggy and me, having three children in diapers was the norm. After the tenth child was born, invariably one of the children would ask when we were going to have the next baby. I told them there would not be any more children; we had planned on ten and now we had ten.

One of the older ones suggested we have a family of twelve, like the couple in the movie *Cheaper by the Dozen,* and then things would be cheaper for us. I rejected the idea and told them they had to believe me; children were not cheaper by the dozen.

Peggy had done an excellent job in designing living accommodations for our children. She had worked with the architects of our home to build a large bedroom and two smaller ones in the downstairs area. Our five sons used the large bedroom, and it contained five bunks. Three of the beds were on one wall and two on another wall. There was also a large closet in the room. The two smaller bedrooms were for our five girls. Three of them shared the larger bedroom, and the two youngest girls shared the other.

Our children never complained that they did not have their own bedrooms or that they wanted more space for themselves. They fully accepted the living arrangements. As they grew older, it was Peggy and I who decided our children needed more space. In 1974 we added an additional one thousand square feet to the house and called it the studio. The studio had two levels. The brick-floored main level was where I pursued my hobby of lapidary and Rick did his artwork and painting. Above was a loft area that we divided into a study, a bathroom, and a bedroom for two boys.

I was busy at Tufts trying to build a high-quality anatomy department. I addressed the physical plant problems by getting the department's offices renovated and new laboratory space built. In 1966 we started a graduate program in anatomy, awarding master's and doctoral degrees. I made known my expectation that each faculty member would have first-class funded research programs, even though we still carried a significant teaching load in the medical and dental schools. The department was responsible for teaching gross anatomy, histology or microscopic anatomy, neuroanatomy, and embryology. I elected to teach human gross anatomy to the medical students. In 1965, the course for the medical students consisted of nearly four hundred hours of dissecting a cadaver under the direction of the faculty. Four students were assigned to a table, each sharing the dissection of the cadaver.

Whenever anyone asked why I taught gross anatomy, I gave them three reasons. First, I enjoyed teaching the subject. Second, there is nothing new in gross anatomy, so, having learned the subject, I could walk into the classroom or the dissecting lab without any further preparation. This fixed knowledge left me with more time to read and stay up-to-date in my field of research. Third, I enjoyed student contact. After spending four hundred hours in the laboratory over a semester, I knew the students pretty well.

I talked to students about many aspects of medicine and science besides anatomy. I was especially sensitive to the reaction of students to dissection. Until about 1990, gross anatomy was the first course a student took when entering the Tufts medical school. Most of our entering students had already taken biochemistry, microbiology, histology, and even physiology before entering medical school. None had taken a course in gross anatomy, so this became their introduction to medical school.

The night before the first anatomy class, the dean of the medical school gave a reception for incoming first-year students. Faculty and administrators as well as the president and provost of Tufts University attended. At the reception, students met their classmates for the next four years and introduced themselves to faculty. When they learned that I taught anatomy, some students asked questions about the laboratory and privately expressed their anxiety about seeing a room full of cadavers for the first time. I reassured them and told them they would be fine.

These receptions provided an opportunity for students to select
their partners for the anatomy course. With four students assigned to a
table, they would work as a team during the entire course. Sometimes
students chose partners they knew as undergraduates, but most of the
time they were meeting for the first time.

After I became dean, I too held a reception for incoming students.
In August 1978 Peggy and I arrived at the reception and soon separated
and worked the crowd, introducing ourselves and talking to students.
After the reception as we drove back to Concord, Peggy told me what a
grand event it had been and that she was very glad she had attended.
She said the students were interesting, and she told me she had the ultimate compliment at the reception.

Peggy said she was talking to three students. It was the usual discussion about the tensions of starting medical school and the tough
courses they would take the first semester. Eventually, she excused herself and moved on, but a few minutes later the three students walked
up to her and said they had something important to ask. They told her
they would like her to be their fourth partner at the dissection table the
next day.

Peggy said she was bowled over and flattered and had told them she
appreciated the invitation to join their team but that she was not a new
student—she was the wife of their dean.

As I drove on, I thought to myself what a compliment the students
had paid Peggy. Here she was the mother of ten children, yet she looked
youthful enough to be mistaken for an incoming medical student.

The first day of medical school, most try not to show emotion as
they approach their cadaver, acting as if it were hardly anything out
of the ordinary. After the first few minutes, most of the students were
fine in the dissection laboratory, but some students became nauseous
and left the room, only to return soon with a sheepish look. Occasionally a student walked out of the "gross lab" and quit medical school on
the first day.

In September 1965, under my direction, the first-year students began their first course in medical school: human gross anatomy. The entering class of students was excellent. In order to ease the students into

anatomy and to minimize the shock of seeing an embalmed cadaver, we started the dissection on the anterior chest wall. The face and head were wrapped with cloths so the first view would not be the face of the deceased.

I approached a table with three students instead of four. I asked why the other lab partner was missing. One student responded that their missing lab partner had told them if he had to take apart a cadaver to get through medical school, this career was not for him. According to one of the students, his last words to them were that he was leaving medical school. He had packed up his dissection instruments, picked up his books, and walked out the door.

The anatomy laboratory was in the basement of the building, so I went upstairs and saw the student who had left the anatomy lab sitting on the steps of the medical school. He appeared dejected and seemed to be trying to make a decision. I sat beside him on the steps and asked if it was true he was quitting medical school. He told me that all of his life he wanted to be a doctor, working hard to do well in college and be admitted to Tufts. Now he discovered that he could not touch the cadaver. He said it had always been his impression that medicine was about healing, and the first thing he had to do was to destroy a body. To him it made no sense, and perhaps medicine was not for him.

I said he was not destroying a body; he was learning not only how the human form was structured but also an important part of the language of medicine. Yes, I agreed, he took the body apart, but nothing was destroyed. In a systematic fashion, I explained, he would do his dissection, learning all the parts of the body and giving the cadaver the same respect he would give a patient. When the course was finished, I told him, all of the dissected parts would be assembled and the body buried. Besides, I added, the privilege of dissecting one of their own was given to few in society. I told him it was time for us to go downstairs to the laboratory and get to work.

The student sighed, got up, and followed me to the dissecting room. He returned to his table, his partner handed him a scalpel, and he went to work.

Years later in the late 1970s, when I was the dean of the Tufts medical school, I was at a fundraiser in California. We gave a reception and invited alumni and parents who had children at Tufts. I gave an update with a slide show on the positive changes at the medical school. After the discussion period, I talked individually with our alumni. Many of them I remembered as my former students. A man walked up to me and asked if I remembered him.

I could not place him. By this time I had taught thousands of medical students, and I told him I could not remember him. He said I had taught him gross anatomy in 1965 and that he was the student I talked out of quitting medical school on the first day of anatomy. Now, he told me, he had a big internal medicine practice in San Francisco.

Then it came back to me, and I told him I did recall sitting on the front steps of the school with him and talking him out of quitting. Since I was on a fundraising trip, I thought to myself that this person would surely make a nice financial contribution to Tufts because I had persuaded him to stay in medical school.

My fundraising hopes were raised when he said that I was the person who persuaded him to stay in medical school, and because of that he was now a successful doctor. Then, with a smile and a twinkle in his eye, he said he would never forgive me for talking him out of quitting medicine.

From the time Peggy and I married and had our first child, we had lived on my salary. Both of us agreed she should not try to work but stay home with the children during these critical growing years. As a consequence of this decision, money was tight.

For many years, until 1972, we had only one car. We did live in an affluent neighborhood, but Peggy and I decided that with all the needs of our family, another car was not possible. Every now and then, one of the children asked about our lack of a second car and why all of the neighbors had at least two cars, and some three. Peggy would reply with a smile that we had made a decision a long time ago that we wanted a large family and that we would rather put our money into raising our family than buying another car.

In 1966 Peggy went to work as a registered nurse at Emerson Hospital in Concord. By this time, Daniel, our youngest child, was almost a year old. Over the years I had been concerned that Peggy had been out of nursing so long she might never return to the profession. I had asked Peggy if she wanted to go back to work now that the children were older. I reminded her that she had studied for years to receive her nursing degree and I didn't want her to lose her skills.

Peggy said she knew I was right. She told me she had been thinking about going back to work for quite a while and she had recently decided it was time to return to nursing. Another reason for going back to work, Peggy said, was that she wanted the children to see her as a professional as well as a mother. Peggy insisted that she was not going back to work to support our family since she thought that I provided more than adequate income on my own. Peggy proposed that whatever money she made would be saved for travel with the children. She wanted them to see some of the world and know that it's not all like beautiful Concord. The education she wanted for the children would be not only what they learned in school but also what could be gained only through travel.

I agreed with Peggy and suggested that she call Emerson and get an appointment to talk to them about a job. I also told her not to worry about the children while she was at work; we would figure it out, and I promised they would never be alone.

Soon after her interview at Emerson Hospital, Peggy was hired as a nurse on the 6:00 to 11:30 P.M. shift. She requested that shift because we had identified a fine sitter who could work for a few hours in the afternoon, and then I would try to get home as early as I could.

Two weeks later, on a weekend, Peggy prepared to go to her first shift at Emerson Hospital. The older children stood in awe as they saw their mother come downstairs in her white nurse's uniform, her nursing cap from Santa Rosa Hospital in San Antonio, and her spotless white shoes. She pulled her blue nurse's cape out of the closet where it had been stored for years and put it on.

Sarita told her mother she liked her in her nurse's uniform. She had never seen her in it, and she thought it looked great. Sarita was so pleased her Mother was going to take care of sick people.

The first few years, Peggy worked on the medical and surgical floor. It was not long before she gained the reputation of being an outstanding nurse with a strong sense of professionalism. For example, it was not unusual for Peggy to see one of her patients on a Concord street. Having a strong professional belief in patient confidentiality, she would give no indication that she knew the person as one of her patients. Often though, former patients would see and greet her, thanking her for her superb care when they were at Emerson. Once when Peggy and I were standing in a grocery store checkout line, the man ahead of her turned and greeted her, telling Peggy how much he appreciated the fine nursing care she gave him at Emerson Hospital. Peggy tried not to acknowledge that she knew the man but returned his greeting with a subtle nod of her head. The man persisted, asking Peggy if she remembered him as one of her patients, and then he said maybe it was because he had his clothes on that she could not remember him. Then, as our faces reddened, he pushed his joke to its logical conclusion, suggesting that if he were *naked*, he was *sure* she would remember him.

In 1973, Peggy moved from the medical and surgical floor to the operating room. There she became a "circulating nurse." Her hours of work were now 7:00 A.M. until 3:00 P.M. She was responsible for the cleanliness of the operating rooms, the sterilization of instruments, counting all of the instruments and needles the surgeons used, and making sure every item was accounted for before the incision was sutured.

Working in the operating room meant she would be "on call." If an emergency surgery was to be performed, the on-call nurse had to go to Emerson and participate in the surgery. Almost without fail, when Peggy was on call the phone would ring late in the night asking her to return to the hospital. Often the surgery was not concluded until dawn, and Peggy would come home exhausted. An hour or so later, she would return to the operating room for her regular shift.

Eventually Peggy took the lead in persuading the hospital nursing supervisor that if the on-call nursing staff was called back to the hospi-

tal and worked all night, they had to have at least four hours of sleep before returning to the operating room. In her own determined and quiet
way, Peggy had changed a long-standing practice.

A TROUBLED JOURNEY THROUGH CENTRAL AMERICA

In July 1969 I traveled to Central America because the Pan American
Health Organization (PAHO), part of the World Health Organization
(WHO), had asked me to evaluate the academic quality and condition
of the anatomy departments in the medical schools there. The trip
would take two weeks, and I was to be accompanied by an anatomist
from Brazil.

The first anatomy department we evaluated was in the medical
school in Panama. We spent the entire day with the chairman of the
anatomy department, and it soon became apparent that the medical
school in Panama needed considerable support. There was no modern
equipment in the department, and the research was quite basic and
hardly of merit. At the end of the day, my colleague and I walked back
to our hotel. It was dark, but the streets were busy. He asked my impressions of anatomy at the Panama City medical school. I replied that
they had practically no resources and the administration really did not
appear interested in the quality of anatomy instruction their students
received. They had only one professor and two assistants in the department to teach all of the anatomy courses to more than 120 medical students. Those of us teaching in medical schools in the United States neither understood nor were even aware of the difficult conditions in
which some of our fellow anatomists in Central America worked.

The next morning we flew to San José, Costa Rica. In 1967 I had visited the medical school there while attending the Central American
Congress of Anatomy. I had been impressed by the high quality of the
basic sciences at the medical school. They enrolled eighty medical students and had a rigorous selection process. The basic sciences building
was quite modern and well equipped. Now, upon my return, I found
four hundred students in the entering class, and some faculties were

unhappy with the selection process. When I was there in 1967, some faculty members were agitating for an open-door policy of admission to medical school. The dean in 1967 had strongly opposed increasing class size or having open enrollment. Now he was gone, and the new dean allowed anyone who showed up for an anatomy lesson to enroll. I was disturbed because the facility was the same size it was in 1967. The school was built for eighty entering students, and I wondered where they put four hundred. I knew that an enrollment increase of that magnitude without a proportionate expansion in faculty numbers and teaching space would result in low-quality medical education.

Early the next morning we flew to Managua, Nicaragua, and took a taxi downtown. After checking into our hotel, we went to the PAHO office and met the PAHO representative. He told us that the medical school and the university had been closed by order of Nicaragua's iron-fisted leader, President Somoza, because of student unrest and some riots. I told him I was sorry to hear about the university's closure, but I asked for permission to go there and visit the medical school. I stated that we had come a long way and wanted at least to be able to report that we had interviewed some faculty and talked to students on campus.

The PAHO representative said that a visit to the school was impossible. We learned that after Somoza closed the school, he sent in troops and they surrounded University City. Then the PAHO representative informed us that because of limited flights, our departure would be delayed for two days. He suggested that we play tourist and see the grand colonial architecture of Managua. It was safe to walk around, he said, but he reminded us not to travel out of the city.

Managua was not a beautiful city. Many streets had deep ruts or were unpaved and muddy. Rusty tin roofs outnumbered the beautiful Spanish colonial tiled roofs. We had been to three countries—Panama, Costa Rica, and now Nicaragua—and in all three the medical schools were in serious trouble.

I knew we were doing the best we could to complete our PAHO mission, but we did not have much to show after visiting three countries. El Salvador was next on our itinerary, and I knew their medical school quite well. I thought perhaps our luck would turn in San Salvador.

I was delighted to be back in El Salvador. It seemed like I was on familiar ground, and the visit gave me an opportunity to see a good friend, Dr. Manuel Sigaron. In 1968 he was a member of the anatomy faculty and had invited me to teach a three-week cell biology course at the medical school in San Salvador. He and his wife went out of their way to see that Peggy, the children, and I were comfortable and enjoyed our visit to his country.

Our PAHO tour arrived in San Salvador on July 19, 1969, and as we taxied to our gate I looked out the window and saw a number of World War II–era P-51 airplanes lined up along the runway. They appeared to be armed with small bombs and machine guns. I told my companion they appeared ready for combat. He agreed and reminded me that there was tension between Honduras and El Salvador, but he didn't think it was too serious and suggested that perhaps the military was just preparing for maneuvers.

Our hotel was a modern one, high on one of the hills overlooking the city. After registering we parted in the lobby, agreeing to meet downstairs in the bar at 7:00 P.M. My room was on the top floor of the hotel, and I took a moment to look out the window just as the lights were coming on. The city looked beautiful at night. It was dusk and San Salvador spread out before me like a lighted quilt. Then the lights went out. I thought to myself that this was just another example of poor engineering in El Salvador. In the dark I managed to find a candle and matches. After lighting it, I looked out the window and saw that the city was almost totally dark.

At 7:00 P.M. I left my room and started down to the lobby and the bar to meet my Brazilian companion. When I reached the lobby there was turmoil. People were shouting or arguing, and others appeared agitated. Candles illuminated the bar and lobby.

I located my colleague and asked what was going on. The place was wild, the city was blacked out, and people were acting strangely. He told me that the Salvadoran air force had bombed Tegucigalpa. He reminded me of the airplanes we had seen when we landed. My companion said people called it an "Israeli-like strike," and people had heard on the radio that the Honduran air force had been wiped out.

I knew that "Israeli-like strike" referred to the Six-Day War between Israel and Egypt, when the Israelis destroyed the Egyptian air force. I said I did not wish death or injury to anyone, but if they had bombed the Honduran air force it was my hope that they had wiped out every one of their planes. If not, I was certain that the next morning they would be over San Salvador to bomb at first light.

This latest setback had me convinced that our academic mission to the Central American medical schools was going to be a failure. Each place we had visited was unsettled and in chaos. I told my companion that if there was a war, we could forget our planned visit to Tegucigalpa the day after tomorrow. Now, only Guatemala was on our itinerary and that was only if we could get out of El Salvador.

As I predicted, the Honduran air force bombed San Salvador early the next morning. I heard the explosions and saw smoke. Later I learned they had tried to bomb the airport, but their bombing was not precise and they had hit some oil storage tanks instead. There was some minor damage to the airport, enough to prevent commercial flights from landing or taking off. This episode was the beginning of the "Soccer War," so named because El Salvador and Honduras had met in the World Cup soccer tournament. The bitter competition in the tournament had supposedly resulted in ill feelings between the two nations. In reality, the tensions between the two nations were the result of large numbers of Salvadorans migrating illegally into Honduras. When Honduras protested, El Salvador made little effort to remove the immigrants. Honduras considered this immigration an invasion of their land and accused El Salvador of trying to annex a territory settled illegally by the Salvadorans.

The day after our arrival in El Salvador, July 20, 1969, we were picked up and driven to the medical school. The place was in turmoil. Young medical students rushed about, clearly agitated and excited. People were shouting orders, and others tried to calm the chaos at the entrance of the medical school.

I asked about the situation, and a faculty member told me the students had been mobilized and sent to the front, and there was considerable ground fighting along the border. He was bitter and said that politicians started wars but did not fight them, and it was the young people who were being killed or wounded.

At the administrative offices of the medical school we were met by several of the school officials and a PAHO representative. As soon as we walked in, he informed us that our visit to the medical school in San Salvador had been canceled because of the war. He also said it would be impossible for us to get to Honduras for a site visit. It did seem like an impossible situation: we were wasting our time in San Salvador and yet we couldn't leave because of the airport closure.

The PAHO representative said he had been working on a plan and had arranged for the two of us to go by Jeep to Guatemala. It was scheduled to leave at 3:00 P.M. He also informed us that we *must* depart on the Jeep because PAHO would not assume responsibility for us after 3:00 P.M. He made it clear that if we were not on the Jeep going to Guatemala, we were on our own.

One of the school administrators who had been listening to our departure plans spoke up and told the PAHO representative it was inconceivable that he would send us by Jeep across the jungle. He said there was fighting going on along the frontiers and in the jungle, and he feared we would be machine-gunned. He was convinced we would not make it to Guatemala.

The man from PAHO responded that he regretted the decision, but he had orders from Washington. The Jeep was to leave at 3:00 from in front of the medical school, and he hoped the two of us would be on it.

My Brazilian companion and I talked over the situation and our options. We decided we had only one option—the Jeep. I told the PAHO representative the two of us would be ready and waiting for the Jeep at 3:00 P.M. He appeared quite pleased that we were leaving and would no longer be his responsibility.

We were told that our Jeep would be clearly marked as a World Health Organization vehicle by a WHO flag flying from the front fender. In addition to the driver and the two of us, there would be one other person from PAHO. One of the administrators who opposed our leaving via Jeep remarked that the WHO flag would not mean a thing. It would, however, make a better target for some soldier, from either El Salvador or Honduras.

At 3:00 P.M. the two of us stood outside the medical school building waiting for our Jeep. I was amazed when it showed up on time, and we had soon loaded our bags and left San Salvador for Guatemala City. Under the best of circumstances, the trip is about four to five hours, but it took us about ten hours. The roads were congested with people leaving El Salvador, and we were stopped numerous times by heavily armed soldiers at checkpoints to have our papers examined. We carried diplomatic passports issued by the World Health Organization, so we were barely questioned and had no problems. At the last checkpoint before entering Guatemala we were stopped again. We had quite a wait as the soldiers checked the cars ahead of us. Finally, we reached the soldiers and they asked for our papers.

An Indian woman, poorly dressed and middle aged, walked up to our Jeep. She said she was a poor peasant woman trying to return to her village close to the border of Guatemala. Her children were waiting for her and she needed to be with them in this troubled time. She asked for a ride to the next checkpoint because everything was confused, and there were many bad people on the roads. The woman said she was afraid to walk through the jungle alone.

The driver told her it was not possible to transport her because the Jeep was an official government car. It was against the rules to transport people without authorization. The driver said that although he regretted it, we could not give her a ride. The woman persisted and was attracting attention to us. Several armed soldiers and some civilians with large machetes were watching and listening to her request. It was apparent to me they were not pleased by our response to the woman's plea for a ride.

In a low voice I told the driver to forget the rules and give the woman a ride. People were watching, and they did not know anything about official rules and regulations. There could be a lot of trouble if we didn't give her a ride. I told him if he got a complaint, to tell them I ordered him to give her a ride. The driver finally said he would take her in the Jeep, but only under protest. He told the woman to get into the Jeep, and she did.

I was anxious to be on our way because I estimated it would be after midnight before we arrived in Guatemala City. The driver said I was right it would be after midnight, but he could not make much speed because the roads were crowded and dangerous.

Just before we reached the checkpoint at the Guatemalan border, the driver stopped the Jeep and the woman climbed out. She thanked us, saying we probably saved her life. Pointing to me, she told me how grateful she was for my intervention and that she would light a candle and say a prayer for me to have a safe journey. With that, she hefted her bundle and walked into the jungle.

We arrived at the Guatemalan border after midnight. Immigration quickly stamped our passports, and we were on our way into the city. We registered at our hotel, and though it was late when we got to our room, I turned on the television looking for news of the war. After the update on the "Soccer War," the station announced that on July 20, 1969, the United States had placed a man on the moon. It gave me great pride we had done so, but I was sure the Apollo landing had probably gone much more smoothly than had our trip through Central America.

The next day my colleague and I went to the medical school at the university. We found the dean's office and went in. After introductions the dean informed us that the federal government had closed both the medical school and the university. The students were on strike, and the faculties were supporting the student strike. I told the dean we were truly sorry to learn of this situation and knew he could not arrange a visit to a university and a school on strike. We thanked him and left.

We had visited five countries and were unable to even get to Honduras because of the war. In country after country, poverty, war, strikes, and closure by the military prevented us from doing our job. Every time I return to Central America to try to help out, the situation is worse.

There is so much work to do in those schools and, if asked again, I would go back to Central America to lend my ideas on how to improve medical education there.

Although our mission to Central America for PAHO was not successful, it emphasized to me, and reminded me again, how fragile medical care and education were in those Central American countries. I took on the PAHO mission because I knew from previous experiences in Central America that most of the population received little or no medical care. On my prior teaching journey to San Salvador, I had seen the long lines of very poor people waiting patiently to receive medical attention. I was told some had been standing in line to see a doctor since 4:00 A.M.

My journey to Central America in 1969 was consistent with my academic career because I had tried for years to advance the quality of medical education there. I believed then, and still do, that if I could improve medical education then eventually the public would receive the health care they so desperately needed. It was also with the objective of improving medical education and thereby health care that I had taught at the medical school of El Salvador and, in 1974, at the one in Ecuador. To the same end, I have done numerous consultations on medical education in two schools in Mexico.

GOING ON SABBATICAL AND ACTING LIKE A DEAN

William Maloney and I met at the Medical College of Virginia when he was dean of the medical school and I was an assistant professor in the Department of Anatomy. He led an effort to restructure the medical education program at MCV, and I was a major participant in the initiative. In 1963, Maloney left MCV and joined the staff of the Association of American Medical Colleges. In 1966 our paths crossed again when he was appointed dean of the Tufts University School of Medicine.

In September 1972 I went to see Maloney in his office. I wanted to thank him personally for approving a sabbatical leave for me so that I could go to a research institute in Paris. There, they were doing some excellent research on the prostate gland. I wanted to learn some of their laboratory techniques and apply them to my work at Tufts. Tufts had granted me a six-month sabbatical leave for that purpose.

I also told Maloney I had decided to resign as chair of the Department of Anatomy before I left on sabbatical. I offered to work with the acting chair so that there would be an orderly transition. When he inquired as to why I wanted to give up the chair, I told him I wanted to spend more time on research and that I would still carry a full teaching load. Then, to my surprise, he asked me to be his associate dean. He told me he knew I was an excellent administrator; he wanted me to be the number-two person in his office and run the day-to-day operation.

I asked for time to talk to Peggy and told him I wanted to get the reaction of some faculty. A few days later I told Maloney I would take the job in late July 1972, when I returned from sabbatical leave.

Peggy, our ten children, and I left Boston for Paris on December 31, 1971. We rented an apartment on the Avenue de Paris in Versailles. It was situated only a few blocks from the Palace of Versailles. The grounds and gardens of the palace became our children's playground while we lived in Versailles.

My sabbatical was productive, and I learned some new techniques I could utilize in my studies of the prostate gland back at Tufts. I had excellent support and tutelage from the director of the laboratory, Dr. Etienne Beaulieu, and I worked closely with Dr. Charles Robel, a scientist in the laboratory. The six months I spent working in the laboratory contributed to my research and thereby to my academic credentials.

While on sabbatical, I was invited to give a lecture in the Department of Physiology at Cambridge University in England. I discussed some of our studies on the fine structure and the biochemistry of a group of endocrine cells of the ovary. Later, after an excellent dinner with members of the faculty, we continued our scientific discussion of physiology while sipping port. I couldn't help but think that for a person who started in a two-room schoolhouse in Texas, it was quite an educational leap to be asked to lecture to faculty at Cambridge University.

Sabbatical leave for me was also a marvelous learning experience for our children. The older ones quickly learned their way around Versailles and Paris. Peggy and I decided not to enroll the children in French schools. Instead, she took on the job of tutoring them. Peggy had talked to each of the children's teachers at home about lesson plans to follow while we were in France. During our stay in Versailles, Peggy faithfully followed the lesson plans. By the time the children returned to school in Concord, they were at the proper grade level in their studies.

In addition to the education of our children, one of the other benefits of our stay in France was that the children spent their time with their brothers and sisters. In Paris, there were no friends and pals to distract them from the family.

The last month before we were to return to Boston, we managed a brief trip to Germany, Holland, and Belgium. I told the children this would be the last time they would all be together as a family. Laurie and Sarita would soon be off to college or at a university, and the rest would quickly follow. They understood what we were saying; during our sabbatical trip, they had drawn even closer to each other. To this day, all of our children have remained close to each other.

We truly enjoyed our stay in France. The time had gone quickly, but we looked forward to our return to the United States and Concord. We landed at Logan International Airport in Boston on an appropriately American date: July 4, 1972.

After returning to Tufts from sabbatical leave, I moved into the dean's area. As executive associate dean, I took responsibility for the day-to-day management of the educational program and working with the faculty. The dean, William Maloney, concerned himself with broad policy issues, hospital relations, and alumni fundraising. Frequently, when the dean was traveling or had other commitments, he would ask me to represent him.

In 1973, six months after I assumed the job of associate dean, I was informed that Maloney was going on sabbatical leave to Germany. Burton C. Hallowell, the president of Tufts University, came to see me one day, told me of Maloney's leave, and asked me to be the acting dean until his return. I was surprised by the news and astonished the university administration would ask me to be acting dean because I had a Ph.D. rather than an M.D. I told him I wanted to think about his offer and would call him in the morning.

I told Peggy the news and asked for her thoughts. I also told her I was inclined to take the job; I knew I could do it. Peggy immediately wanted to know if it was appropriate for me, with no M.D., to take on the job as dean of a medical school. It was unusual, but I did know of several Ph.D.s who had been deans of medical schools. Deans did not make clinical or basic science decisions, relying instead upon the faculty for those functions. My job as acting dean would be to see to it that the medical school functioned appropriately and achieved its mission. I told Peggy most of my work would be developing the faculty, keeping budgets balanced, working with the hospitals, seeking the best education possible for our students, and working with our medical alumni. I added that my appointment would be for only six months because after that Maloney would return from sabbatical.

Peggy was pensive for a moment and then said it was up to me. She would go along with whatever I decided. She asked, though, that I try to limit the nights out and the travel; she didn't want me to wear myself out. Then she asked me to do a few other things if I took the job: to take charge, run the school, and act like a dean.

The next morning I called Hallowell and told him I would take the job. He was pleased with my decision and expressed his confidence in me. He said he would be available to help if I needed him, but otherwise he would stay out of my way. Hallowell told me that most of my interaction with the central administration of the university would be with the provost. The president wished me good luck and reminded me to ask for help if I needed it.

A number of basic science and clinical faculty members expressed confidence in my leadership when my temporary appointment was announced. The Tufts medical school, like the other two in Boston, at Harvard and Boston University, is heavily dependent for clinical teaching on a system of associated teaching hospitals.

I knew the basic science departments at Tufts were strong and stable. My major concern was to continue to provide excellent clinical education for our students. To do so meant I had to solidify relations with our associated hospitals and to continue to look for new clinical affiliations where we could teach our students. Tufts was associated with a number of teaching hospitals in Massachusetts, Rhode Island, and Maine. Our two primary clinical affiliations were with the New England Medical Center, directly across the street from the medical school building on Harrison Avenue, and Saint Elizabeth's Hospital (now Saint Elizabeth's Medical Center) in Brighton.

The New England Medical Center was created by the merger of several hospitals. These included the Pratt Diagnostic Center, the Rehabilitation Center, the Floating Hospital for Children, and the Boston Dispensary, the last being a venerable institution dating to the 1780s that once counted Paul Revere as a member of its board of directors. Samuel Proger, M.D., professor and chair of the Department of Medicine at the Tufts University School of Medicine, was the person who persuaded the hospitals to combine forces and become teaching hospitals under the New England Medical Center name. Recently, the medical center has officially changed its name to the Tufts–New England Medical Center.

We also had clinical affiliations for teaching with the Boston Veterans Administration Hospital and Newton-Wellesley Hospital, and we sent third-year medical students to the Baystate Medical Center in Springfield.

In addition to Saint Elizabeth's Hospital, the medical school was associated with several other Catholic teaching hospitals in Massachusetts and Rhode Island. I decided that I needed to meet with the cardinal of the Archdiocese of Boston, Cardinal Medeiros, to understand his expectations for an academic relationship with Tufts. I did so and as a consequence was able to forge a close working relationship with the Catholic hospitals.

After our first meeting, the cardinal asked me to meet regularly with Father Little, secretary of the board for the archdiocese. At my first meeting with him I asked what the archdiocese expected from Tufts and how we could enhance our affiliation. I made it clear I wanted to keep our relationship strong and growing.

Father Little said the archdiocese knew that Tufts had no money to spare but the archdiocese did want Tufts to recognize the high academic quality of the faculty at Saint Elizabeth's Hospital. They wanted equivalent academic rank with faculty in the New England Medical Center, and he hoped that someday the chair of one of the Tufts clinical departments would come from Saint Elizabeth's. Father Little emphasized that the Catholic hospitals wanted our assistance to continue their academic growth.

During the time I served as acting dean and then as permanent dean, I kept those words in mind and worked to solidify the bond between the Catholic hospitals and Tufts. As a consequence, I involved myself in hospital academic activities. The cardinal appointed me to the search committee for a new chief of medicine at the hospital following the untimely deaths of their chief of medicine, Dr. Frederick Stohlman, and his wife in an airplane accident on September 8, 1974.

I made it a point to be as involved with Saint Elizabeth's Hospital as was appropriate. As dean, I greatly valued their contribution to the Tufts teaching program. Keeping Father Little's words in mind, I worked diligently to ensure that the appropriate academic rank and the dean's attention were given to those in our associated hospitals.

THE AMAZON

Although I was the acting dean, I continued to teach and to do research to a limited degree. I was principal investigator on a federal grant to study the reproductive cycles of male squirrel monkeys, *Saimiri sciureus*. Two of my colleagues from the Department of Anatomy, Duane Belt and James Morehead, were co-investigators on our grant. We were interested in the male squirrel monkey because unlike most mammals, which typically breed year round, it has a reproductive cycle and breeds only in the spring. Following the breeding season, the monkey's reproductive tract atrophies, suggesting that the testes are no longer producing the male sex hormone, testosterone.

We decided that it was not feasible to import squirrel monkeys from their native habitat because removing them from their usual environment would undoubtedly alter their endocrine system, making our results invalid. We decided to go to the Amazon in 1973 to collect tissue and blood samples to bring back to Tufts for analysis.

We made contact with Mike Tsalickis, who specialized in providing animals for zoos, aquaria, and laboratories. Tsalickis's headquarters were at Leticia, Colombia, a small town and inland port and Colombia's only access to the Amazon River. The airport there had one runway but no fuel and was not equipped for instrument landings and takeoffs. Tsalickis agreed to provide the squirrel monkeys for our study and gave us permission to use some of his animal holding areas while we gathered tissues and blood for our studies.

Mike Tsalickis was an entrepreneur. In addition to the animal business, he operated a small one-story inn and provided transportation and guide services. Mike, a Greek American originally from Tarpon Springs, Florida, was in his mid-forties, rather thin, not too tall, and wiry. He gave the appearance of a person who had spent many years in the jungle and a lot of time in the sun. His face and arms were bronzed. Tsalickis moved gracefully and quickly. I noted that he never sat in one place for very long.

After we met up with him in Leticia, we gathered equipment and Duane Belt, James Morehead, and I followed Tsalickis to a one-story wooden barn. Inside were large holding cages for numerous and varied monkeys. I was impressed with how clean the animal facility was and how the animals were not crowded in their cages. Mike had tables and chairs brought in, and we unpacked and arranged the equipment and chemicals we had brought from Boston. We planned to start our studies as soon as possible.

The next day, a local guide took us by a long canoe with an outboard motor to an island Tsalickis owned. We spent the day looking at the animals on the island. The squirrel monkeys were not easy to spot, as they jumped quickly from tree to tree. It was a wonderful day, and it gave me an appreciation for the beauty of the jungle and how difficult it was to move through it.

After returning to Leticia from our trip up the Amazon River, Duane, Jim, and I went to work. Mike arranged for his men to trap a few monkeys for our studies, and we spent the rest of the week gathering and preparing tissues and blood samples for our research. By the end of the week, we finished, packed the materials we had processed, and caught the airplane back to Bogotá. We believed our study was progressing, and we planned to return in three months to gather specimens in the early spring. We gave Tsalickis our approximate date of return, and he assured us all would be arranged for our studies.

The research trip to the Amazon enhanced my academic credentials. Without significant teaching and research qualifications, I would have never have received the administrative appointment as dean of the Tufts University School of Medicine or as president of Texas Tech University. Funding for the Amazon squirrel monkey studies was provided by the National Institutes of Health because of our grant proposal to them. Funding from the National Institutes of Health is given only after an exacting peer review of the grant applications. It is a highly competitive process, and we were delighted when we received the grant for our studies on the Amazon squirrel monkeys.

THE DEAN AND THE PRESIDENT

Soon after his return from sabbatical leave, William Maloney resigned as dean and a national search was launched to seek his replacement. In 1975, after the search committee had considered a number of candidates, I eventually emerged as the choice of the faculty of the medical school and the university administration. On July 1, 1975, I became the dean of the Tufts University School of Medicine.

It was policy at Tufts that each school of the university had to generate all of the funds it spent. Most medical schools fund teaching and research programs with money generated from patient care, research overhead, tuition income, alumni donations, state support, endowment income, and development efforts. My task of funding our programs was difficult because the Tufts medical school had neither significant patient care income nor state support, and the medical school endowment was quite limited.

I struggled to hold down the tuition for our medical students because I did not want Tufts to become a medical school for the sons and daughters of the wealthy. A diverse enrollment that would include economically and educationally disadvantaged students was important and critical to the quality of our medical school. Even though I reduced expenses and cut programs, each year the tuition had to be increased. Not wanting to merely send out a letter about the tuition increase, I assembled the students and, in broad terms, reviewed with them the school's financial situation. I told them how much their tuition would increase the next academic year. Then I went over the projected budget and showed the students where and how tuition money would be spent to enhance their medical education.

I told them of the considerable dollars our alumni gave each year. These monies went to the operating budget and reduced their tuition. Peggy and I spent many nights meeting with alumni to raise funds, urging our former students to support their school. When meeting with the current students, I reminded them of their responsibility after graduation to support Tufts by giving to the annual fund drive.

In 1976, Jean Mayer, the distinguished nutritionist from the Harvard School of Public Health, was appointed the tenth president of Tufts University. Mayer arrived at Tufts like an academic whirlwind and almost immediately proposed several major programs for the medical school. I was concerned that there could be negative financial impact. One of Mayer's efforts was a major emphasis on nutrition, which I welcomed. At our first meeting, he urged me to introduce a new course in nutrition for our students. The curriculum was already filled with course work that the faculty considered important for all medical students. Consequently, there was little room in the curriculum for electives. The clinical and basic science faculties, with some exceptions, were not especially interested in nutrition, and they did not appreciate time being taken away from the courses they taught. Still, we managed to find a few hours to teach principles of nutrition.

To Jean Mayer's credit, Tufts did eventually excel in nutrition teaching and research. Today, it is the only university in the nation with a school of nutrition science and policy. He even persuaded the federal government to build a thirteen-story nutrition research building on the health sciences campus in downtown Boston.

Mayer's actions made it clear he intended to extend the excellence of the university by using the capabilities and resources of the health sciences center. In order to spend more time in Boston, he had a nearby building renovated to house the president's office.

Mayer had excellent ideas, but he carried many of them out with little or no consultation. I was worried that he would start involving himself with our affiliated teaching hospitals. I explained and reviewed with Mayer our teaching hospital structure. I emphasized that we had no extra funding to go to the hospitals, and we held them in the Tufts teaching orbit by goodwill and commitment to their academic programs. I told Mayer it was a finely tuned system, and the only coin we had to give the hospitals was academic rank for the clinical faculty at the hospitals.

Consistent with his desire to be involved in almost every aspect of the medical school, Mayer, to my dismay, soon was visiting our teaching hospitals. When I questioned him about this activity, he told me he only wanted to know the system and understand the hospitals and their needs so he could help me with the teaching program. He assured me he did not want to interfere.

I said to Mayer it was all right to go to the hospitals but asked him to promise he would not make commitments to them before he talked to me. I did say that, should he visit one of our hospitals, I wanted his impressions of the teaching program.

It wasn't long before word came back to me that Mayer was making financial commitments to some of the hospitals without telling me. The president had no funds to put into the hospitals, and the medical budget was stretched to the limit. One day I took a call from one of the hospital administrators in our teaching system who wanted to know when they would receive the funding promised. With a sinking feeling in my stomach, I told him there was no money for his hospital in the budget. Then the hospital administrator told me Jean Mayer had stopped by for a visit, reviewed the teaching commitment to Tufts, thought it substantial and of high quality, and said he would see to it they received money from the medical school to support the program. I told the administrator I would check with the president and get back to him as quickly as possible.

After I hung up the telephone, I sat at my desk and thought about the problem Mayer had created for me. If we started sending substantial funding to one hospital, the others would expect an equal amount of money or more. I picked up the telephone and arranged an appointment with Mayer. The next morning I arrived at the president's suite in Ballou Hall before 8:00 A.M. and a few minutes later was ushered into Mayer's office. It was elegantly furnished and had a spectacular view of Boston. On the conference table were coffee, tea, and croissants.

Mayer invited me into his office and offered breakfast. I declined and told him frankly that I did not have much appetite. Mayer said I worked too hard and hoped I was not getting ill. He wanted to know what brought me to Ballou Hall so early in the morning.

I told him we needed to talk about our relationships and his expectation of me as dean of the medical school. I reminded him that I had already explained, in painful detail, the financial situation of the school. While charged by the administration and the trustees with generating every cent the medical school spent, I was proud that we had not run a deficit during my years as acting dean and now as dean.

As Mayer buttered a croissant, he said that he had reviewed my leadership of the school and that I had done an excellent job keeping the budget balanced.

Then I told him of my call from the hospital administrator asking when the funds would be transferred. Frankly, I said, his meddling with our system of hospitals was making my job much more difficult. Mayer said that I had misunderstood, that he was trying to help me. He insisted that he needed to know the hospital system so that he could help me.

My response to Mayer was an admonition that he stay out of the Tufts hospitals because his going there did not help me—it caused trouble for me. Further, I had learned that some members of the faculty had been going to him with financial and program requests, bypassing me altogether. I reminded Mayer that I had asked him not to talk to faculty about such things before I had had a chance to do so. Bluntly, I said that his seeing faculty and making financial commitments to hospitals had to stop. Then I said to Mayer that if he wanted to be dean of the medical school, to come downtown and be my guest.

Mayer blanched, and then his face became florid. For a moment I thought he was going to fire me on the spot. He muttered a few words and made it clear the meeting was over. I excused myself and left. I am convinced that once Mayer understood how far he could push me, he backed off. I had drawn a line, and he understood he was to stay on his side of the line. To his credit, and my relief, he never mentioned the breakfast incident to me. After our meeting, Mayer greatly tempered his involvement in the hospitals and with the medical faculty.

In addition to his wanting nutrition as a high-profile discipline at Tufts, Mayer wanted to start a veterinary school. I was not convinced there was a shortage of veterinarians in New England and saw no reason to establish a veterinary school. As Mayer laid out his vision of the new school, I became greatly concerned for the medical school. He spoke most convincingly about "one medicine." The Tufts health sciences campus in downtown Boston would be the place where medicine, dentistry, and veterinary science would come together and promote the concept of "one medicine." Under this banner, each school would be a resource for the others, resulting in a synergistic process for solving health problems, enhancing research, and providing education.

I tried to persuade Mayer that creating a veterinary school was not a good idea. I told Mayer a veterinary school and his "one medicine" concept might be a grand idea, but I was afraid it was going to take resources away from the medical school. I reminded him that over the years the medical school had purchased and renovated the buildings it occupied using money from its endowment. I wanted to know if the vet school planned to purchase space from the medical school and if it would be expected to pay the operating costs of the space it utilized. I also pointed out that I expected our basic science faculty to be compensated for teaching veterinary students. I told Mayer that these and other financial matters needed to be resolved before we committed to starting a veterinary school.

Mayer told me not to worry, that the answer to all my questions was in the affirmative. According to him, the medical school would be compensated and all we had to do was add a few more faculty members to teach veterinary students. Mayer promised that the vet school would not have a negative financial impact on the medical school. I was still not convinced we needed a vet school, but if it paid its way, that would be fine, and if it advanced his "one medicine" concept, that would also be fine with me. I said, however, that if the medical school was not reimbursed for expenditures resulting from establishing a vet school, we were going to be one of the most, if not the most, expensive medical school in the country. I assured Mayer our tuition would go sky high.

To my dismay, the trustees approved the creation of the veterinary school, and soon Mayer hired a dean, who, in turn, started recruiting faculty. It was only a matter of days after the arrival of the new veterinary dean that I had my first quarrel with him. Many more were to follow. My greatest worry had been borne out in fact. Mayer had not addressed the financial reimbursement of the medical school for space and faculty.

After the veterinary school became a reality, it was an almost daily struggle to avoid its financial impact on the medical school. There were numerous meetings, sometime contentious, with the veterinary school dean and the provost. Still, Mayer and I maintained a cordial and close working relationship. Although we disagreed on some matters, he had come to respect my leadership. I, in turn, recognized Mayer's genius of generating ideas and making them happen on a grand scale. Often I found the problem to be in the details of implementation. To Mayer's credit, his dynamic style of leadership brought Tufts University national and international recognition and led it into the ranks of the academically elite universities in this country. Tufts University owes much of its excellence today to Mayer. He awakened the academic potential at Tufts, and his ideas and vision became the catalyst for markedly enhancing its reputation.

Twenty-five years after Mayer proposed his "one medicine" concept, the entire veterinary school moved from the health sciences campus in downtown Boston to the Grafton campus, forty miles away. Today, as I predicted, the medical school tuition is among the highest in the nation.

Jean Mayer served as president of Tufts University from 1976 until his retirement and appointment in 1992 as the first chancellor of Tufts. He died in 1993.

CHAPTER 8

⷟⷟⷟

Back to Texas

In 1979 Dr. Maurice Cecil Mackey resigned as president of Texas Tech University and the Texas Tech University Health Sciences Center, and the board of regents launched a nationwide search for his replacement. Peggy and I were spending a week on Nantucket when I received word of Mackey's resignation and the presidential search.

I asked Peggy if I should try for the job as president of Texas Tech. It would be a great job, it was a fine school, and it had significant resources that could be used to enhance programs. I also knew that the medical school was struggling and had once been on probation.

Peggy said it was my decision. I had done an excellent job at Tufts, she said, since I had managed to launch a capital campaign to build a new library and teaching building and had already raised enough money to buy the land, with some funds left over for endowment. The academic programs were strong, she added, but she knew the veterinary school continued to be a problem to me. She was of the opinion that, after my eight years as acting dean and dean, it might be a good time to leave.

Peggy also knew that Tech meant a lot to me. I had two degrees from Tech, and two of my brothers had graduated from there. Three of our children—Lisa, Victoria, and Rob—were going to school at Tech. It was also where I met Peggy. I had always been proud of my Tech degrees, and the education I received there made me competitive in science and academics. My only real concern was moving the children from New England to West Texas. So a week later, in Concord, Peggy and I sat down to decide whether or not I should apply for the Tech job. We talked about the job for quite a while, focusing on the impact the move would have on our family. Then, together, we did an analysis of our situation, listing the positives and negatives. We determined there were more pros than cons.

The next day I sent the Tech search committee my curriculum vitae and credentials and I called Jean Mayer, telling him I was looking at the Tech job. I didn't want him to read about it in the newspaper or hear it as a rumor.

A few weeks later, I received a call from Freda Pierce, the secretary to the board of regents. She said she was calling to let me know that the presidential search committee wanted to have an interview with me at a meeting being held at the Dallas/Fort Worth International Airport (DFW).

Two weeks later, I flew to DFW and met with members of the search committee. The committee was large and included several members of the board of regents as well as faculty, student, and community representatives. They asked probing questions about my academic and administrative experience. It was in my favor that I had a thorough knowledge about medical education, possessed an excellent record in teaching and research, and was a Tech graduate. I returned home and told Peggy I thought the interview had gone well and that I had a feeling I was still a candidate for the job.

A month later, Peggy and I were both asked to travel to DFW for another interview. This time I met with the search committee and all of the members of the board of regents. Peggy was not with me in the room because she had been asked to meet with the spouses of the board members.

When Peggy found out she had a meeting with the spouses, she was not pleased by the idea of being screened by a selection committee. Peggy said she would make it clear she was not much for teas and coffees and that the most important thing on her agenda was her family.

My interview by the presidential selection committee and Peggy's with the committee of spouses must have gone well because several weeks after the second interview at the airport, Freda Pierce called again. The board was inviting me to the Tech campus as one of the presidential finalists. I thanked her for the good news, and then she asked that I keep the news about the meeting confidential because the board wanted my visit kept secret.

I was somewhat taken aback by the request. I explained that meetings such as these could hardly be kept secret. After all, my wife knew I was being considered for the president's job, our children knew and had probably told their friends, and I had already informed the president of Tufts that I was in the running. I pointed out to Mrs. Pierce that their biggest problem was going to be keeping my visit a secret in Lubbock because the search committee and other faculty and staff would know of my visit.

Mrs. Pierce agreed with my analysis of the situation but again asked that I keep my visit secret. She said she would book a room for me at an inn not far from campus but that I would need to use a fictitious name when I registered. Quickly I tried to come up with a cover name that I wouldn't easily forget. I decided on "Murdock," Peggy's maiden name. A week later, as I prepared to leave for the airport, I told Peggy I was off to Lubbock and covert operation "Murdock." I said I would telephone her in the evening and would take Lisa, Victoria, and Rob out to dinner while I was in Lubbock.

I had no idea what the outcome of the presidential search would be. I knew there was one local candidate, John Bradford, the longtime dean of engineering, and another outside person. I was sure they were both highly qualified or they would not be finalists.

As my flight approached Lubbock, I looked out the window and saw below me the beautiful high plains, the Llano Estacado (Staked Plains). I recalled the legend of how the Llano Estacado, stretching a hundred miles across Texas into New Mexico, got its name. In 1541 Francisco Vasquez de Coronado, the Spanish conquistador, traveled eastward across the area. Inasmuch as there were few landmarks to guide the explorers, he ordered that stakes be driven at intervals as they crossed the plains.

As I left the plane in Lubbock, I glanced down the jetway toward the exit into the terminal. I saw a television photographer accompanying a woman I assumed was a reporter. I wondered who had come in on this flight that was important enough to justify TV coverage. Then it occurred to me that they were here to interview me. My cover had been blown; so much for Mrs. Pierce's insistence that this visit be a secret. I knew there were no secrets at a university, and indeed there should not be. I decided to walk quickly past the reporter and photographer.

As I went by the two journalists, I looked for the exit from the terminal. Then a voice asked if I was Dr. Cavazos, and the lights on the television camera came on. Not given to lying, even for the board of regents, I stopped, turned, and faced them, and said that I was.

The reporter introduced herself as Pam Baird, of Channel 28 News in Lubbock. She wanted to ask a few questions on camera about my visit and if my being there was related to the presidential search. I told her I would not answer any questions or make a statement, and I knew she would understand. By evening a large part of the population of Lubbock would see me on the news, declining to answer questions. I smiled at the reporter and the photographer, waved, and walked to the exit. I did not learn how they knew I was arriving in Lubbock.

I rented a car and drove to the Lubbock Inn, where Mrs. Pierce had made a reservation for me. My covert arrival was shattered a second time when I walked up to the registration desk and said my name was "Murdock" and that I had a reservation. The clerk welcomed me to Lubbock, Texas, as "Mr. Murdock," and said he needed a credit card and my signature on a form.

I sheepishly handed him a credit card with my real name on it. The clerk glanced at the name on the card, smiled, did an imprint of it, and handed it back to me with the key to my room. He acted as if it were an everyday occurrence that guests had fake names or credit cards with someone else's name on them.

The next morning, I arrived on the Tech campus and went to the suite of the board of regents. Here I met Mrs. Pierce, who took me to a nearby conference room and said that Mr. Robert Pfluger, chairman of the board of regents, would be right in.

As I sat sipping coffee, I couldn't help thinking about Peggy and my family. I knew there was a strong possibility I would not get the job at Tech, but if I were to be appointed it would mean uprooting them from the home they loved. Still, I really wanted the Tech job, and I knew I could do it.

Then a man with a friendly smile on his face walked in. He was quite tall, wore horn-rimmed glasses, and although there was strength of character in his face, he was somewhat modest in demeanor and rather soft-spoken. I liked him immediately. He said his name was Robert Pfluger, we had met at the DFW airport interview, and he was chairman of the board, part-time; full-time, he was just a rancher from San Angelo. He welcomed me to the Tech campus.

I asked for the agenda and what was to follow. Pfluger told me they had just finished interviewing the other finalist; they had selected three, but one had recently withdrawn from consideration. He said that across the hall was a room filled with faculty, students, alumni, business people from town, and lots of reporters. Every member of the board was there for the final interview.

I told Pfluger that I was on the Tech campus because I wanted the job, I knew I could do it, and I would answer the questions from the search committee to the best of my ability.

With a smile, Pfluger expressed confidence that I would do a good job answering questions and said that I would get to ask questions as well. He asked that I make a statement about how I saw the university and what kind of leadership I thought I could bring to it. Pfluger said that after the interview was over, about noon, the board would go into executive session. He said that the session might take a few hours, but he asked that I be at my hotel by early evening and to expect his telephone call there.

As Pfluger had promised, the room was filled with people. He introduced me to the crowd and asked me to make an opening statement and to review my academic background, my management skills, and my plans for Tech if I were selected as president. Pfluger especially wanted to know why I wanted to be president of Texas Tech.

I described my academic background, but I especially focused on my expectations for Texas Tech and the Health Sciences Center. I tried to keep my statements positive but spoke about areas needing attention. My opening comment was, "I want this job because nine other presidents have made Tech great. I want to extend what they started."

I did an assessment of the university and the Health Sciences Center based on reading material provided to me, noting there was considerable excellence at the two institutions, but, like most human enterprises, they could be improved. I gave examples of where there needed to be improvement in academic programs, but I also spoke about the strengths of the two institutions. After my opening statement, the questions and answers went on for almost two hours.

Finally, the interview ended. Pfluger said he appreciated my comments and forthright manner. He adjourned the meeting, and the board began their executive session.

After a light lunch at the Lubbock Inn, I spent the afternoon walking about the Tech campus. I was amazed at the growth of the university and the magnificent new buildings. I couldn't help thinking about my student days. When I came to Tech as a student in 1948, enrollment was about forty-eight hundred, a marked increase over previous years because of returning veterans of World War II going to college on the G.I. Bill. I was one of them.

When I enrolled at Tech, there were only a few buildings bordering the central campus. Most had been built in the late 1920s and early 1930s, and each was built in the Mission/Spanish Revival style. As a student, most of my time was spent in the Chemistry Building. In addition to the chemistry department, this building housed three other departments: biology, geology, and physics. Those three departments were now in the Science Quadrangle, across from the expanded Chemistry Building.

I also drove to the enormous Health Sciences Center on the northwest side of the campus. Although it had some unfinished shell space, the medical school building was about a million square feet. I couldn't help but think about our space problems at Tufts Medical School. There, the smallest office or lab was considered prime space.

Later that day, I went out to the small house that Peggy and I had bought for our children to live in while attending the university. I explained to Lisa, Victoria, and Rob that I had to be back at the Lubbock Inn early in the evening because the chairman of the board had promised to call with a decision.

After returning to the Lubbock Inn, I called Peggy and gave her an update on the children and my meeting with the search committee and the board. I did some paperwork while I waited for the telephone call. By nine o'clock I still had not heard from Pfluger, and I began to suspect that the board had failed to agree on whom to select for president. I pulled a book from my briefcase and started to read. About an hour later the telephone finally rang.

It was Pfluger, and he said the board hadn't made a decision yet. He told me I had most of the votes for president, but two board members were opposed. They were going back into executive session to continue the discussions. He said he would call as soon as he had something definite to tell me.

I was quite disappointed in the news Pfluger delivered. The board consisted of nine members appointed by the governor of Texas. Seven members in favor and two opposed was not a resounding vote of confidence in my ability to lead Tech. I turned back to my book, but it was difficult to concentrate. Finally, about eleven o'clock, I went to bed.

About half an hour later I was still awake. Then the telephone rang again. This time it was Pfluger calling to tell me that the board had selected me as the next president of Texas Tech. He extended his congratulations, and I told him I was delighted with the news. Then Pfluger told me my selection was not unanimous; board members Fred Bucy and Don Workman had voted against my appointment. Pfluger assured me, though, that the board had every confidence in my ability. He asked if I would take the job. I told him I would and asked about the next steps.

Pfluger said he wanted me to meet with him, board member Fred Bucy, the general counsel to the university, and the vice president for finance at the Lubbock Inn at 9:00 A.M. We were to discuss the compensation package, academic appointment, and any other matters I might wish to bring up. Then we would go to the campus, the board would convene in open session, and they would vote on my appointment.

As soon as I finished talking to Pfluger, I dialed Concord and awakened Peggy. I gave her the good news, and she said she was pleased for me, knew I would do a great job, and Tech was lucky to get me.

The next morning, January 12, 1980, I went downstairs to breakfast. The local newspaper, the *Lubbock Avalanche-Journal*, had my selection as the lead story. It also ran a large photograph of me on the front page. Now, I thought to myself, my cover was totally blown. A number of people stopped by my table to congratulate me on my appointment and to offer their support. I was touched by the friendliness of the Lubbock people and the commitment of so many to the university.

At 9:00 A.M. I met with Pfluger, Fred Bucy, Dr. Marilyn Phelan, who was the university's general counsel, and the acting vice president for finance, Dan Williams. Pfluger opened the meeting by congratulating me that I was going to be the next president of Texas Tech. In reality, I had two presidencies: one at the university and the other at the Health Sciences Center. I would have an office at each place. Williams proceeded to describe my salary, benefits, car allowance, and the requirement that I live in the President's Home, which was not far from the campus. The annual salary offered for two presidencies was almost the same amount I received as dean of Tufts Medical School, but I was so pleased to be appointed president that I was not about to quarrel over the pay.

Phelan said I would have an academic appointment as a professor with tenure in the university and in the Health Sciences Center. It was my decision as to the academic departments in which I would have my appointment. I chose the Department of Biology in the university and said I would like to hold similar rank in the Department of Anatomy in the medical school. Phelan had mentioned tenure, but I said I didn't want automatic tenure. I was professor of anatomy, with tenure, at Tufts, and I intended to go through the same probationary period for tenure as any full professor would have to go through at Tech and the Health Sciences Center. This proposal meant that at the end of three years I expected to come up for consideration of tenure in both institutions.

Phelan advised me to take the tenure offer, because it was important for my security and I certainly was qualified for it. I thanked her for her concern but told her that I preferred to go through the tenure appointment process.

We returned to campus, and while waiting for the formal board meeting to begin I telephoned Jean Mayer at Tufts to let him know that I had just been selected to serve as president of Texas Tech and expected to leave in February. Mayer said he was pleased for me but that my leadership at the Tufts medical school would be missed. We arranged to meet after my return to Boston and discuss transition. He concluded the call by saying, "Congratulations, Mr. President."

"Thank you, Mr. President," I responded.

A few minutes later, I was escorted into the Board Room and introduced as the next president of Texas Tech University and the Health Sciences Center.

TRANSITION, INAUGURATION, AND CAMPUS LIFE

In early February 1980 I resigned as dean of the Tufts University School of Medicine, and Murray Blair, my associate dean, was appointed acting dean.

I arrived in Lubbock in late February, and my inauguration as president was set for April 15. Peggy and I decided it would be best if she and the children stayed in Concord until the school year was over.

I began my Tech presidency by being up early and in my office by 7:00 A.M. The trip from the President's Home to my office was only eight minutes, a real delight after the forty-minute commute from Concord to Boston.

By habit, I keep a clean desk and try to follow the efficiency rule of not touching a piece of paper more than once. I made decisions quickly and moved on to the next problem or issue. My work was enormously facilitated by Clyde Morganti, the assistant to the president. He had worked for the former president, so he knew the university and the functions of the office quite well. Morganti was a retired air force officer and former commander of Reese Air Force Base near Lubbock. Clyde was the most organized and efficient person I had ever met. He had a wonderful sense of humor, had the highest of ethical standards, and worked hard. Without fail, Morganti's advice was sound and practical. Soon I counted him as a trusted colleague and friend. The two of us usually arrived at the same time in the morning, about 7:00 A.M., and my day started by meeting with him to review the schedule for the day and any issues needing to be resolved.

My administrative assistant was Sharon Nelson. She had worked for the two previous presidents of the university, Grover Murray and M. Cecil Mackey, as well as Lawrence Graves, during his time as interim president. She knew the operation of the office well and had in-depth knowledge of the university. Like Morganti, Sharon Nelson was efficient and diligent in her work, and the office ran smoothly.

After I left the presidency Sharon Nelson was the administrative assistant to two other interim presidents and two other presidents of Texas Tech. So she worked for a total of five presidents of Texas Tech and three interim presidents. This is quite a record of accomplishment and testimony to Sharon Nelson's excellent administrative skills.

I was fortunate to have Clyde Morganti and Sharon Nelson working in my office. They eased my transition from Tufts to Tech, and in the years that followed they were of enormous assistance to me.

A couple of days before my scheduled inauguration as president Peggy and the children flew in to attend my inauguration. My mother, my sister Sarita and her husband, Albert Ochoa, and all my brothers and their spouses followed. Peggy and I were delighted that so many of our relatives were able to be at the inauguration. It was a grand moment for all of us.

Mother said it was a happy moment for her, but she was sad that Dad was not there to see me installed as president of a university. We all talked about Dad and how we missed him. Careful not to let me get too comfortable basking in my glory, Mother told us how proud she was of *all* of her children: Dick, a three-star general in charge of Fort Hood,

Bobby and Joe, successful in their business, and Sarita, a beloved teacher in Laredo. Mother said Dad would have seen this list of his children's achievements as payoff for those early years of struggle to raise and educate us.

The day before my inauguration, I was in my office working on my speech when the intercom buzzed. Sharon Nelson said there was someone to see me. I opened the door to Sharon's office, and there stood Dr. Robert Melampy, my major professor and mentor through my Ph.D. degree. Iowa State University had designated Melampy as its official delegate to my inauguration. I told him how delighted I was he was there. I asked why he didn't call so I could have picked him up at the airport.

Melampy said he wanted to surprise me and that it was his honor to be there. He told me he had known when I was his student that I had a great academic future. Melampy added that achievement was what happened when one worked sixteen hours a day, seven days a week. He had predicted it, and he was very proud of me.

The next day was inauguration. Near the close of the ceremony, Robert Pfluger, as chairman of the board of regents, placed a Tech medallion around my neck signifying I was president of Texas Tech University and the Health Sciences Center. In my inaugural address, I thanked Peggy and the children for their support and love. I had a catch in my voice and felt a tear of joy in my eye.

Then I spoke of three major areas where I believed we could achieve excellence if we stayed focused on our mission and worked together. First was nutrition, through the cooperation of the Schools of Agriculture and Home Economics and the Health Sciences Center. Second, I asked that we seek ways to use solar and wind to augment oil and natural gas, an area in which the Schools of Architecture and Engineering could take the lead. The third area was improving the health of the public, in which the Health Sciences Center and its regional campuses would take the lead.

In the years of my presidency I kept these three initiatives in mind and reminded the faculty and staff of them. I believe we made some progress on nutrition and energy, but the most progress was in improv-

ing the health of West Texans. I directed the growth of the medical
school, built the new regional academic health center in Odessa, Texas,
and expanded the centers in El Paso and Amarillo. I persuaded the
Texas legislature to fund the School of Nursing and the School of Allied
Health. These two new schools opened midway though my administration and became part of the Health Sciences Center.

As I entered the president's job, I found considerable excellence at
the university and the Health Sciences Center. Both had fine faculty
and first-rate students, but much more needed to be done to improve
the overall merit of the two institutions.

In the spring of 1980 two of our children, Lisa and Rob, were enrolled at
Tech, and Cat (Victoria) was in Lubbock although she was not enrolled
at Tech that semester. Laurie, our oldest son, was already in West Texas,
too. A few months before, he had been hired as a pilot by Permian Air-
ways, which was based in Midland. Laurie flew twin-engine Navajo airplanes over most of the western part of the state. Rick was still a student
in his last year at Tufts University. Sarita lived with us in Concord while
working at Harvard Dental School.

During the trip to attend my inauguration, Sarita took time to visit
the campus and talk to several people about programs. She had been
thinking about her future and told Peggy she wanted to move with the
family to Lubbock. She said she would miss us if she stayed in Boston
and had decided to work on an MBA at Tech's College of Business,
which had an excellent reputation. She felt the tuition was manageable
and was confident that she could find a job in one of the banks in Lubbock and go to school in the evening.

Finally, after considerable effort, Peggy and I moved our younger
children, three dogs, and three cats from Concord to Lubbock.

In a couple of months Peggy had everything unpacked and arranged in
our new home, and Peggy said that since the house was in order and the
children in school, she was going back to work. Lubbock General Hospital was hiring surgical room nurses, and she explained she wanted to

work there part-time, so that she could be home or traveling with me in the evenings. Peggy asked what I thought of the idea. I told her it was grand.

A few days later, Peggy was hired at Lubbock General Hospital to work as a nurse in the operating room. Soon after, while meeting with one of the regents, I mentioned that Peggy was going back to work as a nurse. He looked at me, somewhat startled and surprised that the wife of the president of Texas Tech was going to work. He was not sure how the other regents would react to my wife working. He informed me that the president's wife had certain official duties and that her working could interfere with them.

I told the regent I was not asking for permission for Peggy to work. I was just informing him. I assured him that Peggy would do a splendid job meeting her obligations as the president's wife. I told him Peggy had her own mind, and I for one would support her if she wanted to go back to nursing.

The conversation ended, and no one ever raised the issue again.

A few weeks after my inauguration at Tech, I attended my first meeting of the Texas College and University System Coordinating Board. Beryl Milburn chaired this board, and earlier in the year she had said that other than the University of Texas and possibly Texas A&M University, no other state-financed Texas university or college even approached being a quality school.

Not many people in Lubbock agreed with Milburn's assessment of the public higher education system in Texas. Constructing a building with state funds on a college campus had to be approved by the coordinating board. The exceptions to this rule were the University of Texas at Austin and Texas A&M University when using money from the Permanent University Fund.

Milburn opposed Tech's plan to construct an addition to the Music Building, calling it "unnecessary." The addition was a high priority for the university because music education classes and rehearsal space were in the old Music Building and two wooden buildings. These wooden buildings were declared army surplus after the end of World War II. The university, pressed for temporary space to accommodate a surging enrollment after the war, had bought and erected them on the Tech campus. They were officially designated "X-buildings," but the students called them "X-Shacks." When I was a teaching assistant in the Department of Biology, I had taught several zoology laboratory sessions in "X-19."

Bill Parsley and Mike Sanders, my legislative assistants, were instrumental in educating me about the coordinating board and explaining to me the strategy we should use to gain approval for the Music Building addition. They suggested "space replacement," meaning that Tech would offer to demolish enough square footage to equal the amount of space the addition to the Music Building would contain.

The day that the coordinating board met, I presented the space replacement proposal, explaining that in the late 1940s and early 1950s I had had a number of classes in the X-buildings and later taught in one of them. I recalled the wind whistling through the building and the West Texas dust settling in the room. As teaching space, these were terrible buildings, and our music faculty had no alternatives. I recalled that my fellow students had a saying about the X-buildings: "They'll be here until we have grass on the campus." We were wrong, though, because now the beautiful Tech campus had grass, but the X-buildings were still there.

The coordinating board approved construction of the Music Building addition, and on July 8, 1980, I participated in the groundbreaking ceremonies. With my commitment to the coordinating board, I saw to it that all of the X-buildings be razed except one, which had a concrete basement that housed a linear accelerator for the physics department. I decided it should be left because of the high cost of removing it.

After the X-buildings were gone and the Music Building addition was under construction, I asked Dr. Glenn Barnett, my vice president for planning, to give me an update on the square footage of the university. This statistic was important to me because one of the formulas the legislature used to budget funds for an institution was based on square footage. He gave me the numbers and I thought about them.

If we were going to build any more new buildings at Tech, I told Barnett, we would have to find ways of reducing the square footage. Barnett replied that he had to tell me I was the second president who had traded off the X-buildings. Grover Murray (the eighth president of Tech) had made the deal with the coordinating board years before, but the university never got around to tearing them down.

As president of the Health Sciences Center, I spent considerable time there because I believed improvement of its academic quality required my attention; it was not because I had taught at and led a medical school for more than thirty years. The need was obvious. The school was created to train physicians who would provide health care in West Texas, the most medically underserved area in the state. I knew that most physicians tend to practice close to the area in which they spent their residency or received specialty training. To me this fact meant that the medical school had to improve graduate education as well as enhance undergraduate medical education.

In creating the medical school at Tech, the state legislature decreed that Tech would not only build the Health Sciences Center in Lubbock but also establish regional academic health centers in El Paso and Amarillo and in the Permian Basin at either Odessa or Midland. As a result, Tech sought to provide health education and medical education for an area of 128,000 square miles, about the size of the state of Kansas.

Medical students would complete their first two years on the Lubbock campus. For the last two clinical years, one-third of the students would go to Amarillo, one-third to El Paso, and the remainder would stay in Lubbock. It was envisioned that eventually students would be rotated to Odessa.

On August 21, 1972, the medical school had started with thirty-six first-year students and twenty-five third-year students transferring from other medical schools. It is remarkable that in less than two years the medical school administration and the faculty put together an educational program. In 1974, the transfer students became the first graduating class. The Liaison Committee on Medical Education (LCME) formed by the Association of American Medical Colleges and the

American Medical Association was the accrediting agency. The LCME visited Lubbock twice in 1973. In 1974 it granted full accreditation to the medical school, but for one year only.

Late in 1974, six years before my arrival at Tech, the LCME had placed the school on probation. The reason for probation was a concern that the medical school did not have adequate clinical teaching facilities. When a new medical school such as the one at Tech opens, its curriculum tends to advance more rapidly than its facilities. The too-rapid startup of the medical school resulted in an inability to fulfill some of its commitments because of a lack of clinical facilities and resources. In 1976, after considerable work was undertaken to develop clinical and research facilities and to recruit faculty, the school was again fully accredited.

I especially enjoyed working with the dean of the medical school, George S. Tyner, M.D. He had told me the reasons why the school had been on probation and what changes had been made since re-accreditation. I told Tyner that in the months ahead we would work to improve our relations with the hospitals so that they would give us more clinical teaching opportunities. I noted that all of the clinical departments now had a chair, but we still needed to recruit additional faculty.

Tyner told me they were currently admitting 80 first-year medical students, and next year the school was scheduled to admit 120 entering students. I told Tyner we did not have the capacity or the programs to take 120 students. After all, four years ago when there were only 80 new students the LCME had put the program on probation. I suggested that 100 students would be a reasonable goal for the next few years, which would give us time to solidify the El Paso and Amarillo teaching programs, as well as the one in Lubbock. Also, in about four years we planned to build the Regional Academic Health Center in Odessa.

In the following months I worked with Tyner to correct deficits cited by the LCME and to restructure and improve many aspects of the educational programs. Credit goes to many, especially George Tyner, for improving the quality of the school and attracting top-flight faculty.

Years later, on November 8, 1993, Peggy and I returned to Lubbock for the unveiling of two commemorative plaques, one on the university campus and the other at the Health Sciences Center. During my tenure as president the board of regents had decided that for each president of the university and Health Sciences Center a commemorative plaque should be affixed in an appropriate place. The dedication of the plaque would take place five years after the president left office. My plaque at the Health Sciences Center reads as follows: "Lauro F. Cavazos, Third President of Texas Tech University Health Sciences Center, 1980–1988. Lauro Cavazos, fifth [actually, sixth] generation Texan and the first Texas Tech alumnus to serve as president, led the Health Sciences Center from infancy to maturity. He guided expansion that nearly doubled the operating budget, and provided the means to expand the academic programs at the HSC. He oversaw more than $27 million in facilities development at all four campuses. The Schools of Nursing and Allied Health joined the School of Medicine to create the Texas Tech University Health Sciences Center during Cavazos' tenure. Dr. Cavazos resigned to become U.S. Secretary of Education."

DOSES OF DISCRIMINATION

Midway through my presidency at Tech, discrimination and racism surfaced again in my life. Not since my early days at Flato, when I fought a bully who did not like "Mexicans," had it been so blatant. One day as I passed through Sharon Nelson's office on my way to mine, I saw her return her telephone receiver rather forcefully to its cradle. She was an excellent assistant with wonderful skills and always polite. I knew something had upset her.

With some hesitation, she told me that a woman had called my office about her daughter's problem at Tech. Sharon told her she would transfer the call to the vice president for student affairs, but the caller wanted to speak to the president and have him handle the matter personally.

Finally, my assistant suggested that she send me a letter explaining her daughter's problem. Sharon told the woman I always answered my mail and that by sending a letter, her daughter's situation would automatically be brought to me personally.

The caller said, "Oh, the Mexican can read?"

Sharon terminated the telephone conversation. I sighed when she told me the nature of the call. I knew that even as a university president, I was not immune from racist remarks.

About midway through my presidency at Texas Tech, there was another incident. I agreed to speak at a chamber of commerce dinner in a small town about seventy miles northwest of Lubbock. A member of the Tech board of regents ran a business nearby, and he asked me to speak at this special occasion for the local chamber. He drove me to the town, and I was glad he did the driving because we were in a blinding sandstorm, a frequent springtime occurrence in West Texas. My talk was scheduled for 7:00 P.M., and there were about three hundred people in attendance. Prior to the beginning of the program, I met many of them and we talked about the weather, crops, cattle, and education. It was a delight to visit with them. They struck me as typical West Texas people, hard working and honest. Most were Anglo, but there were a few Hispanics. A few of the Latinos told me how proud they were that a person of my heritage headed a big and important university.

Then the program began, and the master of ceremonies, a local Anglo rancher, introduced me. My office had sent him my curriculum vitae, and he used it to frame his introduction, telling the audience about my academic degrees, my presidency of Texas Tech, on what national and state commissions I served, how many years I had been dean at the Tufts medical school, and my numerous academic publications.

I presume he thought he was being complimentary or perhaps humorous, for as he finished his introduction, he said, "For a Mesican, you sure done a lot."

Though startled by his comment, I did not respond to his bigoted, racist remark. I ignored it and gave my talk. Afterward, there was a reception; I again exchanged pleasantries with many of the people in the audience.

The next day, my mind kept going back to my experience the night before in the small West Texas town. Certainly the "Mesican" remark pained me, but I was even more troubled that no one in the audience was indignant or had extended an apology for the introduction and overt racism to which I had been subjected. A week or so later, though, I was pleased to receive a letter from a woman who had been in the audience. She wrote that she was appalled that the master of ceremonies had made the "Mesican" comment, and she apologized for her neighbor's rude behavior. Of the three hundred or so people in the audience, she was the only person who wrote or called about the incident. I appreciated her letter.

The lesson I learned from these two instances is that none of us, regardless of station or status in life, is immune from racism. I recognized that the racist beatings at Flato Elementary School were but a prelude to future acts of bigotry. These latter incidents, coming from adults, were far more disturbing and hurtful to me than a split lip or a bruise on the cheek inflicted by a school bully.

MOTHER'S HEALTH

Peggy, more than any other person, is responsible for whatever I have achieved in life. She has been, and continues to be my constant support and advisor. In my childhood years, it was Mother who shaped my life. From the earliest days I can remember on the ranch, she worked on shaping my attitude, my behavior, and my values. Dad did his share, perhaps far more than many fathers, but because of his job, I rarely saw him during the day. He left the house on the ranch before the sun came up and usually did not return until we children were in bed.

Mother and I talked on the telephone often, and she would keep after us to visit her, telling us how much those visits meant to her. So Peggy and I frequently drove to Kingsville to see Mother.

For years I had been trying to get Mother to quit smoking, but to no avail. She smoked about a pack a day of unfiltered Lucky Strike cigarettes. As far back as I could remember she had used tobacco. In later years, I lectured her about the health problems resulting from smoking when I was urging her to quit. Obviously, my talks about lung cancer and other ills due to tobacco had little effect on her. She continued to smoke, and by the time she was seventy years old, I gave up trying to get her to stop.

Soon after Mother turn eighty she was diagnosed with gallstones, and the doctor recommended surgery. In those days, that meant about ten days in the hospital. Soon after her operation, I went to see Mother in the hospital. She was doing fine, and there had been no complications.

Mother said that the doctor told her she could go home the next day. Then she surprised me by saying she had quit smoking. She was proud that she had gone ten days without a cigarette. Now, she said, she didn't even want one.

As I walked out of the hospital, I thought to myself that stopping smoking just proved that once Mother made up her mind to do something, nothing could stop her. For the rest of Mother's life, she never smoked another cigarette.

A few months after her gall bladder surgery, Mother called me one evening at our home in Lubbock. After the usual inquiries about children and our well-being, she said she needed some advice. Mother told me that while she was in the hospital they had checked her completely, giving her x-rays exams and many tests. Mother told me they had found a balloon on the big artery in her stomach. Mother asked if I knew what the doctors meant by a balloon. I told Mother it sounded as if they were saying she had an aneurysm. The doctor had told her if she did not have an operation, it could pop like a balloon and she would die in a few minutes. Mother made it clear she did not want another operation and asked me what I thought she should do.

Although the news of the aneurysm was a shock so soon after her surgery, I had to be honest with her. More surgery would be a considerable risk, especially with her blood pressure and heart problems, and the aneurysm could burst at any time, even today—or five years from now. I told Mother if I were in her situation, I would not have the surgery, but it was her call.

Mother said she was glad to hear what I had to say because she had just gotten off the telephone with Dick, who had told her exactly the same thing. She informed me she was not going to be operated on, and if she died the next day it didn't matter. She decided to forget about the balloon in her stomach and have a good time.

During the next few years, Mother enjoyed relatively good health for a person in her eighties, but when she was eighty-six, her health began to fail, and there were several hospitalizations. Peggy and I drove from Lubbock to the hospital in Corpus Christi, Texas, and we always found her in good spirits.

After her last hospitalization in Corpus Christi, she was started on renal dialysis because of failing kidneys. Hypertension and cardiac enlargement were taking their toll on her body. Once a week, she traveled from Kingsville to Corpus Christi, about forty miles, for dialysis. She disliked the procedure immensely.

One day in early April 1987, my sister Sarita called, upset because she had driven from Laredo to take Mother to the renal clinic in Corpus and Mother had announced that she would not go again. Sarita told her she would die in a few days if she did not have treatments, and Mother told her she didn't care.

I told Sarita that Peggy and I would be in Kingsville in a day or two and that I had to be in Dallas the next day for a conference. I told Sarita to keep working on Mother and to call Dick. He had a way of fussing at Mother, and she might pay attention to him.

Dick called Mother and threatened to put her in a nursing home. Because she dreaded nursing homes, she agreed to one more round of dialysis.

The next day I traveled to Dallas for my conference. It had been a long day, and I was troubled by Mother's refusal of treatment. I went to bed, planning to return to Lubbock in the morning and drive with Peggy to Kingsville.

That night at 11:00 P.M., Saturday, April 4, 1987, the telephone rang, and it was Peggy. She told me Dick had called, telling her that Mother had died. According to Dick, Peggy said, the aneurysm let go, she passed out, they rushed her to the hospital nearby, she received the final sacraments, and she was gone.

I knew Dick and I had given Mother sound advice the time she had asked about the aneurysm. Mother enjoyed seven years of relatively good health, she was at home when the aneurysm ruptured, she avoided a nursing home, and the Church ushered her out with all of its blessings.

Mother is buried next to Dad in a small cemetery overlooking the Santa Gertrudis Creek.

TENURE, RESIGNATION, AND A CALL FROM THE WHITE HOUSE

At Tech, as at most universities, there is a committee within each college or school to review faculty members' qualifications to receive tenure. Generally, three criteria are used to make the judgment about awarding tenure: teaching ability, research and publications, and public service. Faculty must excel in all three areas in order to qualify for tenure. If the recommendation from the tenure committee is positive, it goes to the dean of the college or school. If approved by the dean, it goes to the academic vice president for review, and then to the president. If the president concurs and agrees to award tenure, the recommendation is sent to the board of regents. Tenure gives the faculty an appointment at the university without limit of time. It ensures that a faculty member will have academic freedom to teach without constraint.

While tenure protects the academic freedom of the faculty member, it also requires that the professor maintain a high level of excellence in teaching, research, and public service and to continue to grow academically. Of concern is the tenured faculty member who does not continue to do high-quality teaching and research.

Once granted tenure, a faculty member has a lifetime appointment and can only be removed for moral turpitude, or if the department is abolished, or if a financial exigency is declared by the university. If there are too many tenured faculty members in a department, there is little or no room to bring in new young faculty. Put another way, the department, if "over-tenured," will grow old together.

I considered tenure recommendation to be among the most important and serious duties I had as president of the university and the Health Sciences Center. I read every tenure application folder several times and reviewed the percentage of tenured faculty in the departments. To my dismay, I found a few departments at Tech that were 100 percent tenured. Some departments, although close to being fully tenured, continued to submit faculty for tenure.

The board of regents at Tech had the ultimate responsibility for awarding tenure, and each year I gave them my recommendation of those faculty members who deserved tenure. Each year when I took tenure recommendations to the board, I heard the same discussion. Some argued that there was no such thing as tenure in their businesses; if people didn't do their jobs, they could be fired. Some regents thought the same principle should apply to the faculty.

Always, during tenure discussions some board member asked what assurance I could give that a faculty member I was recommending for tenure would continue to be highly productive for decades to come. I told the board I couldn't answer the question but that we needed tenure at our university. I said that if we did not have tenure at Tech, we could not compete nationally for excellent faculty. I insisted that if Tech was to continue to grow and excel academically, we needed a sound tenure system in place. I pointed out, however, that we must not let departments become over-tenured or have too large a percentage of our faculty tenured. If this happened, we would be unable to bring in new faculty. I told the board we had to be able to assure the faculty and the American Association of University Professors (AAUP) that we supported the tenure concept. I reminded the board that the AAUP had put Tech on probation some years back when the university fired several professors without cause; it was several years before the university was taken off of probation.

Although the tenure matter was an issue every year, in the sixth year of my presidency the board truly focused on the tenure issue and insisted I do something to keep Tech from becoming top-heavy with tenured faculty. I promised the board I would examine where we were with tenure numbers and percentages and project the impact of significant numbers of additional tenured faculty on our efforts to enhance the quality of the university.

After the board meeting, I met with one of my administrators and told him the tenure issue would blow up in our faces if we didn't go about it properly and in a fair manner. The faculty senate was already concerned that we were even having discussions about tenure, and I understood their concern. I didn't really believe that the board was opposed to the concept of tenure as such; I believed that they were simply bothered by the high numbers of tenured faculty, and so was I.

A few months later I met again with the board to discuss the tenure issue and told them I believed I had a mechanism by which we could both preserve the tenure system and ensure that the university had a balance of tenure and untenured faculty.

A board member asked me to outline my recommendation, and I told them that first we had to assure the faculty that no one already tenured would lose their tenure and that the tenure concept at Tech would be preserved. Second, I said that we should think about setting limits on the percentage of tenured faculty in a department. Non-tenured faculty in a department that was approaching its maximum of tenured positions would have contracts, perhaps one- or two-year appointments, renewable many times. Then, I explained, if a tenured position opens up because a tenured faculty member moves, retires, or dies, the non-tenured faculty in the department could compete for the tenured slot. Those competing would go through the tenure review currently in place. Third, to maintain quality I suggested that tenured faculty undergo a thorough review of their academic performance once every five years. I made it clear that the objective of the review would not be to terminate tenured faculty but to help faculty improve their teaching and research.

After considerable discussion, the board agreed that I should move ahead. I said that if we moved in this direction or even had extensive discussions on the tenure issue, the faculty would vote "no confidence" in me. But I believed that we had to find ways to control tenure numbers if Tech was to continue to improve. I told the board that the days ahead would be difficult for me and that they too were going to take a lot of heat.

In the months that followed, the pressures on me were significant, with the board wanting tenure review and limits and the faculty senate wanting me to stay out of the tenure issue entirely. Finally, as I had predicted, the faculty senate called a confidence vote on the president. It was overwhelmingly negative. I should have taken solace that it was not 100 percent "no confidence," but it was the saddest and most troubling day of my entire academic career.

The next day the board of regents met in an emergency session and publicly voted their confidence in the president. Frankly, their vote, though well intended, meant nothing to me. It did not help alleviate the deep hurt I felt from my alma mater and my colleagues on the faculty.

The proposal to limit tenure never went to the board for a vote, and in essence, nothing came of the tenure matter. The AAUP was called in to investigate Tech. Their concern was preserving academic freedom and tenure. I met with the site visit team, and after a thorough review the AAUP found no cause to take action against Tech.

As a postscript to the tenure issue, in the last weeks before I left the presidency at Tech to become U.S. secretary of education, I called in my academic vice president and told him I wanted to meet with the faculty of each of the colleges and schools before I left for Washington. I did not want a general faculty meeting; I wanted to discuss issues specific to each of the colleges and schools. I also said I did not want any other administrator at these faculty meetings; it would be just the faculty and I.

The faculty meetings were arranged and went even better than I expected. We had wide-ranging discussions on education and the future of Texas Tech. If memory serves me correctly, no one mentioned the tenure issue or the no-confidence vote. The final faculty meeting was scheduled with the College of Arts and Sciences. This college had been the most vocal and sensitive to the tenure issue. I knew it was going to be a difficult meeting, but I looked forward to clearing the air on the tenure issue.

The auditorium was almost full; perhaps 250 to 300 faculty members were in attendance. I talked about my expectations and hopes for Arts and Sciences. I reminded them that as a zoology major, I was a graduate of what was then the Division of Arts and Sciences. There was no rancor from the faculty, nor were there confrontational questions. I responded to their queries. As the meeting came to a close, I brought up the tenure issue and the no-confidence vote, saying that it distressed me. I hoped that the faculty now understood that I wanted only the best for Tech and for them.

One faculty member rose and asked to be recognized. He said he wanted me to know how much he appreciated and admired my courage in meeting with the faculty, and they wished me well. There was a standing ovation as the last faculty meeting I held at Tech came to an end.

By 1988 I had been president of Texas Tech and the Health Sciences Center for almost eight years, longer than the average time for a university president and second only to Grover Murray among Tech presidents. The years had been interesting, challenging, fun, difficult, rewarding, and sometimes heart-breaking and disappointing. I was constantly focused on faculty matters, the academic quality of the university and the Health Sciences Center, finances, and budgets. The collapse of oil prices worldwide had had a major financial impact on Texas. As a result, all of the state's institutions sustained severe cuts in their operating budgets.

My efforts to reform tenure at Tech had been costly to me in terms of professional status. Those months had taken a toll, and I was tired. In addition, although the Ranching Heritage Center, part of the Museum at Texas Tech, had seen significant growth, the relationship between the Ranching Heritage Association, an external group supporting the center, and the university was strained. It took much time and effort to reestablish a cordial working relationship with the association, but I eventually did.

On the Health Sciences Center campus, I was often at odds with our teaching hospital, Lubbock General Hospital, over academic and fiscal matters. Those issues consumed much of my time and energy.

Still, I believe there were many positives in my presidency. In 1985 I launched the first capital campaign in the history of the university, the Enterprise Campaign. It had been successful, exceeding our goal of $65 million. I oversaw the creation of the School of Architecture by moving it from under the College of Engineering. We acquired a large plant and considerable land and moved our Textile Research Center into more spacious and useful quarters, and several other new buildings were constructed during my time as president. I also led the move to a tougher admissions policy, which went into effect in the fall of 1989. This change required much debate and discussion among the administration, the regents, and the faculty.

Throughout the university and the Health Sciences Center, there was now a major commitment to research. Research funding increased markedly from both the State of Texas and the federal government.

At the Health Sciences Center, I oversaw the creation of the School of Nursing and the School of Allied Health. We also obtained permission from the legislature to start the School of Pharmacy and the School of Veterinary Medicine, although the legislature did not provide funds for these two schools. I am pleased, although it was years after it was authorized, that the School of Pharmacy opened at the Amarillo Regional Academic Health Center in 1996. The Academic Health Centers at El Paso and Amarillo were expanded, and the Odessa Regional Academic Health Center was constructed during my time as president. I persuaded the legislature to complete the shell space in the Health Sciences Center in Lubbock, which provided almost a million square feet of finished teaching, research, and administrative space for medicine, nursing, and allied health.

Looking at photographs of me when I was appointed in 1980 and how I appeared in 1988, it is obvious the presidency at Tech exacted not only an emotional toll but also a physical one. Peggy reminded me that when I came to Tech as president, I was a vigorous man with black hair, and eight years later it was almost all white. She said the bags under my eyes were pronounced, and I had a tired look on my face that wouldn't go away.

On May 11, 1988, I called a press conference to announce my decision to resign the presidency of my alma mater in July 1989. Peggy was at the press conference, and it was a sad day for both of us. I was leaving nine years after becoming the first Texas Tech alumnus to become president of the university. I stated that I planned to return to teaching; I held a tenured position as a professor of anatomy in the School of Medicine. I explained that the average tenure of a university president in the United States is four and one-half years. I had exceeded that by quite a margin, but I still wanted to give the board fourteen months' notice so that it would have adequate time to find a replacement.

Wendell Mayes, a longtime friend, classmate, and chairman of the board of regents, insisted that neither a group of regents nor an individual regent had prompted or influenced my resignation. Regent Wesley Masters pointed out that he had chaired the evaluation committee in late January, and I had received the highest marks given in his six years on the board.

I emphasized that Tech needed a new president, suggesting that those in positions of leadership should recognize when it is time to leave. My time had come. I had paid my dues to Texas Tech for my education, and it was time for a change.

Neither Peggy nor I had any idea of the magnitude of the change. Two months later, I got a call from the White House, and four months later, on September 20, 1988, Vice President George Bush swore me in as the U.S. secretary of education. I was the first Tech graduate and the first Hispanic appointed to the Cabinet.

CHAPTER 9

Recruited to Washington

On a bright sunny day in Lubbock in July 1988, Sharon Nelson entered my office at Texas Tech University and told me a Mr. Robert Tuttle was calling from the White House. Tuttle was the White House director of personnel, and he told me President Reagan was seeking a replacement for William Bennett, who had recently announced his decision to step aside as secretary of education. Tuttle asked if I was interested in being considered for the post.

Although I was taken aback by the question, it was not the first time I had been approached about the job. Soon after the election of President Reagan in 1981, the Reagan transition team had inquired about my interest in the post. I pointed out to them that I had recently assumed the presidency of Texas Tech University and did not think it appropriate to seek another post so soon. I did not hear from the White House again until I received the call in July 1988.

By then the situation was quite different, since I had recently announced my intention to resign as president of Texas Tech. I told Tuttle I was not sure of my answer, that I needed to give it some thought and discuss it with my wife. I asked Tuttle to give me the weekend to think it over and that I would call him the following Monday.

Peggy and I had planned a trip the next day to Taos, New Mexico, which would give us a weekend with plenty of time to discuss the possibility of a Cabinet appointment without the typical interruptions occurring when I was on campus or in Lubbock. As we drove through the beautiful West Texas plains and into the mountains of New Mexico, we talked about the opportunities and pitfalls the post of secretary of education would present. Peggy and I became excited by the prospect of going to Washington.

I reminded Peggy that since President Reagan had only a few months left in his term, I might, if confirmed, have only three or four months to serve in the Cabinet. Although my term of service could be brief, it would be a grand experience and an opportunity to learn about education at the national level.

Peggy agreed and said that even if George Bush won the presidency, there was no assurance he would appoint me to his Cabinet. Still, she thought it would be an interesting time, regardless of how long or short my appointment would be. Then she reminded me that President Reagan might not even appoint me to his Cabinet, but it was still an honor to have even been considered.

I told Peggy she was right. No matter how brief our stay in Washington, it would give us an opportunity to focus national attention on some of the fundamental needs of education. We had talked a lot about education improvement, and this opportunity gave us a chance to do something besides talk. On Monday I telephoned Tuttle and told him I was indeed interested but had a lot of questions, and I was sure he did as well. Tuttle asked if I could come to Washington the next Sunday afternoon to meet with him at the White House.

I checked my calendar and told Tuttle I could make the trip to Washington that week and that I would bring my wife. The following Sunday afternoon Peggy and I were at the White House. In the Office of Personnel we met Tuttle, whose job was to screen candidates and recommend Cabinet-level appointments. I immediately liked Tuttle, and during the time we worked together in President Reagan's administration, I considered him a colleague and a friend.

Tuttle told Peggy the interview was going to take time and that there was an empty office across the hall where she would be comfortable. He asked if she brought something to read. Peggy told Tuttle she was studying for the National Certification Board exam in perioperative nursing. She said she would use the empty office and stay out of the way.

After making Peggy comfortable in the nearby office, Tuttle and I moved to his office. The initial interview went on more than two hours. He did a thorough job of learning about me and searching for problems and issues in my past life that might be a barrier to my confirmation. He wanted to be assured that the president would not be embarrassed when he nominated me for the Cabinet. Tuttle explained that the administration was sensitive about the nominee's past, especially after the 1987 failure of Robert Bork's confirmation as a Supreme Court justice.

We finished for the day, and then Peggy and I had dinner with Tuttle at the Willard Hotel. It was a delightful evening, with Tuttle continuing our discussion from the afternoon. I asked Peggy if she had any questions, and she queried Tuttle about the role of a Cabinet officer's spouse. He replied that there was none at all. In our excitement that evening, neither Peggy nor I read between the lines of Tuttle's response. Had we done so, we might have discerned that a Cabinet member's spouse would be effectively widowed by the job.

The next day I made the rounds of the White House staff and was interviewed by a number of White House personnel, including Kenneth Duberstein, the chief of staff. I thought the interviews went well, and we talked about strategies to address education problems. I was honest and forthright in the interviews, and when asked about Bill Bennett and how the higher education community saw him, I responded that there was a gulf between them. Bennett had alienated the colleges and universities to the extent that there was hardly any dialogue between the Department of Education and post-secondary education. Bennett's style, outspoken and colorful, was a delight to the national press but was not well received by the higher education community.

I said that I agreed with Bennett on many of his higher education statements but that universities had difficulty accepting his solutions. I would try to find ways to bring all of us together—the education community, the federal and state governments, and the students and parents. I knew divisiveness would not solve education problems.

During these interviews, I had an opportunity to visit briefly with Vice President George Bush. I wished him well on his campaign for the White House, and I was pleased that he had moved education into the forefront of his campaign. I told him I was delighted he wanted to be known as the "education president."

Tuttle informed me that the administrative staff would discuss and consider my candidacy for the Cabinet post. If they agreed I could do the job, they would review it with President Reagan for his decision. Peggy and I returned to Lubbock and waited for a decision from the White House.

A week later the White House called to seek my permission for a thorough probe of my background by the Federal Bureau of Investigation. I gave them permission to proceed on the background check and assured them they had my full cooperation. I completed innumerable questionnaires and gave consent for a thorough review of my federal income tax returns. Later I learned that the FBI investigation had been accelerated by order of the president. The FBI gave me a clean bill, and I was asked to return to Washington for further discussions.

On my return, the first meeting was with Tuttle. He asked about my political affiliations. Most had assumed I was a Texas Democrat. I informed Tuttle that I was registered to vote in Texas, where one does not have to indicate party affiliation. I told Tuttle I had sometimes voted in the Democratic primary and at other times in the Republican primary. When I lived in Massachusetts, I was registered as an Independent.

This answer seemed to satisfy Tuttle, but the press and others continually questioned me about my party affiliation. I did not consider party affiliation terribly important, but I soon learned differently in Washington. Conservative Republicans were suspicious of my agenda and of me. The Heritage Foundation, a conservative think-tank in Washington, was constantly critical of my leadership. The conservative *Washington Times* blasted my education leadership almost daily. This newspaper seemed to especially enjoy printing malicious gossip about Peggy and me. I did not want politics to interfere with my efforts to improve the education of all children.

On August 10, 1988, I met with President Reagan in the Oval Office. It was the third time we had met. In 1984, during his first term of office, he had presented me with a certificate for outstanding leadership in education, and I met him again when then Secretary of Education Terrel Bell invited a small group of Hispanic educators to meet with him and the president.

President Reagan asked me a number of questions about education and then asked if I would serve in his Cabinet as the secretary of education. I said I would be deeply honored and delighted, and I promised I would do an excellent job for him. I especially appreciated his comportment and kindness to me. He was so gallant and cheerful when he told Peggy, who had joined us in the Oval Office, that I had agreed to serve in his Cabinet.

Peggy and I were awed by the occasion. Pride, joy, humility, and a bit of fear were some of the emotions I remember. This moment was the culmination of an educational career that had started in a two-room schoolhouse on a ranch in Texas. During the visit to the Oval Office I realized I would be the first Hispanic appointed to the Cabinet in the history of the United States. It was a personal honor but also a telling statistic that bore witness to the lack of education achievement by so many Hispanics and to the discrimination they have suffered.

Bill Bennett joined us in the Oval Office. It was the first time I had met him, and I was immediately impressed with his manner and ideas. I liked him from the start, and to this day I admire his thoughts on education and his dedication to educational excellence for all. I greatly value his friendship. During my time as secretary, I had several meetings and discussions with Bennett on education strategies and policy. He and I agreed on many education issues but disagreed on others. Nevertheless, it has always been a pleasure to work with him. To his credit, Bennett wants everyone to excel in his or her education. His books and essays on ethics and behavior have attracted the attention of the nation, as well they should. They are thoughtful, scholarly, and to the point. Over the years our personal friendship has grown. As former Cabinet officers, we have participated in several education forums. It is always good to see him, and I enjoy our lively debates on national education issues.

After I left the Oval Office and President Reagan, the chief of staff told me there would be a press briefing by the president at which he would announce my appointment as the next secretary of education. President Reagan, Bill Bennett, and I proceeded to the White House press room. I insisted that Peggy be invited to witness the announcement in the briefing room, and a staff member arranged for her to stand along the wall.

The briefing room of the White House was jammed with television cameras and reporters. The president stood between Bennett and me and announced his intention to nominate me as secretary of education.

The *San Antonio Express-News* quoted President Reagan as saying, "Dr. Cavazos will be the first Hispanic-American member of the Cabinet. That says a lot about him and about Americans of Hispanic heritage. This is a proud day, not just for Dr. Cavazos, for his family, and Hispanic Americans, it is proud day for all Americans." When the president was asked if he had nominated me because of my ethnic background, the newspaper reported that Reagan said, "I selected him because he seemed to be the best fitted man to follow Mr. Bennett." In introducing me, the president said, "Dr. Cavazos has been a leader in helping minorities gain educational opportunity. It is work where he believes progress has been made, but where much remains to be done. I share that view, and Dr. Cavazos, you'll have my every assistance in carrying on this important work for America's minorities."

The newspaper also quoted me telling Reagan, "Your administration has clearly demonstrated that education is one of its highest priorities and the initiative that you have begun in this vital area will be of tremendous benefit to this nation and to this nation's future. I share your views and I look forward to serving you."

The national response to my nomination as secretary of education was mixed. Some praised the nomination based on my education experience, while others saw it only as a political move on the part of the Republicans. Jose DeLara, president of the League of United Latin American Citizens (LULAC), called the appointment political but that Hispanics would welcome progress wherever they could find it. He said my appointment was an excellent choice but that it was a move by the Republicans to gain Hispanic votes. He cited the Reagan administration's opposition to affirmative action, an attempt to dismantle the Civil Rights Commission, and some Republican support for the movement to make English the official language as examples of the failure of the Republican administration to be supportive of Hispanics.

Many Hispanics in the United States knew of my commitment and efforts on their behalf to improve their educational achievements. A number of the Hispanic leaders in the nation expressed hope that I would be reappointed no matter who was elected president in the fall.

Many criticized the Republicans and the Reagan administration for appointing a Hispanic to the Cabinet in the final months of the election campaign, thereby suggesting political motivation for my appointment. I responded to the press that the Democrats, during their long hold on the White House, could have appointed a Hispanic to the Cabinet but chose not to. I disregarded the political posturing by Democrats and many members of the press.

Still, some Hispanics continued to be dismayed at my nomination and my acceptance of the job. They continued to characterize the appointment as one aimed at garnering the Hispanic vote. I remarked to Peggy how I wished they would quiet their strident voices and be pleased that one of their own had finally been appointed to the Cabinet.

No doubt some element of politics did enter into my appointment to the Cabinet. What else could one expect from Washington? Even after I was sworn in as secretary of education, the issue of political motivation in my appointment continued to swirl in the press. During a press conference in Corpus Christi, Texas soon after my swearing in, I was asked if my appointment was a politically motivated effort to get the Hispanic vote. Again I responded that the administration thought I was the best person for the job.

Some suggested I had a commitment from Vice President Bush, that if he were elected he would keep me in the Cabinet. The vice president and I never discussed it, and I only expected I would serve a few months, until the next president was sworn into office. Even with this short tenure, I saw it as an opportunity to continue my efforts to improve the education of minorities, the educationally disadvantaged, and the disabled. I had commenced these efforts as dean of Tufts University School of Medicine and continued them as president of Texas Tech. The Cabinet post now gave me a national platform from which to speak on behalf of the improvement of education for every person in America.

I started preparing for the Senate confirmation process. Under the able direction of Nancy Kennedy from the White House Office for Legislative Affairs, and Francis Norris, assistant secretary for legislation in the Department of Education, I made the rounds of key members of the Senate Committee on Labor and Human Resources. Sen. Orrin Hatch (R-Utah) and Sen. Nancy Kassebaum (R-Kans.) were most helpful.

I knew and had worked with Sen. Edward Kennedy (D-Mass.), chairman of the Committee on Labor and Human Resources, when I was dean of the Tufts University School of Medicine. He was supportive of my nomination, although we differed on the amount of funds needed for a quality education. As secretary of education, I came to appreciate Senator Kennedy's grasp of education issues and his commitment to helping students in financial need. I believe we always worked well together, despite a few disagreements on some issues. Whenever we disagreed, we would sit quietly in his office and resolve our differences.

Another person I soon learned to admire and enjoy working with was Sen. Arlen Specter (R-Pa.). His insight into education problems was most helpful to me. He was especially interested in providing education for the incarcerated. We worked well together on several projects, and I knew I could depend on his counsel and direction. After my resignation as secretary was announced in 1990, he was one of the few who took time to write to me. I appreciated his kind and generous letter. Also, Senators Hatch and Kennedy contacted me by telephone and expressed their disappointment that I had left the post of secretary of education. I will always be grateful for those calls.

In my legislative rounds preparing for confirmation, I also stopped by to see Sen. Lloyd Bentsen (D-Tex.). He was a longtime friend from South Texas, and he was now running for vice president on the Democratic ticket. He told me to go lobby someone else because I should know I had his vote.

In early September, I spent many hours studying the briefing books prepared in the Department of Education. These voluminous books contained considerable data and were organized as questions and answers on education issues. The answers, of course, represented or agreed with the administration's viewpoint on the education issues. Peggy repeatedly quizzed me from these books and evaluated my responses relative to the answers in the briefing books. This activity was to be the beginning of a working system the two of us developed and used to prepare me for the many House and Senate committee hearings at which I testified.

The confirmation hearing before the Committee on Labor and Human Resources was held on September 9, 1988. Overall, the hearing went well and lasted an hour and a half. In addition to discussing education matters, Senator Kennedy used the occasion to point out the need for considerably more funding for education. He acknowledged that federal funding was not always the answer to improving education but pointed out how frequently the administration tried to cut education spending. In our exchange (quoted from Senate Hearing 838, 100th Cong., 2d sess., 1988), Senator Kennedy said, "With the exceptions of the 1985 and 1989 budgets, which were submitted in 1984 and 1988, the administration has consistently tried to cut education spending. Notice

how big the proposed cuts have been in some years, 17 per cent, 15 percent." The charts he used to illustrate his point graphically showed the
pattern of request for education funds from the administration. Senator
Kennedy continued, "That is why many of us find it so hypocritical that
this Vice President talks about being an education president when for
the last seven years we have seen this administration consistently request less than the Congress has requested over the period of years."

The chairman then made a telling point: "Now, again, the amount
of request does not mean everything, but even the administration seems
to increase their budget in years divisible by four. Every other year it has
been cut, cut, cut when Vice President Bush has been a part of this administration. . . . Again, this is the pattern: Propose education spending
in election years and push for cuts in every other year."

Senator Kennedy then said to me, "It is that kind of activity that has
to bring cynicism and skepticism about who is for education and who is
not. And at this time, one of our prime concerns is whether you will be
a forceful advocate for adequate federal funding."

I tried to assure Kennedy and the committee that I would be a
forceful advocate for education. I did point out that we had to set priorities for our education goals and then determine budget needs. I promised I would do everything I could do to obtain the best funding possible
for education. But I continued to emphasize that improving education
required more than simply adding funds to the budget: "[F]unding is
not the total picture, as far as I am concerned. We need strong advocacy
for education, in general, for all of our students. That is another part of
that same equation, Senator."

During the remainder of the hearing, I promised I would provide
strong leadership for the Department of Education, with reform and restructuring high on my agenda, along with quality education for minorities and the disabled. In retrospect, I believe I kept my commitment
to the Committee on Labor and Human Resources during my tenure as
secretary of education, although others might argue differently.

At the close of the hearing, Senator Kennedy said, "But I want to
say that I have been, again, very impressed with your responses." His

next remarks pleased me: "But your responses, I think, have been enormously helpful, and as one who has had the good opportunity to work with you in the past on other issues, health and manpower issues and other questions in the health area, I know that you are a man who follows through with your statements and your commitments, and I will look forward to supporting your nomination and seeing that we do everything we can to get early consideration of it."

Peggy and I were greatly relieved the hearings were over. We had done all we could to present an honest assessment of the state of education and some of the strategies to bring about improvement.

After the confirmation hearing, we returned to Lubbock to wait for the Senate committee's vote. We were delighted when we later learned that the vote had been unanimous. The next step was for the full Senate to vote on my confirmation.

The Senate vote would be on September 20, 1988, and Peggy and I started preparing for our move to Washington. We had only a few more weeks before we left Lubbock, and we had much to do. I sent the board of regents my resignation as president of Texas Tech University and the Health Sciences Center effective September 19, 1988. We had lived in Lubbock for more than eight years and had met and worked with many wonderful people whom we greatly admired and counted as friends. During the last weeks in Lubbock, Peggy and I received numerous invitations for dinners and receptions in our honor. We turned them all down, but thanked everyone for their kindness.

Time went quickly as we were getting organized for the move. One day Peggy said I seemed down, and she wanted to know my problem. She told me she was sure I was going to miss Lubbock and Tech, but this ·job in Washington would be interesting and exciting. I admitted that I was a bit down; I was bothered and disappointed that the board of regents had yet to publicly acknowledge my presidency and service to Tech and the Health Sciences Center. There had been not one word of thanks for eight years of work. I told Peggy I did not understand the board's nonreaction to my appointment to the Cabinet, or to my being the first Tech graduate to be appointed to the Cabinet. The board's silence baffled me.

Peggy told me I was being overly sensitive, but she admitted that a few words of recognition and appreciation from the board were in order. She said not to let it bother me, though, because the board would probably express its appreciation at the last meeting before our departure.

The final board of regents meeting I attended was held at a hotel near the Dallas/Fort Worth airport just a few days before we left for Washington. Most of the agenda dealt with setting up the search for a new president and the appointment of an acting president. After the board adjourned, I flew back to Lubbock, disappointed that the board had not passed a resolution for the minutes of the meeting thanking me for my service and leadership. Perhaps it was an oversight, but it is difficult to believe it did not occur to one board member to offer a resolution of thanks for my eight years as president.

In 1993, the board of regents invited me to the unveiling of a plaque at the university and the Health Sciences Center in recognition of my years as president. It was the board's policy of placing a plaque for each of its presidents, five years after the president left office. The invitation was the first communication from the board of regents since my departure in 1988.

Returning from my last Tech board meeting, I told Peggy there had been no action taken acknowledging my service as president. I said I hoped that some day, maybe before I died, some member of the board would acknowledge my work for the university and my appointment as secretary of education by placing resolutions in the minutes. Even if they did it after I died, that would be okay, too.

Peggy and I went to my office and in one afternoon, packed and moved all of my personal books, papers, and mementos. I borrowed our son Tom's pickup truck, and Peggy and I carried the boxes and loaded them. After we cleared the office of my personal belongings, I placed my keys to the office and the university car on my desk and walked out.

On a return trip to Tech a month after I became secretary of education, Peggy and I did receive a wonderful sendoff from Tech faculty,
students, and staff. It was a great public expression on their part of appreciation for my leadership over the years. We will never forget the
event and everyone's kind words. The students gave their tributes to us
in the format of a political party nomination. Fifty campus organizations voiced their best wishes and thanks for my work. There were tributes from faculty, staff, and the alumni association.

The great Texas Tech marching band was there, and Peggy and I
held our tears of joy and sorrow about leaving almost to the end of the
Texas Tech alma mater—then the tears flowed.

On September 20, 1988, Peggy and I sat in the vice president's office in
the Capitol. On television we watched the Senate go into executive session to consider my nomination to be secretary of education. Senator
Kennedy obtained passes for our family to watch the Senate vote from
the visitors' gallery. They listened to Senator Kennedy speak about the
confirmation hearing. With appreciation we heard him praise my leadership in education. From the *Congressional Record*, September 20, 1988,
volume 134, number 130, one can read Senator Kennedy's words: "It is
readily apparent that Lauro Cavazos knows a great deal about American education and that he has the perspective to be a superb Secretary
of Education."

He went on to describe the Committee on Labor and Human Resources confirmation hearing in which I noted that "the Federal Government is part of the solution" to America's education problems. Senator Kennedy quoted me as saying, "The Federal Government has a
responsibility to provide resources for those students who are most vulnerable. The Federal government must provide leadership and ideas. It
must be an ally in the education reform movement."

Heady words—and I truly meant them. I would work vigorously to
make them come true during my term of service. In the time ahead, I did
not let political consideration sway my judgment about any education
decisions. I remained focused on trying to do the best I could for the

education of children. Still, others insisted on discussing and analyzing the political implications of my decisions.

In the vice president's office, Peggy and I sat tensely as the roll call was taken, and to our delight the vote of the Senate in favor of my confirmation was unanimous.

Later in the day, Vice President Bush swore me in as secretary of education at the White House.

On my research trip to the Amazon, 1973.

A Cavazos family portrait, Concord, Massachusetts, 1975.
Front row (left to right): Lauro III, my wife Peggy, and myself.
Second row: Daniel, Alicia, and Roberto. *Third row:* Tomas, Victoria,
and Rachel. *Fourth row:* Ricardo, Veronica, and Sarita,
holding our dog Max.

My official Tufts portrait, painted during my last days
as dean of the School of Medicine, 1980.

My inauguration day at Texas Tech, 1980. *Front:* My mother, Tomasa Cavazos, and my sister, Sarita Ochoa. *Back (left to right):* My brother, Gen. Richard Cavazos, myself, and my two youngest brothers, Joe Cavazos and Bobby Cavazos.

My swearing-in ceremony at the White House, with my family,
President Reagan, and Vice President Bush, 1988.

Official White House photograph, courtesy of the White House
and the Ronald Reagan Presidential Library.

President Reagan and Vice President Bush greet me and
Peggy in the Blue Room at the White House prior to my
swearing in on September 20, 1988.

Official White House photograph, courtesy of the White House
and the Ronald Reagan Presidential Library.

A Cavazos family portrait of Peggy and me with our
ten children on our fiftieth wedding anniversary, 2004.

CHAPTER 10

༺ ༒ ༻

Serving as Secretary

Peggy and I moved to Washington at the end of September 1988. Although we were excited about my new job, we quickly missed our children and grandchildren. It was the first time we had been by ourselves since before our first child was born in 1956. This move and these circumstances meant major adjustments for Peggy and me.

Peggy asked what was first on my agenda in the Department of Education. I told her I wanted to talk to the departmental employees, thank them for what they had done in the past, and tell them I looked forward to working with them in the future. I delayed my first general press conference until after my meeting with the people in the department.

Dr. Linus Wright, the former superintendent of schools for Dallas, was the deputy secretary of education. He convened the department meetings and introduced me to each group. Wright had done a great job working for Bennett. He was a knowledgeable and capable educator, and during those first few months under President Reagan I relied heavily on Wright for guidance and ideas on education issues.

I told the departmental employees there were four steps we needed to take to improve education. First, we needed to raise the awareness of the nation to its education problems, and we needed to let the people know how they could bring about educational change and improvement. Second, I said we must care about the education of all of our children. Meaningful change starts with caring. I added that I did not see enough caring in America. I told the department we must teach the illiterate to read, work with dropouts and keep in school those who were vulnerable to dropping out, and help the disabled child learn. Third, I said, I needed to emphasize how important it was to raise the expectations of children by telling them they can learn and that they will be successful in school. If we tell a child he or she will fail, they will fail, and we need to emphasize success. Fourth, I wanted us to work together to educate every child in America to his or her fullest potential. The latter became a mission statement for me as secretary.

My first day in the office was one of briefings by staff on issues, procedures, and functions of the department. I was determined to learn all I could. Although the Department of Education was relatively new, having been spun off of the Department of Health, Education, and Welfare by President Jimmy Carter, it had about five thousand employees, and our budget was $27 billion.

The first week I was in the office, Linus Wright, the deputy secretary, briefed me on travel and the security system. He said that when I traveled, everything would be arranged well in advance; all I had to do was show up. Flights, tickets, seating, and hotel reservations would be done in advance, and a security person would travel with me, make sure everything worked smoothly, and coordinate with local security people when I arrived at my destination. I told Wright I didn't need security and people looking after me; I had traveled the world by myself and never had a problem. I asked if I had to use the security system provided by the federal government, and if so, why.

Wright explained that I had no choice in the matter of security. It was required. He reminded me that as a Cabinet officer I was in the line of succession to the presidency, should something happen to the president, the vice president, then the Speaker of the House, and, after them, the other Cabinet officers, depending on the date their department was created. I was thirteenth in the line of succession—among the Cabinet officers.

At the inauguration of President Bush in 1989, I had another civics lesson. There were three holdovers from President Reagan's Cabinet: Attorney General Richard Thornburgh, Secretary of the Treasury Nicholas Brady, and me. We were each assigned military escorts for the entire inauguration period. I had a Coast Guard petty officer as my driver, and a lieutenant commander in the Navy was in charge of the detail. They took excellent care of Peggy and me during the inauguration period. Two days prior to the inauguration there were a number of social events. Peggy and I managed to avoid as many as we could but did enjoy a few.

The last event of the inauguration is the grand parade after the swearing in of the president and vice president. Peggy and I sat through most of the parade, but it was a bitterly cold, wet day in Washington. After an hour or so, we excused ourselves, said good-bye to President and Mrs. Bush, and slipped out of the grandstand. Peggy and I met our military escorts in the parking lot and asked them to drive us to our apartment near American University.

As we pulled into the parking area in front of our building, I thanked them for a job well done, and we wished them the best in their military careers. The naval officer said it had been their privilege to help me, adding that the two of us certainly had been easy to take care of, hardly asking for a thing. He told me after dropping us off he had to go to his office and shred these papers. I asked, "What papers?"

The naval officer said the documents detailed where he was to take me in case of an emergency or a disaster. He said that because I was a Cabinet holdover, I would be third in line from the Cabinet for succession to the presidency; none of the new Cabinet officers had been sworn in yet, so the usual order didn't apply.

I learned another rule about security when President Bush spoke to a joint session of Congress on September 11, 1990. Peggy and I were traveling in Texas at the time, and I was planning to give a number of speeches. Because of my travel commitments, I was going to be away from Washington when the president gave his speech. A friend of mine and regent of Texas Tech, J. L. Gulley, had asked me to give a talk to a civic group in Tyler. The invitation fit my travel schedule and gave me an opportunity to talk about academic choice and the right of parents to choose the school their son or daughter would attend.

On our way to Tyler, I received word from the White House that I was the "designated absent Cabinet officer" during President Bush's speech to Congress. Federal law prohibits everyone in the line of succession to the presidency to be together in the same place, at the same time, at a public meeting. I was told I had reservations at a small motel on the outskirts of Tyler, Texas, and I was to go there as soon as I finished my talk. A Secret Service agent would contact me at the motel, and I was to follow his directions.

After the talk in Tyler, Gulley invited me to a reception, but I turned him down, pleading a tight schedule. I could not tell Gulley I was going to the edge of town to spend the night. We took our leave and went to the motel. After we had checked in and had been in our room for a few minutes, there was a knock on the door. The man standing there introduced himself and handed me his Secret Service credentials for my inspection. I told him to come in.

He laid out the plan for the evening. Just before the president started his speech to Congress, he would join us in our room. He had ordered some Cokes and sandwiches for us, and we could watch the president's talk together. He asked that I not leave the room until he told me it was okay. Peggy and I turned on the television set, and just before the president entered, the Secret Service agent returned to our room. A few minutes later, the sandwiches and Cokes were delivered, and we watched the president give his speech.

Soon after the president's address was over, the agent asked to be excused because he had to make a telephone call. In a short while, the agent came back and said I was off the hook. The president had returned to the White House, and my temporary role as "designated absent Cabinet officer" had ended. He thanked me for my cooperation and said good evening.

He walked out of our room and we never saw him again. The next morning Peggy and I returned to Washington.

In December 1988 Peggy and I attended a Christmas reception at the White House. The beauty of the Christmas decorations dazzled us. I led Peggy to one of the windows in the East Room. From there we could see the Washington Monument, the snow on the ground, and the Christmas lights. It was a grand sight. Peggy agreed and said few would guess that a country girl and a man raised on a ranch in South Texas would someday be at the White House attending a Christmas party and seeing the wonderful scene from the East Room window. I told Peggy both of us had worked hard enough to earn the view.

That Christmas I did not yet know whether I would be reappointed to the Cabinet by President-elect Bush, so I told Peggy that we would probably be leaving Washington soon, since President Reagan's term was ending. I expected a lot of changes in the Cabinet, and I doubted there would be many holdovers from the present Cabinet. Then Peggy suggested I might be one of the holdovers.

I told her I really doubted it. There had been several newspaper articles recently speculating on the composition of the Bush Cabinet, and many journalists didn't believe I would be reappointed. Although I had campaigned for the vice president in Texas, some felt that my lack of solid Republican credentials would eliminate me from the new Cabinet. I suspected that the education post would go to someone with mainstream Republican ties. I said to Peggy I could name three current or outgoing Republican governors who had led education reform in their states and might want to be secretary of education.

Peggy said for me not to be too disappointed if I didn't end up in Bush's Cabinet. Peggy reminded me that although both of us had enjoyed our brief stay in Washington, we missed our children and our many friends in West Texas, and she knew I was anxious to get back to teaching and research at Tech.

Peggy was right about my wanting to return to university life. We hadn't been in Washington long before I realized that long-term involvement in the Washington scene was not for us. I told her I suspected I could be more effective at bringing about change in education as a private citizen than I could as secretary of education because in Washington, politics got in the way. I told Peggy I just hoped we would have the opportunity to congratulate the vice president before we left the White House that evening.

Later in the evening, Peggy and I did run into President-elect Bush and his spouse, Barbara. We exchanged holiday greetings, and I congratulated him on his election as president. He then said he would like to talk to me and to arrange an appointment as soon as possible.

I did, and on a bright sunny Saturday morning in early January 1989 I was admitted to the vice president's residence on the grounds of the Naval Observatory. He and Robert Teeter, his chief of staff, met me in the library. The president-elect was in casual clothes and was warm and friendly in his greeting. After an exchange of pleasantries, he said that he had invited me to visit because he wanted me to remain on the job as secretary of education in his Cabinet. Before I could respond, he said he wanted me to listen and think about his viewpoints on education.

The president-elect reviewed for me his commitment to improve the education system in America. He believed academic choice was an important strategy for improving schools. We talked about vouchers, and he ruled them out. I told him how pleased I was to learn of his stand on vouchers, as it was similar to mine. I was opposed to a federal voucher program. As secretary of education I had maintained that a state-funded and state-provided education was the responsibility of the states.

Vice President Bush spoke of his support for bilingual education, and his views were also compatible with mine. I was pleased he also opposed the "English Only" movement gaining momentum in America, especially in the western states. I often spoke out against the "English Only" movement because I considered it divisive and anti-intellectual.

The president-elect covered other points on education, and I found myself in agreement with him on those as well. It was significant to me that in his campaign for the presidency he had repeatedly said that he wanted to be known as the "education president." I told him that I would be pleased, honored, and delighted to serve in his Cabinet. I promised to work hard to improve education, but if I were to succeed, I needed his support in the days ahead.

I liked what the president-elect had said to me about education. He told me to recruit quality leadership in the Department of Education, and he wanted to see minorities and disabled persons in leadership positions. In his warm and gentle manner, he asked me to let him know if people were making it tough for me to do my job. He said he would try to protect me from political attacks.

I thanked him and suggested that early in his administration he should convene a national summit on education, bringing together education leaders and policy makers to work on education problems. Maybe they could suggest ways of bringing about improvement. I added that such a meeting could focus the nation on how to have better schools.

Bush agreed, and on September 27 and 28, 1989, he brought together the governors of the states and territories for the third domestic summit in the nation's history. Focused exclusively on education, it was held at the University of Virginia in Charlottesville. The president, the governors, and the Cabinet members came together and pledged to improve education for all children in America. It was agreed to establish national education performance goals and to urge restructuring of our public schools in a framework of flexibility and accountability.

I am pleased that the establishment of the National Education Goals occurred during my term as secretary of education. Credit for developing these goals belongs to a number of people, including President George H. W. Bush, the National Governors Association, the White House Office of Domestic Policy, the Department of Education under my leadership, and the Education Policy Advisory Committee. This last group consisted of business and professional people appointed by the president to work on reaching the goals.

In his State of the Union address on January 31, 1990, President Bush described the six national education goals. They focused on raising the level of educational achievement for all students. At the time, I believed these goals could promote a new beginning for education in this country because they committed the nation to a decade of changing and improving our education system. The goals were to be reached by the year 2000. They ranged from early childhood education, to increasing the high school graduation rate, to excellence in challenging subject matter, to being first in the world in mathematics and science achievement, to literacy and lifelong learning, and to schools being free from drugs and violence.

Unofficially, I added a seventh goal that I had often included in my talks to educators and parents. My goal was that by the year 2000, every child be educated to his or her fullest potential. I was unable to convince others that this should be our seventh goal. Still, my seventh goal is inscribed on a plaque on a monument in front of the Department of Education building in Washington. The monument is a large school bell, symbolizing that the Department of Education is the nation's schoolhouse and that America is committed to providing an excellent education for all of its citizens. The school bell had been donated to the Department of Education by the town of Milford, Pennsylvania, which had preserved the bell after renovating a school. We placed the school bell monument at the front door of the Department of Education, and one of the plaques at the base of the monument reads:

> Milford School Bell. Dedicated November 13, 1989, as an enduring symbol of the United States Department of Education goal to educate every American to his or her fullest potential.
> George Herbert Walker Bush   ·   Lauro F. Cavazos
> President of the United States   ·   Secretary of Education

Inscribed on the other plaque are words from one of my speeches:

> I'd like to place an old fashion school bell in every school in America. That bell would toll and say "America, something important is about to happen. Send your sons and daughters prepared to learn." We must heed the tolling of the school bell.
> Lauro F. Cavazos
> U.S. Secretary of Education
> November 13, 1989

I am pleased the school bell stands in front of the department today and that it will be there far into the future as a reminder of our need to educate all children to their fullest potential.

After my discussion with President-elect Bush about my continuing as secretary of education, I hurried to our apartment and told Peggy the good news. She was pleased for me, but she knew both of us were looking forward to getting back to the real world and university life. With almost a sigh, Peggy said it appeared that our return to West Texas would have to wait a while longer.

I suggested to Peggy that we stay in Washington for two years, no more. By then we would have the education reform agenda on the plate of every politician and educator in this country, and maybe some improvement would commence.

Considering the shape education was in, Peggy suggested I go back to the office immediately, because two years wasn't a lot of time in which to get a big project started. She told me she could stand anything for two years, and she would help me in every way possible. Time would pass quickly, and soon we would leave Washington with its politics and unrealistic views of what was beyond the Beltway.

Some labeled me as "the only Democrat in a Republican Cabinet." This characterization of my political beliefs was neither fair nor accurate, however. Growing up in South Texas in the 1930s and early 1940s, I never once met a person who claimed to be a Republican. That political species was so rare in my world that I even remember the first Republican I met, and meeting him made quite an impression on me. The year was 1945, and I was in the army, training as an infantry scout dog handler at Fort Robinson, Nebraska. During a political discussion in the barracks, I said to another soldier that I had never met a person who said or admitted they were Republican. In the town where I lived, there was one person rumored to be a Republican, but he was the town drunk. I added that candidates who won the Democratic Party primary in Texas always won the election.

My fellow soldier said I had lived a sheltered life, and then he announced that he was a Republican and proud of it. Furthermore, he said there were lots of Republicans in Newton Lower Falls, Massachusetts.

I may have grown up in a solidly Democratic region, but my adult years as a registered Independent in Massachusetts and as a Texas voter free to cross party lines made my "Democrat in the Cabinet" label a myth. To this day, Peggy and I are registered voters in Texas, and we vote for the person whom we think is best qualified for the job, regardless of political affiliation.

Soon after I had first arrived in Washington, I found out that one had to have a political party affiliation. Without one, it is difficult to get a political appointment or to make significant contributions to one's government post. The local newspapers in Washington could not decide to which political party I belonged. As a result, I was battered on the left by the *Washington Post* and on the right by the *Washington Times.*

I also quickly learned that from the first day after getting elected, the politician's first thought is how to be reelected. Every move, speech, and program appeared to be designed for that purpose. I recall a Cabinet meeting early in the Bush administration when I discussed some program ideas about early childhood education. Present in the room were the president, the vice president, and all of the Cabinet officers. One of my colleagues in the Cabinet asked how this program was going to get the president reelected.

I did not respond, but I thought to myself, "I'm just trying to get children educated. Reelecting somebody never crossed my mind." Still, my colleague's question was a valid and appropriate one as far as a politician was concerned.

After my appointment as secretary it did not take me long to learn about the realities of "political pork." This term is applied to special items or funding for programs of specific benefit to the constituency of a representative or senator but to no one else. As secretary of education, I had to review all bills approved by Congress that dealt with education matters. There were many such bills, and most were handled by staff, who then kept me informed. Then I would give my recommendation to the director of the Office of Management and Budget (OMB), and the OMB director, in turn, would write comments and pass the bill on to the president for veto or signature.

I was especially sensitive to bills bypassing the competitive peer-review system, which is in place in many federal agencies. For example, bills for funding health research programs require review by health professionals not working for the federal government. Panels of non-federal education peers read and judged grant applications competing for education program funds.

One episode of politics and pork I recall with particular clarity. Staff had asked me to review a recently approved bill to fund a new university library on the West Coast. I did so and then called in my very capable chief of staff, Chino Chapa, to write the brief. Chino had come to work in my office in mid-1989, after I recruited him from Rep. Charles Stenholm's office. I had known Chino during my time as president of Texas Tech because he had been editor-in-chief of the *University Daily*, the student newspaper at Texas Tech. After he graduated from Tech in 1982 with a degree in journalism, he had gone to work in Washington as a legislative aide for Stenholm.

Chino was from Kingsville, Texas. His parents' home was only a few blocks from where my Mama Grande Rita and two of my aunts and uncles lived. He was an enormous help to me. He was loyal, wrote well, was thoughtful, and had good ideas; he was extremely capable and committed to education. I was fortunate to have found someone with his abilities. We worked well together, and I depended upon him to take the lead on reviewing proposed legislation. He asked which bill concerned me.

I told Chino that I could not support the appropriation of $12 million to build a new library at a university on the West Coast. I didn't care that it was a project of their senator, who was also a very powerful Republican. I saw it as pure political pork. I told Chino there were other universities needing libraries and that there was a federal agency to build libraries—but only after the peer-review panel recommended funding for a project considered the most deserving in the competitive cycle. So I asked Chino to write the brief recommending that OMB decline to fund the library and ask the president to veto the bill.

Chino told me he would have the write-up on my desk by morning for my signature. He also told me to expect a call from the senator who was pushing this library bill through.

Two weeks later, I took a call from the director of the Office of Management and Budget. He asked if I remembered a bill I didn't like, one that was for funding a library on the West Coast. I said I did and that I didn't like it because the library program had not gone though the peer-review system. It was pure pork, and I didn't care if the senator pushing this through was a Republican and quite influential.

The director told me my recommendation was right on target because it was pork and a capital expenditure for new construction. Those he normally turned down, but in this case he had approved it and sent it to the president. He told me that I needed to understand that there was "Republican pork" and "Democratic pork," and I needed to learn the difference.

Cabinet members are expected to campaign for members of their political party seeking election or reelection. It seemed to me the White House was constantly asking me to campaign for a Republican running for office. Before I agreed, I examined the candidate's record and ideas, and if they were good ones, I agreed to a visit to the home district. If, however, I thought the candidate a poor choice, I refused the White House request to go on the campaign trail.

Chino Chapa had the job of dealing with the political office of the White House and their requests for me to campaign for candidates. He would come and tell me that I had to have an answer on whether I would do a campaign visit for this or that candidate running for the House. The White House was after Chino for my answer.

I would tell Chino I had been thinking about the request. When I looked at a candidate's record and found it was not stellar, I would tell him to inform the White House that I would not go out there to work for the candidate. I didn't like the candidate with the weak record, and I wanted to stay out of it. I would ask Chino to tell the White House I would go anywhere, anytime, if they sent me a candidate I could support without reservations.

Chino would point out that I was correct but that my stance was not politically realistic in Washington. I was expected to work for Republican candidates. A lot of the Cabinet officers were on the campaign trail. There were some tight races, and I was supposed to work for Republicans running for office. Chino told me that he didn't want me in trouble with the administration.

I told Chino he was right and that I appreciated his concern and words of caution. I asked him to tell the White House to continue sending me their campaign requests, but they needed to understand that I reserved the right to accept or refuse depending upon the candidate's qualifications.

Chino said he understood and respected my position, and he would find a tactful way to deliver my message on campaigning to the White House.

CHOICE, TESTIMONY, AND RETURN TO KINGSVILLE

I am sure Mother and Dad did not fully understand what an enormous step they took when they transferred their children from the Santa Gertrudis School to Flato Elementary School. They saw it simply as an effort to get the best education possible for their children. I, however, now see it as an example of academic choice. During my tenure as U.S. secretary of education, I pushed for academic choice in public schools and for the right of parents to choose the school their child would attend. I gave many speeches throughout the country arguing for choice programs.

One day in early 1989, as I was being driven to give a talk on academic choice in public schools at the National Press Club in Washington, I was reviewing my speech. A staff writer had prepared it, and I found it rather boring, somewhat political, and not terribly well written. As I thought about my speech before so many press people, I remembered my parents' struggle in the 1930s to enroll us in one of the public schools in Kingsville. I realized that it was a perfect example of the kind of choice I had been recommending nationally: parents making a decision about their children's education and the school they would attend, without regard to school district boundaries. Academic choice was controversial in the 1980s and 1990s but unheard of in the 1930s. As I was being driven to my speech, I realized that I was a product of academic choice. My parents were far ahead of their time. They wanted to partner with the school administrators and teachers in obtaining the best education possible for their children. I did not give my prepared speech, instead working from an impromptu outline and telling my audience of my parents' experience with academic choice and their struggle to educate their children.

During my term as secretary of education, I put an emphasis on academic choice in public schools. In the final days of the Reagan presidency, on January 10, 1989, the White House convened a conference on school choice. Although choice had been adopted as a concept and pushed by education conservatives, many saw it as a mechanism for giving vouchers to attend private and parochial schools. I found it deplorable when school choice was linked with vouchers. I considered public school choice as one of the major tools with which we could restructure and improve education. Unfortunately, during my time as secretary of education an excellent idea to improve the education of children became embroiled in politics and failed to spread nationwide.

The choice program arranged by the White House was of high priority; both President Reagan and President-elect Bush participated. We heard about the success of choice from students in East Harlem District 4. These students spoke with enthusiasm and eloquence of their choice program.

During the choice program, I presented a review of school choice and some of its advantages. I was the first to label academic choice "the cornerstone for restructuring education."

In the early days of President Bush's term, I told Peggy of my plan to push academic choice. I said that I had decided if we were going to bring about some restructuring of schools, we needed a major effort to promote school choice.

For a decade prior to my appointment as secretary, there had been no significant school reform. Any changes that had been made were cosmetic or marginal. I believed that an initiative on choice would open the doors to major changes resulting in improved education. No single cause had diminished American educational achievement, and I was convinced no single action would correct it. Yet, I saw choice as the single vehicle to bring about some improvement in our schools.

Americans have choice in many things affecting their lives, with housing, religion, and work or career being a few examples. It is thus unfortunate that when it comes to the education of our children, we have little choice at all. For the most part, children are assigned to a school district, and there is little discussion about it with parents.

I consider magnet schools an example of choice. In those schools, students from differing neighborhoods and backgrounds go to a school because of common interests in particular subjects, such as science, the arts, or technology. Magnet schools were originally a desegregation strategy, and many are of excellent quality. Their success has encouraged choice advocates to apply the same principle to solving some of the educational problems we face today, especially in the inner-city schools.

As secretary, I insisted that academic choice was not only good for students but also for the school. The more options open to students and their parents, the more competitive each school must be in order to attract students. When they are offered choice, most can determine which schools are best able to meet their needs. Those schools least desirable will eventually be forced to improve.

It seems to me that choice works best as part of a comprehensive strategy of education reform, including school-based management. Choice means that schools have to listen to parents, and school-based management lets teachers and administrators respond with innovative educational improvements.

When I pushed the concept of choice, I ran into opposition from Rep. Augustus Hawkins, then chair of the House Education Committee. As a Democrat, he was against many of the ideas I proposed as a member of a Republican administration. It was his honest belief that academic choice would impede the education of minorities. I did not agree and strongly believed the opposite. I tried to persuade him that a choice program would improve education for minorities and other educationally disadvantaged students. I said that the affluent had always had choice in the education of their children by moving to suburban school districts with the best schools or by sending their children to private schools. I wanted to give disadvantaged parents the same opportunity as affluent parents to select the public school best suited to educating their children.

Representative Hawkins remained vocal in his opposition to my choice initiative. In a congressional hearing before which I testified, he said my ideas about school choice were "snake oil." Over and over, he repeated that choice would hurt the education of minorities, especially those from the Watts district in Los Angeles he had so capably represented for forty years.

I decided to take the case for choice to the American people. I asked Deputy Secretary Ted Sanders, Chino Chapa, and the Department of Education staff to plan regional meetings on choice to give parents, teachers, administrators, and the business community an opportunity to learn about choice and its educational advantages. We decided on five regional meetings, to be held in New York City, Charlotte, Denver, Milwaukee, and Richmond, California. I would chair each of the meetings. We used the same format in each city; education experts made presentations on choice, and we took comments from the audience. This plan provided citizens an opportunity to discuss education issues face to face with the education secretary.

Teacher unions and principals voiced opposition to our choice initiative, and they dominated the meetings in New York and Charlotte. By the time we held the Denver and Richmond meetings, organized parental groups had made a strong case in support of choice.

Representative Hawkins had a staff member at each of the choice meetings. We provided a forum for their viewpoints, and they were articulate in their opposition to choice. Frequently, as a choice meeting approached or was being held, Hawkins would fire off a scathing press release in opposition to choice.

In Denver, after one of Representative Hawkins's press releases, Lon Anderson, my press aide, and Chino Chapa came to me about preparing a response to Hawkins's release. I asked them to draft one for me. They wrote an equally contemptuous press release. I tried to edit the response so that it would be more diplomatic, knowing we would have to work with the chair of the Education Committee. I decided to go ahead with my staff reply, but because of Peggy, the press release was never sent.

Peggy, who was with me at this meeting, persuaded me that it was pointless for Hawkins and me to air our differences in the media, and she said it was a spectacle to see two minorities fighting each other about education. She insisted we should unite and find ways to provide the best education possible for our minority children.

Later, I told Chino to arrange a meeting with Hawkins in his office with no staff present, either his or mine. A few weeks later I went to Hawkins's office. For forty-five minutes we met in private. Each of us talked about our expectations and hopes for the education of minorities. Clearly, both of us had the same goals. I pointed out that it would not benefit our cause if we continued our public battles. Our discussion was frank and thoughtful. Neither of us expressed rancor. I told Hawkins I greatly admired his lifetime commitment to education. We agreed to open lines of communication and continue to work toward the goal of enhancing education. All my time in Washington, I counted him as a friend. Hawkins's ideas and leadership continued to help improve education until his retirement from Congress in 1991.

By the time I left Washington on December 15, 1990, the choice concept had spread to at least ten states. Today, many states and school districts provide choice for students. I am convinced the widespread appeal of choice is because of its simplicity and commonsense approach to education. Academic choice, coupled with school-based management, uses competition to ensure accountability, respects the role of parents in education, and restores autonomy to teachers. To me, choice and school-based management can help bring about educational improvements in an era of unprecedented social and economic diversity.

Although some people have associated school choice with school vouchers, believing the latter to be a means of giving federal funds to private and religious schools, during my time in Washington I vigorously opposed vouchers for use in private and religious schools. I continue to oppose this idea today.

Today, many strategies are being proposed to improve education. The Supreme Court has now ruled that vouchers are constitutional, and they are widely used in a number of states. Vouchers allow students to transfer from public schools to private or parochial schools. Home schooling and charter schools have also emerged. While these may be valid ways of improving education, I urge that we not abandon our public school system, especially those schools in the inner city. We must continue to seek ways to improve public education. Historically, it has educated the general citizenry, and this educated population made this nation the greatest in the world. There is no need to create a new school system. Our energies, skills, and resources should be focused on markedly improving our present system of public education. Walking away from a failing school system is not the answer.

When our parents enrolled my sister Sarita and me in Flato Elementary School, I am sure they were not thinking in terms of grand concepts of restructuring education. The term "academic choice" was not in their vocabulary, and it was unheard of in most education circles. They were simply far ahead of their time in deciding to take a necessary step to improve their children's education.

As secretary of education I testified before congressional committees on major pending legislation or funding for education. During my time as secretary, both legislative branches were controlled by the Democrats. Inasmuch as the executive branch was Republican, not much progress was made passing education legislation.

I made it a practice to meet privately with the committee chairs before a public hearing. This practice afforded me the opportunity to clarify the administration's viewpoint on specific issues, or I could answer questions the chair might have of me before the hearing commenced. One of my favorite committee chairs was Rep. William H. Natcher of Kentucky. He headed the House Appropriations Subcommittee on Labor, Health, and Human Services.

My first private meeting in Natcher's office went well. He was most gracious and spoke gently. I liked him immediately. I later learned that Natcher never accepted political contributions; he used his own money to fund his election campaigns. His staff was small in number, and I understood that he read his own mail. Natcher also never missed a vote. He came to the House of Representatives on August 1, 1953, and retired on March 3, 1994, amassing a congressional record of 18,401 consecutive votes.

I was pleased Natcher took time to show me the many fine mementos and autographed photographs he had gathered during his long legislative service. Then we talked about the hearing the next day. I, of course, was going to defend the president's budget proposal for the Department of Education. I knew that once the budget was approved by the Office of Management and Budget and the president, a secretary could not negotiate funding levels with the appropriations subcommittee.

I told Natcher of my hopes for the Department of Education, and I told him I thought the president's budget recommendations were quite adequate for our needs to further education. Natcher leaned back in his chair, looked at me, and told me not to worry because we were going to have a fine hearing the next day and he was certain we were going to work out a good appropriation for my department.

I asked Peggy to come to the hearing with me. These were public hearings, and I knew she would enjoy seeing the committee meeting and hearing the discussion. I asked her to take notes, to give me her impressions, and to let me know how I could do a better job in front of the committees.

The next morning when we arrived at the hearing, my staff was already there, and I had fine backup from them. The program and finance people in the department were very capable and provided me with data and information should I need it in the course of the hearing.

Before we started, I introduced Peggy to Natcher. He said he was delighted to have her there and invited her to sit in the front row, just behind me. Peggy declined.

The hearing was a long one. We started just after nine in the morning, and I testified, or staff responded, for about three hours without a break. Finally, the chair thanked me for my testimony and suggested we adjourn for lunch and start again at 1:30 in the afternoon. The chairman said that after lunch he wanted me to come back and tell him how I was going to spend an extra $2 billion, because he was going to add to the department's appropriation.

I was delighted at an extra $2 billion for the Department of Education, but my position required me to defend the administration's recommendations. I needed to find a way to convince Natcher we did not need the money. I asked Chino to arrange a meeting during the lunch break between our finance people and OMB staffers. Their job was to work out a compromise with the committee staff.

And so they did. I only got an extra $1 billion, which I was not supposed to want, added to my department's budget.

On another occasion, in 1990, while testifying before a House committee, I reviewed the recently established National Education Goals. There were six goals to be reached by the year 2000. I started my review with the first one: "By the year 2000, all children in America will start school ready to learn." I went on and described goals two and three. Then I announced the fourth goal: "By the year 2000, U.S. students will be first in the world in science and mathematics achievement."

I was asked how well our students were currently doing in math and science compared to students from the industrialized nations. The answer was disheartening: last in the world in mathematics and next to the last in science.

One of the Democratic committee members asked if I believed that by the year 2000 our children could move to the number-one ranking. I thought to myself that Americans would not accept a goal stating "second in the world in math and science." I also knew I was under oath, and I was not about to commit perjury. So I answered that I did believe the goal could be reached but only if we restructured our educational system in order to improve the teaching of math and science.

Although I equivocated in my answer, I believed we had the capacity and ability to reach our goal but that it would take enormous effort and dedication to change our educational system. Major restructuring of our public education system did not occur, and to date we have not reached excellence in math and science.

In early March 1990 Peggy and I flew to Mexico City from Washington. The visit to Mexico had two purposes: to meet with the president of Mexico and to receive an honorary degree. During the days we were in Mexico City, Peggy and I stayed at the home of the U.S. ambassador to Mexico, John D. Negroponte. He later served as U.S. ambassador to the United Nations and to Iraq and as director of national intelligence.

The president of Mexico, Carlos Salinas de Gortari, invited me to visit with him at the president's home, Los Pinos. On his first official visit to the United States after his election in 1988, President Salinas de Gortari had asked for a meeting with me. We had met at Blair House in Washington where he was staying as the guest of President Bush. At Blair House, we had talked about education, which was a centerpiece of President Salinas de Gortari's new administration. He wanted to encourage me to work with Manuel Bartlett, his minister of education, to develop educational programs beneficial to both Mexico and the United States. Later I told Peggy that I was impressed with Salinas de Gortari's ideas about improving education in Mexico and that he had invited us to visit Los Pinos the next time I was in Mexico City because he wanted to continue the education discussion.

After our arrival in Mexico City, Peggy and I were deeply honored to meet with the president. Again, he encouraged me to work with his administration on education problems, especially along the Mexico–United States border.

I was able to arrange this visit with the Mexican president close to the date I was to receive the *doctor honoris causa* degree from the Autonomous University of Guadalajara, on March 23, 1990. As part of the award ceremony, I was required to give a speech. I chose to talk about education, some of the issues and some of the solutions to the problems. I planned to give my talk in Spanish, and the day before we left for Guadalajara I was in the study still working on and polishing my speech.

Chino Chapa came into the study and told me he had taken a call from our office. Earlier the White House had telephoned about having the president give a commencement speech at a university or college with a large Hispanic enrollment. I had sent the White House the names of three or four schools with large Hispanic enrollments that the president might consider talking to at some point. We had also sent the graduation dates for those schools.

Chino said that the White House had almost made a decision but wanted to talk to me first. When I did, I was informed that the president wanted to speak at Texas A&I University (now Texas A&M University–Kingsville). However, the White House needed the commencement to be rescheduled from the afternoon to the morning.

Otherwise, the president's schedule would not permit him to be at the university.

I placed a call to Dr. Manuel Ibanez, then president of Texas A&I University. He was a good friend of mine, and I had known him for several years. I told him that I had good news for him, that President Bush had decided to attend his spring commencement and give a talk. Ibanez said it was great news and wanted to hear the details. When I told him that the time of commencement would have to be shifted to accommodate the president's schedule, he said that it might be a problem, but he really wanted the president there. He said he needed to talk to his board of directors and would get back to me soon.

I told Ibanez I needed his decision at that very moment because I had to let the White House know immediately. So he told me he would move the commencement to morning and simply tell the board. He told me how much he appreciated my convincing the president to come to Texas A&I. I remarked to Ibanez that he wouldn't believe how a presidential visit upsets routines and places. There would be a lot of demands, and he would have to meet them to the satisfaction of the White House.

On the day of the commencement speech in June, 1990, Peggy and I flew with the president on Air Force One. It was her first trip on the president's airplane, and she was excited by the prospect. We left from Andrews Air Force Base, headed nonstop for Kingsville. We were to land at the U.S. Naval Air Station.

Peggy and I were seated in the second compartment. The first was occupied by the president, and the other compartments were for dignitaries the president had invited and for staff. There was also considerable seating for the press. It was the president's custom to invite his guests to his compartment for a brief visit. Peggy and I watched as they moved forward and returned to their seats.

At one point Peggy said we had been flying quite a while and that we must be getting close to Kingsville. I told her we were due to land shortly. Then the steward came to our compartment door and said the president would like to see me.

As soon as I entered the president's compartment, he asked about Peggy and said he wanted to see both of us. He wanted us to visit and tell him about Kingsville. After I returned with Peggy, the president told her to sit at his desk because the chair was quite comfortable.

The president and I sat on a sofa and talked about A&I, Kingsville, and the King Ranch. I told him we would be flying over the ranch soon, and he would have a grand view of the ranch and see a beautiful part of the world.

The three of us chatted about Texas and the upcoming visit. The steward came to say that we were getting close, and he needed to ask the president to get ready for landing. The president acknowledged the steward's statement but kept on asking questions of me. I told him I thought it was time for Peggy and me to get back to our compartment, but the president kept asking me to show him the sights as we approached Kingsville.

Soon, the steward returned and said they were on final approach and that the secretary and Mrs. Cavazos needed to return to their seats. I rose, but the president told me to stay and buckle my seat belt and for Peggy to remain in his desk chair; it had a seat belt.

We landed at the Kingsville Naval Air Station, and the president insisted I ride with him in his automobile into Kingsville. It was quite a return for a native son, to come back to Kingsville on Air Force One and ride in a motorcade with the president of the United States.

Later, I asked Peggy how it felt to sit at the president's desk on Air Force One as we came in for a landing. Peggy said she had to admit it was quite a thrill for a country girl.

CHAPTER 11

⟨⟩

Education for Hispanics

Improving the educational attainment of Hispanic Americans has long been one of my major goals. It was a special focus of mine during my time as secretary of education, and to this day I continue in the effort. Long before my arrival in Washington, I was troubled by the often minimal educational achievements of Hispanics and worked to improve their education.

In January 1983, while president of Texas Tech University, I was in Brownsville, Texas, a bicultural city at the tip of Texas in the Rio Grande Valley. I was concerned about two issues. One was the low minority enrollment at the university I led, and the second was the failure of so many Hispanics to educate themselves to their fullest potential. In Brownsville, it was my hope that I could persuade school administrators and teachers to help me recruit more Hispanics to Texas Tech.

After my visits to a number of schools, the superintendent of the Brownsville Independent School District, Raul Besteiro Jr., invited me to see some of his schools. As we were driving around town, he told me that because of the massive immigration from Mexico, he built a new classroom every fourteen days to accommodate the rapid growth in enrollment.

Although the winter temperatures in Brownsville are generally mild, that day was an exception. It was bitterly cold, and a few days before my trip the Rio Grande Valley had suffered an economically devastating freeze, destroying the citrus crop for years to come.

As Besteiro drove past one of the schools, he called my attention to the construction, but something else caught my eye. I watched a group of Hispanic children, perhaps seven to ten years old, cross the road in front of us. I saw that they were not properly dressed for the cold. Their coats were thin, and some appeared to be wearing two or more shirts. None had gloves. I was saddened by the plight of those children on a cold winter day. As I thought about their discomfort, I also thought about the enormous education deficit suffered by so many Hispanics. I was certain that only half of those children I saw on their way to school would graduate from high school. I knew that less than 10 percent of those children who did finish high school would graduate from college. Even for those completing college, professional or graduate school was almost out of the question.

The memory of those children in the cold has stayed with me. It haunts me to this day. It did strengthen my resolve to work toward improving the education of Hispanics for the rest of my life. As secretary of education I had a platform from which to help the nation address the education deficit of Hispanics.

During the years when I was secretary of education, the Hispanic dropout rate from school was between 9 and 11 percent each year, the highest dropout rate of any major ethnic or racial group. Among Hispanics over the age of twenty-five, an alarming 52 percent had not completed high school, compared to 24 percent of non-Hispanics. Only 10 percent of Hispanics over the age of twenty-five had completed four or more years of college, compared to 21 percent of non-Hispanics. Every major report on illiteracy among adults found the rate much higher among Hispanics. My concern was well justified when viewed from a leadership position in Washington. Low educational achievements coupled with the growth of the Hispanic population could have a serious economic, social, and political impact on the nation.

Compounding the troubling data on the education of Hispanics are their increased numbers in American society. Between 1980 and 1995, the white non-Hispanic population in the United States grew by about

12 percent, but the Hispanic population increased by 83 percent. In 2000 there were approximately 40 million Hispanics, and they are now the nation's largest minority group. In the southwestern United States, Hispanics are 55 percent of the total population. By 2010, it is estimated that the number of Hispanics will increase to 50 million. By 2050, demographers estimate Hispanics will be 25 percent of the nation's total population.

In 1989, the Department of Education forecasted that by the year 2000, about 12 percent of school-age children would be Hispanic. I told Chino Chapa to look at the data we had used to establish the National Education Goals we hoped to reach by the year 2000. If we didn't improve the education of young Hispanics, I assured him, we were not going to reach our goals. I added that the high-tech industries were going to need even more advanced skills and education than those possessed by many Hispanics looking for entry-level positions.

Chino asked what I planned to do to improve the education of Hispanics. I told him I'd been thinking about the problem quite a bit for the last few months, and I wanted him to contact the White House and set up a meeting for me with President Bush to discuss improving the educational outcomes of Hispanic children. I believed we needed a national effort. I was delighted when, on December 6, 1989, I received a memorandum signed by the president. In it, he asked me, as chair of the Domestic Policy Council working group on education policy, to form a task force on Hispanic education. We were ordered to complete our work promptly and report our results to the president. The president wrote in the memo, "We must step up our efforts to ensure the education of Hispanic Americans as a vital part of our overall commitment to excellence in education."

I called a meeting with the deputy secretary of education, John Theodore "Ted" Sanders, as well as several of the assistant secretaries, and Chino. I told them of the president's memo asking me to head up a task force on Hispanic education. We were to do a comprehensive study and develop an implementation plan to correct the education disparities of Hispanics. Also, the president wrote that he wanted the Department of Education to assess participation of Hispanics in federal education programs and to identify barriers limiting Hispanic involvement in those programs, and he wanted suggestions and alternative strategies to improve Hispanic participation in federal education programs. I emphasized to the staff that I was determined to keep politics out of the study.

Sanders suggested we use a format similar to the one we had used for the choice study, utilizing regional public hearings. I agreed, because the choice meetings had been successful and given us a lot of information to extend the effort. I suggested that for the Hispanic study we would hold regional public hearings in cities having a substantial Hispanic population. I wanted to arrange them so people could testify on the educational needs of Hispanics and present some of the problems and possible ways to improve Hispanics' education. To me, it was important that parents, teachers, administrators, students, and others who wanted to help improve education be able to attend.

We decided to hold these Hispanic Education Forums in Boston, San Antonio, Los Angeles, Chicago, and Miami. I would chair the meetings in Boston, San Antonio, and Los Angeles, and Sanders would chair the Chicago and Miami sessions.

I wanted to use the same general format at all of the sites: public testimony, visits to schools with large Hispanic enrollments, and meetings with students, teachers, principals, and as many parents as possible. I said we needed to give people an opportunity to meet and discuss educational issues with a Cabinet officer or with someone who has major responsibility in education, such as the undersecretary.

I asked Sanders to go ahead and start the planning process and to spread the word that the Hispanic education study would be the priority of the department until completed. I wanted to meet with the leaders of the different groups in Washington representing Hispanics, so I asked Chino to set up the meeting and find a mechanism to keep the groups informed as we progressed through the study. They were not, however, to write the report.

Just before we went public with the work of our Hispanic education task force, the president convened a meeting of about forty Hispanic leaders at the White House. In the East Room prior to the president's arrival, I told the group of our plans to improve the education of Hispanics. For thirty minutes I listened to their comments and answered questions. It was a useful exchange. Then the president arrived, and he announced the formation of the Task Force on Hispanic Education. His remarks, as well as mine, were well received by the audience.

On March 6, 1990, a month before the first Hispanic Education Forum was convened, I addressed a joint meeting of a special session of the Texas legislature. Gov. William Clements called the session in order to reform the public financing of Texas schools. Texas was under court order to ensure equity of education funding throughout the state.

As a native Texan, I considered speaking to the legislature an honor. Unfortunately, while an honor to me, my talk was not well received or appreciated by several of the Hispanic legislators. Just before I was to speak, Carlos Truan, the senator representing the district where I was born, took me aside and told me how pleased he was that I was there to speak to the legislature. Then he asked me to emphasize the need for more funding for education in Texas, especially for the predominantly Hispanic school districts.

I told him my speech was about the need to restructure the education system in Texas, and it had nothing to do with financing education—the reason they were in special session. I said the speech was written, and I could not change it at this stage.

I knew Senator Truan was upset with my response. During my speech, I said (and I quote from the text), "It would be neither appropriate nor prudent to offer a specific prescription for the public finance question. President Bush and I are strong supporters of the principles of federalism, and believe that matters such as these are for the states to decide, within the framework of the United States Constitution."

I did touch briefly on funding in my talk to the legislature. I said, "Now I don't deny that some schools in some districts might need additional resources, but the real answer lies in better utilization of existing resources." I urged restructuring the schools, but my message was lost on some legislators. I was very disappointed to see Senator Truan lead a walkout of mostly Hispanic legislators in protest of my remarks.

After my speech, in back of the legislative chamber, Senators Truan and Carl Parker berated me because I had not supported additional money for education. Senator Parker, in what I considered a bit of an overstatement, said that I had destroyed education in Texas.

In the months ahead, many Texans wrote or told me of their support for my ideas about restructuring and agreed that simply providing more money for education was not the answer to the education deficit of so many students.

The problem of school financing in Texas goes back to 1968, when parents of children attending the Edgewood Independent School District filed a class-action suit. They contended that the state's system of funding public schools was unfair, resulting in wide disparities among school districts. In 1989, the Texas Supreme Court found for the plaintiffs and ordered Texas to correct the inequity in school funding.

As the Texas legislature closed its special session in 1990, it passed a new funding plan designed to satisfy the court. The legislature ordered that education funds be taken from the more affluent school districts and distributed to the poor school districts. The plan became known as the "Robin Hood Plan."

In 2005, after a decade of the Robin Hood Plan, Texas was still struggling to develop another plan to equalize school funding, one that would do away with the "Robin Hood" approach.

The first public forum on Hispanic education was held in San Antonio on April 10, 1990. I considered it an excellent start to our study. In opening the meeting, I emphasized that I did not want another study nor did I just want to gather statistics about the educational failure of Hispanics. I asked for constructive, original ideas for better meeting the needs of Hispanic students.

During the meeting we heard testimony from teachers, parents, community leaders and activists, and students. At the close of the forum, Chino said he thought the meeting had gone well, he had heard some good comments and ideas, and he already had staff working on the minutes of the meeting. Then he said that a group of reporters wanted to talk to me about the meeting. I agreed to meet with them.

The outcome of the press conference was troubling to me. One reporter asked why so many Hispanic children were failing and dropping out of school, as well as lagging behind educationally. I replied that education had always been an important part of Hispanic heritage and culture. I pointed out that the Spaniards had established universities at Lima and Mexico City in 1541 and had opened five more in the New World before Harvard opened its doors in 1636. This history suggested to me that Hispanics greatly valued education, but over the years we seem to have lost our commitment to excellence in education.

Another reporter asked whose fault it was that Hispanics didn't seem to care about quality education. I responded that I held Hispanic parents responsible for the educational failure of their children and added that we were all responsible for the educational failure of young Hispanics—the schools, society, and me.

The next morning, the *New York Times* ran a front-page story with the headline, "Cavazos Blames Hispanic Parents for Education Failure." In the press, Hispanic advocacy groups roundly criticized me for my remarks.

When she saw the story, Peggy asked if I had used the word "blame" in my statement to the press. I told her I had not. Apparently some people don't see the difference between the term "blame" and the one I used, "responsible." It galled me that the press did not mention that I had also included society, the schools, and me as being responsible for the educational failure of so many Hispanic children.

On April 25, 1990, we traveled to Boston for the second public forum on the education of Hispanics. It was to be held the next day. Soon after we arrived in Boston, I gave a columnist from the *Boston Globe* an interview. I had always admired the insightful and thoughtful articles this reporter wrote. During the interview, I was asked about the San Antonio story and my blaming Hispanic parents for their children's educational failure. I emphasized to the reporter that I had talked about "responsibility" not "blame." Though the story printed the next day was accurate, I was dismayed when I saw that the headline writer for the *Boston Globe* had used the words, "Cavazos Blames...."

I told Peggy that when I saw the newspaper headline, I was reminded of the old adage about not fighting with those who buy ink by the barrel. I said I was going to forget the blame game and focus on the Boston forum. Before the meeting, we were going to visit one of the high schools in Chelsea. The Chelsea schools were troubled academically but improving.

The Chelsea school system had attracted national attention by asking Boston University to operate and improve its schools. Hispanics made up 90 percent of the enrollment in the high school we were visiting. As we walked up the steps to the school, the superintendent of the Chelsea school district, Diana Lam, and the school principal, Mary Raimo, greeted us and invited us into the building. The building was quite old, probably built in the late 1930s, but it was clean and neat. Students stood in the hall, and I briefly spoke to a number of them. They were a handsome, polite group of young people.

Prior to going to the classrooms, I had an excellent session with the teachers. They were an impressive group, determined to do their best to educate their students despite limited resources. Almost all of the teachers were white, but I was not surprised. Despite the growing minority representation in America's population and its schools, at the time of our visit the proportion of minority teachers was about 10 percent. To date, the percentage of minority teachers has not increased substantially.

We talked about Chelsea High School and some of the problems they had encountered and their success in dealing with them. I could sense they were truly dedicated to teaching. I was pleased the students at this high school had such an understanding group of teachers and administrators.

I thanked them and said that when I visited a school, I asked to meet with students in a classroom setting, without teachers, administrators, or the media present. I said that I learned much about education by listening to students in such a setting. I was informed that I was to spend twenty minutes in an English class with twenty third-year students.

Peggy and I went to the classroom. I started out by introducing Peggy and telling them a little about my background. All of the students in the classroom were Hispanic. As the class started relaxing, I said I had been told there were twenty students in this class, but I counted only thirteen. I asked where the rest of the students were.

One student responded that they were "skylarking." When I asked for a definition, a young man in the third row replied that it meant running and playing and skipping school because it was a beautiful day and tough to stay focused on learning. He wished he were skylarking. I asked why he wasn't.

He replied that his mother would kill him if he did. I gave him an understanding smile and nodded my head. I liked the youngster explaining "skylarking." When he said his mother would kill him if he went skylarking, I thought to myself that I had just heard the epitome of parental involvement in education: "My mother would kill me."

Peggy, who was sitting in the back of the room taking notes that I would use to help me write a report, later said that she had never heard parental involvement explained in such a succinct and precise way. On our way back to Boston I told Peggy that the young man was going to do all right in getting an education; he would not drop out of school because his mother would see to it that he stayed in school and graduated.

Our visit to Chelsea High School was in 1990. Years later, I found out what had happened to the student who said, "My mother would kill me." In 1995, I was invited by a group of Latino students at Harvard Medical School to discuss delivery of health care to a community of Hispanics. On the day of the talk, Peggy and I were at a reception, meeting the students and faculty. Out of the corner of my eye, I saw two young Hispanic men and an older Hispanic person enter the lecture hall. I recognized one of the young men as the student who had given the great definition for "parental involvement."

He walked over, told me his name, and said we had met before. I looked at him, nodded, and said we had, but it had been a while. It was 1990, at Chelsea High School, and I said that he had been sitting in the third row.

The young man looked at me with amazement, saying I was right. I didn't tell the young man why he impressed me so, but I asked what he was doing now.

He replied that he had finished high school and was taking some

college courses, but he spent most of his time working with a group trying to keep Latinos from dropping out of school. He said that when he
heard I was speaking, he decided to come with his friends because I had
made a big impression on him at Chelsea.

My prediction about the young Chelsea High school student staying in school and graduating was accurate. I was very pleased for him
and his mother.

A few weeks after the Boston regional forum on Hispanic education, we
held our third meeting, this one in East Los Angeles. The evening before the forum, I met with a group of parents, and as usual, I asked that
there be no press or staff at the meeting. Peggy also attended and took
notes for me.

I made a few introductory remarks, telling them how much we appreciated their being present and what my hopes were for the regional
hearing. Then I asked for their comments and thoughts. I promised I
would respond as best I could. There were about forty people in the
room, and they were very quiet. They stared at me, and not a question
was asked. No one made a comment on my talk or on educational matters. I looked at the group of parents and realized that almost all were
Hispanic, and I had been speaking in English. I switched to Spanish, re-
stated my expectations, and a flood of comments and questions came
forth from the audience. We had a great evening talking about education. They shared with me their hopes and expectations for the education of their children and the barriers they faced.

At the close of the third regional forum, as we were flying back to
Washington, Peggy asked me to tell her the most important thing I had
learned from the three hearings. I told her I already knew what was important but that the hearings had emphasized that parental involvement was essential if a child was to succeed educationally. To me, it is essential that children be exposed to an educationally stimulating and
caring environment as they mature.

Peggy agreed but pointed out that parents sometimes don't feel welcome in schools; even with as much education as she had, she felt in awe
or tense at a conference with one of our children's teachers. She told me

if a person can't speak the language, it is easy to understand why he or she would be uncomfortable meeting with a teacher.

I agreed and told Peggy the forums had made it clear that Hispanic parents often were not comfortable in their children's school. They saw the school as the exclusive territory of teachers and administrators. I told Peggy that at the close of one of the meetings, when I was signing autographs and greeting people, one woman quietly had told me she was ashamed to go to her child's school, even though she wanted to, because she was a dropout. Others told me they didn't like to go to school conferences because they couldn't speak English or had had almost no education at all.

I told Peggy the parental involvement matter was going to be an important part of our report to the president. In it, I wanted to make it clear to teachers and school administrators that education was a two-way street. I would insist in my report that if parents don't want to be involved, then teachers needed to find ways of getting parents into the schoolhouse.

Peggy often heard me say that if parents would not come to the school, teachers must reach out to them and visit with them in their home. Further, if parents could not speak English, the school should hire an interpreter to facilitate communication. I told her there was nothing magical about enhancing education; it only required goodwill and commitment to a child's learning.

Peggy told me I expected too much from people.

We were talking about one of the most important issues in society, the education of children, so I believed it was critical that we find ways to get parents involved. I knew that if parents did not encourage their children to attain high academic achievement, those children would do only the minimum required. Schools could help parents develop the academic and social skills they needed to guide their children through school.

Peggy commented that she really got me going with her question about the most important thing I had learned from the hearings on Hispanic education.

I agreed with her and pointed out that both of us realized undereducated parents were sometimes not aware of their abilities and potential as teachers of their children and how much they could help their child learn if they would speak out. If they were not a part of all aspects of their children's education, learning would be difficult or impeded for their children.

Based on the findings of our public forums on the education of Hispanics, my colleagues in the department and I developed eight options to include in our report. The Domestic Policy Council, after considerable debate and some modification, approved them. On September 21, 1990, President Bush approved all of the options. Two of the options approved focused on parental involvement, and two others emphasized language development and early English-language proficiency. Two of the other options were aimed at removing educational barriers to academic success. Testimony at the forums pointed out that some schools remove underachieving Hispanic students from their regular classroom to work on their academic deficiencies. I doubted this practice was an effective remediation strategy. It probably stigmatizes children early in their schooling and may have a negative effect on their subsequent education.

As we were working on the two options regarding barriers, I said that we needed to urge schools not to hold students back; they needed to have education success, and failing a grade must have a negative impact on a student's progress. Research suggests that if a student fails two grades, there is an 80 percent chance he or she will drop out of school. If a student is not up to grade level in one subject but is in all of the others, then we should promote the student and focus on bringing him or her up to grade level as they move ahead in school.

I had been quite insistent that we include support for migrant students in our report. Large numbers of migrant students drop out of school each year and are educationally disabled by the various and differing requirements for a high school diploma in the state or states where they work. Seventy-five percent of migrant students are Hispanic, and ten states currently enroll 75 percent of all migrant students. The option we proposed urged a compact between the states enrolling large numbers of migrant children to develop agreements helping those students receive a high school diploma.

Our seventh option focused on adult education and urged the Department of Education to develop strategies increasing the role of community colleges, post-secondary institutions, and community-based organizations in helping Hispanic dropout students to earn a high school diploma.

The eighth option was an executive order on educational excellence for Hispanic Americans.

Once the Task Force on Hispanic Education finished its work and the options for the Domestic Policy Council were prepared, we started to work in my office drafting the Executive Order on Hispanic Education.

Gilbert Roman from our Office of Civil Rights wrote the first draft and submitted it to me. I decided it was time to prepare the final document as part of the eighth option. We went to work drafting the final version of the executive order, and I kept the effort within my office. I was determined to keep politics out of the report and to stay focused on educational improvement.

Chino Chapa asked who should be involved in writing the executive order. I said to keep Roman and Deputy Secretary Sanders in the loop, and I wanted Wade Dykes to be part of the effort as well. He was a former White House Fellow, and he was my chief staff member on the Hispanic education effort. Dykes had great writing skills and good ideas about education. I told Chino we needed to have our people critically read and edit the report. I instructed Chino to pull the team together and to start them thinking about the format of the report. I emphasized that I wanted all of the options through the Domestic Policy Council and on the president's desk by early September.

The executive order we drafted markedly increased federal support for the education of Hispanics. I told Peggy that what I liked about our order was that it expanded participation of Hispanics in educational policymaking at the highest level of the federal government, a first, and major, step.

The order established the President's Advisory Commission on

Education Excellence for Hispanics. This commission would advise the secretary of education on efforts and strategies to enhance education for Hispanics. It would also assess the participation of parents in the education of their children and promote early childhood education. The commission would advise on ways to remove barriers to success in education and work, thereby helping students achieve their potential at all education levels.

Of the eight options we took to the Domestic Policy Council, the executive order generated the most discussion and debate. Some members of the council thought it would appear bureaucratic and burden federal departments with paperwork. Others did not think it added anything significant to the accomplishments of the task force.

I argued that such an order by the president provided an identifiable implementation measure on Hispanic education. Hispanic advocacy groups had been lobbying vigorously for such an executive order, believing that it would allow them to participate in planning and make them part of the implementation process.

Finally, after rewrites, changes, editing, review by the Justice Department, and acceptance by the president's chief of staff, John H. Sununu, the executive order went to the president.

I was pleased with the executive order and the options we moved through the Domestic Policy Council. To me, they were concrete steps toward further empowering Hispanics to obtain a quality education. We made sure the options reflected the testimony gathered at the five regional meetings, emphasizing enhanced parental involvement and English-language competency.

On September 24, 1990, on the South Lawn of the White House, President Bush signed the executive order. There were about two hundred Hispanics present. I was on the platform with the president as he signed the order, as was Manuel Lujan, who was secretary of the interior and the only other Hispanic in the Cabinet. I was delighted that we had been able to move the executive order all the way from the Department of Education to the desk of the president.

As I watched the president sign the executive order, I thought back on our public hearings. The testimony on Hispanic education was valuable and formed the base for the options we eventually presented to the president. I knew that our hearings throughout the nation raised the expectations of many people committed to improving the quality of education young Hispanics receive. As I stood by the president, I again had a mental image of the hopeful and anxious faces of mothers and fathers as they quietly explained to me in Spanish the educational needs of their children. I remembered caring and devoted teachers and their students telling us strategies we might use to improve learning for Hispanics.

After we left the White House that day, I told Peggy that for the first time in history we had an executive order recognizing the education needs of Hispanics. It would give us a framework to develop the programs we needed to improve education for them.

Two days after the president signed the executive order and accepted our strategies on how to improve education for Hispanics, I put into motion the mechanism to bring to fruition each of the options.

We created an office for the White House Initiative on Hispanic Education in the Department of Education. The office still exists today. Each option was assigned to one of the primary operating centers in the department. I planned the publication of the task force report. I wanted it to serve as a primer for the education of Hispanics. On several occasions, as we worked on the proposed strategies to improve education, I told Chino Chapa that if the ideas were good ones and enhanced the education of Hispanics, they should be applicable to improving the education of all children, minority or majority.

I did not see the final publication of our report because I left the department in mid-December 1990.

In 1994 I was at a meeting at the U.S. Health Resources and Services Administration in Maryland because I was seeking funding for a program to improve communication between non-Spanish-speaking physicians and their Hispanic patients. One of the people at the meeting asked if I had seen President Clinton's executive order on Hispanic education. I said I had not, but I was quite interested to know what it was about and asked if she had a copy. She immediately went and got her copy. I looked at its title: Executive Order on Educational Excellence for Hispanic Americans. It was almost identical, but not entirely, to the one we had written for President Bush's signature on September 24, 1990. William J. Clinton had signed this executive order on February 22, 1994.

As I studied the document, I couldn't help but take pride in the knowledge that the executive order we had written in my office several years earlier had survived into the administration of another president. To me, this was validation of the work of the Task Force on Hispanic Education.

CHAPTER 12

ᏇᎯᎯᏇ

The Rear View Mirror

It was a bright, sunny December day in Washington, D.C. John Cleveland, my driver, skillfully and quickly moved the car from downtown Washington to the West Wing of the White House. Earlier in the day I had spoken to the commission appointed by President Bush to push the White House Initiative on Historically Black Colleges and Universities (HBCUs). Many of these colleges had been in existence for more than one hundred years, and a presidential advisory board on HBCUs had been established during my term as secretary to enhance the educational capabilities of these schools.

I thought the talk had gone well and that the response from the commission had been warm and generous in praise of my efforts for minority education. I did not realize that I had just given my last speech in Washington as secretary of education. I was on my way to meet with John Sununu, the president's chief of staff. I had known John for some time. In the 1970s, both of us had been on the faculty of Tufts University, Sununu in engineering, and I in the medical school.

John had requested this meeting, but he had canceled it several times. Today, the call from his office had come again, and he wanted to see me in the afternoon. I could not imagine the topic, but a call from the White House did not concern me. Sununu and I had worked well together, and we had met on many occasions to discuss educational initiatives. I had never had a major disagreement or confrontation with him during my time in Washington. I thought perhaps he was going to chastise me because I had turned down a number of invitations to do fundraisers or campaign for Republican candidates. The White House had been persistent in its attempts to get me on the political campaign trail, but I still turned down a number of invitations. I believed we had a more important agenda in the Department of Education than continuous efforts to elect Republicans to Congress.

I walked into Sununu's office. It was decorated for Christmas; a beautiful tree stood in one corner, and there were blazing logs in the fireplace. It was the season of good cheer in Washington, but suddenly I had the feeling that Sununu had not invited me to his office for holiday greetings. In fact, John had the misfortune of giving me my Christmas lump of coal from the White House. To this day I remain convinced that he was most uncomfortable and did not welcome his task.

After preliminary words on the weather and the season, Sununu said that the president wanted a change in the Cabinet composition because he wanted to bring in some new people at mid-term. I knew then where this discussion was going. The president's domestic agenda was in trouble and his popularity was declining just as he was starting to gear up for reelection.

Sununu told me the president had just returned from the economic summit in Europe. It was a long trip, and it had given him time to think about the composition of the Cabinet. He wanted a change in the leadership of the Department of Education.

Sununu said he was asking for my resignation, but before I answered he asked me to consider an ambassadorship to the Dominican Republic or Costa Rica. He said there was no hurry to make a change; we could take six to eight weeks to announce my resignation.

I knew there were no secrets in the White House; staff delighted in leaking news or spreading rumors. Later I learned that Chino had been told by one of my staff that the topic of my meeting with Sununu was my resignation.

Sununu urged me to think about the ambassadorship, but I told him I didn't have to because I didn't want one. I added that if the president wanted my resignation, he could have it right away.

John said I had done a good job in the Department of Education, and if I hadn't, he would have let me know about it in no uncertain terms. Again, John asked me to take the ambassadorship, and again I said no to being an ambassador and that the president could have my resignation immediately.

Sununu told me to wait in his office while he checked to see if the president could see me right away. While Sununu was out of the room, I sat in his office and thought how superficial the White House analysis of the education programs had been. I was troubled and saddened by the lack of appreciation of the efforts of so many in the department to improve education. I honestly thought I had done a good job, under the circumstances. Years later, looking back, I still believe I would have done the job much as I did in those days in Washington. I did learn I needed to be much more political if I was to be perceived as a success in Washington, but that was not acceptable behavior to me.

I had planned to resign from my post as secretary in the fall of 1990, but Peggy had persuaded me to wait until March 1991. I had agreed because the department had so many new education programs and initiatives under way, and I wanted to bring closure to these efforts. I especially wanted to see the "Indian Nations at Risk" study completed, because I knew that American Indians suffered even greater education deficits than Hispanics.

President Bush saw me a few minutes later. I thought I had done the job for him in education, but I had failed to serve his political agenda. The president was kind and gentle to me, as was always his manner. He, like Sununu, emphasized change was needed in the composition of the Cabinet. As it turned out, there was none. The Persian Gulf crisis and war followed, and as a result the president's popularity soared. The president urged me to stay on a while longer and to take my time about a public announcement of my resignation. I told him if he wanted change, it was my duty to give it to him as soon as possible. The president asked me to think about the proposed change and give him a call the next morning.

As I was leaving, the president told me if I ever needed a reference, to give him a call. He said he would be pleased to write of my honesty and integrity.

I thanked him, excused myself, and left the Oval Office for the last time.

I returned to my car and told Mr. Cleveland to please drive me home instead of back to the Department of Education. When we arrived at our apartment, I told Mr. Cleveland not to pick me up the next morning. I thanked him and said good-bye.

When I walked into our apartment, Peggy asked why I was home so early and was I feeling well. I told Peggy I was fine, in many ways. I described my meeting with Sununu and explained that the president wanted change in the Cabinet as he geared up for the reelection campaign. Peggy said she was very sorry for me and that the administration had made a dumb decision in asking for my resignation. She said she wished she hadn't talked me out of resigning in the fall and then asked what I was going to do. I told Peggy I didn't want to be an ambassador; I wanted to get out of Washington as soon as possible. I would call the president in the morning and tell him of my decision to leave by mid-December.

Again, Peggy told me I had done a grand job; politics had just gotten in the way.

I suggested that we pack a few things and go to Concord until I had to give a commencement speech in West Virginia. Then we could go to our home in Port Aransas, Texas. We had purchased it in 1989, expecting to live there after we left Washington. Peggy agreed that she wanted to go to Port Aransas and leave Washington as quickly as possible. She asked about the future.

I told her both of us should continue to work to improve education in this country, and I believed we could be more effective seeking changes in education from outside of Washington rather than from within an administration. That way we would be free of political agendas and considerations. I wouldn't have to clear my speeches with the Office of Management and Budget, and I wouldn't have to deal with Congress. I would be a private citizen free to say what I wanted, without worrying about the political consequences.

Peggy said I always managed to look on the bright side of things. In a few months or even years from now, she said, we would still say we had made a wise decision to get out of Washington as soon as possible. As usual, Peggy was right.

Early the next morning, I called the White House and told the president that my resignation would be effective December 15. I told him that I had a commencement address to give at the centennial celebration of West Virginia State College and then I was through. My letter of resignation would be on his desk later in the morning.

Again, the president expressed his friendship, and then our conversation was over. I had not been an insider at the White House, nor part of the inner circle working with the president. It was difficult for me to keep the education agenda in front of him because of the many pressing matters he dealt with every day.

Within an hour after I talked to the president, Peggy and I were driving north to Concord and she was asking me for my thoughts.

I told her I was relieved and pleased to be leaving and that I realized little was done or said in Washington without weighing the political outcome. To some in the administration, education was a public relations and political issue. As we left Washington, I told Peggy I remembered a country ballad, "Lubbock in My Rear View Mirror." It was about a cowboy really glad to get out of Lubbock, Texas. I said I was going to write a song titled "Washington in My Rear View Mirror." Peggy said it would sell a million records, then told me to drive on, head north, keep my eyes on the road ahead, and forget what was behind me.

I had come to Washington without a political agenda. My only motive was to improve education in this country. As an academician, I cared nothing about politics. I now know my attitude was a mistake. Being neither Republican nor Democrat didn't help in terms of moving the education agenda ahead. Perhaps I should have been more political in pushing the education agenda, but to this day I believe I did a fine job as secretary of education. I did my job honestly and without regard to political consequences, remaining focused on educating all children in America to their fullest potential.

Soon after I left the post of secretary of education in mid-December 1990, Peggy and I returned to our home in Port Aransas, Texas. Port

Aransas is a lovely fishing village, population about three thousand, on Mustang Island, one of the barrier islands off the Gulf Coast of Texas. Fishing and birdwatching are major activities there. For several months I had quiet time to think about Washington, education, and our future. I rested, fished, watched the birds, alligators, and dolphins, and read.

It was winter in South Texas, but the temperature is quite mild in January and February. There are miles of beautiful sandy beaches on Mustang Island, and Peggy and I walked a couple of miles each day on them. We waded in the surf and strolled on the beach.

During our walks, Peggy and I talked about Washington and my education successes and failures. We speculated about the outcome of my job if I had been more political in my decisions. But as the days passed, we talked less of Washington. Soon, our greatest challenge and competition on our walks was which of us could pick up the most sand dollars or the prettiest seashell. Slowly, we were mending from the education battles. Both Peggy and I agreed that every politician in Washington, whether in the executive or legislative branch, is an instant expert on education the moment elected.

Unfortunately, this instant expertise seems to give them license to tell the secretary of education, and all of the educators in America, how to do their jobs. Congressional session after session, legislation for educational reform and more testing passes, and yet the system has not improved overall. Reforms mandated from Washington will not improve education. I am convinced the solutions to the education deficits are in the hearts and minds of parents, teachers, school administrators, and others who care about schooling and who live with the problems and successes of education on a daily basis. They must be heard in the national debates to improve education.

During those quiet days in Port Aransas, I did not read the national newspapers. I found the local weekly newspaper, *The South Jetty*, excellent, its editorials and articles thoughtful and well written. The newspaper kept Peggy and me knowledgeable about what was going on in our town. We were informed about important activities such as fishing, birding, and boating.

At Port Aransas, I reflected on my educational involvement and achievements. In 1991, I could look back to twenty-six years of teaching and research in medical schools, eight years as a university president, and twenty-seven months as secretary of education. During those years I became quite knowledgeable about medical, graduate, and undergraduate education, as well as primary and secondary education. In the Department of Education, I learned much about early childhood education.

In March 1991 Peggy and I agreed it was time to leave the sands of Port Aransas and return to education. I knew I had much to offer on improving education at many levels, and I wanted to be of service to this nation in solving its education problems. I decided, and Peggy agreed, to dedicate the rest of my academic career and my life to improving learning. I was especially determined to better the education of minority children. I also wanted to markedly increase the numbers of minorities in higher education and in the health professions. To this day, I continue the effort.

Shortly after departing from our retreat at Port Aransas, I again joined the faculty of the Tufts University School of Medicine, this time in the Department of Public Health and Family Medicine. I arranged for limited teaching and administrative responsibilities, thus allowing me time to help those who are educationally disadvantaged.

Since my return to academia, I have kept my commitment to work on improving the education of minorities. My quest will continue until failing health or diminished mental capacity hinder me in my work. As to knowing when I no longer make sense, I've made a pact with Peggy. She is to tell me when my statements or thoughts are no longer sensible. Peggy has agreed to tell me, but I suspect she would have told me anyway, pact or no pact.

REFLECTIONS

When I look back, I see a life of education and public service. I am a sixth-generation Texan, born on the King Ranch where my father was foreman of the Santa Gertrudis Division. My education commenced in a two-room schoolhouse on the ranch. Eventually, I earned bachelor's and master's degrees in zoology from Texas Tech University and a doctoral degree in physiology from Iowa State University. I have received twenty-one honorary degrees.

My academic career has been in medical education. I have also worked vigorously to enhance disadvantaged students' access to the health professions by improving the quality of education they receive. I am author or coauthor of numerous scientific and education publications. I taught at the Medical College of Virginia and at the Tufts University School of Medicine, where I was the dean for five years. In 1980, Texas Tech University named me its tenth president, the first Hispanic and first graduate of the university to hold that position. At the same time, I was appointed as the third president of the Texas Tech Health Sciences Center. I served as president of the two institutions until 1988, when President Ronald Reagan asked me to be U.S. secretary of education in his Cabinet. On September 20, 1988, after unanimous confirmation by the Senate, then Vice President George H. W. Bush swore me in. I was the first Hispanic appointed to the Cabinet in the history of the United States.

President George H. W. Bush appointed me to his Cabinet following the 1988 presidential elections, and I served as his secretary of education until December 15, 1990. While secretary, I worked to improve education in America for all students. I encouraged students, teachers, and parents to demand the best possible school systems, and I wanted all students to receive a high-quality education.

As I write these words, I am a professor in the Department of Public Health and Family Medicine at the Tufts University School of Medicine.

I consider myself fortunate to have journeyed from the King Ranch to the White House. Many helped me make the journey, and I thank them. They gave of their time, energy, and wisdom so I could achieve the major post in education and thereby help improve it in this nation.

I must acknowledge the support and guidance given to me about life, education, values, and service by my parents. They obviously were visionaries because they taught me the essentials of living, preparing me for a life of education and public service.

Equal to them in shaping my life, Peggy has been my love and support for more than fifty years. She has borne our ten marvelous children. They, in turn, taught and continue to teach me, even today, much about life and love.

When I think about others who had a positive influence on me, I remember my brothers and sister, and Vallejo, and my relatives and friends from the barrio of Kingsville. Also, many of the men and women living on the King Ranch taught me much. My teachers at the ranch school and in Kingsville and my university professors contributed to my education and thereby shaped my life and its outcome.

The road has been long, and now I am in the twilight of my life. I find myself thinking about and trying to understand the many lessons about life taught to me on the ranch so long ago. In this memoir I have written about learning on the ranch the necessity of taking risks, commitment to just causes, and hard work; I also learned the importance of education, service to country, honesty, and being optimistic about living. Perhaps most important, I learned always to hold the highest ethical standards. Clearly, all of these lessons helped me achieve success in my later life. They made me what I am today. In other words, the ranch taught me how to live.

I marvel at some of the education matters my parents taught me. They did this by example and by extensive and repeated counseling. I am convinced those lessons from my parents guided me and aided my decisionmaking in my service as secretary of education.

In this memoir, I wrote about my parents telling me to speak English to Dad and Spanish to Mother. As a consequence, I grew up speaking two languages, which I have retained to this day. When I entered first grade at the schoolhouse on the King Ranch, I was one of the few children in my grade who could speak English. All of the rest spoke Spanish only and underwent what educators today call "immersion into English." I consider the experience in learning another language on the ranch as my "bilingual education," as taught to me by my parents.

In Washington, it was important to me that I could speak about bilingual education from a practical as well as theoretical viewpoint. As secretary, I was able to articulate my support of bilingual education. It was, and still is, educational, controversial, and political. It evokes strong emotions among its proponents and its opponents. In Washington, however, my background permitted me to speak about it in an informed and caring manner. I maintain that my language learning on the King Ranch was the basis for my decisions and pronouncements about bilingual education during my service in Washington.

From my first days as secretary of education until I left the post, I spoke to the departmental staff and to others of the importance of raising the expectations of children and young people, that is, telling them that they could succeed in educating themselves. I recall my parents telling me as a child that I could learn and do well in school. I remember my father's insistence when I was growing up on the ranch that I *would* go to college. At first I did not think I had the potential, nor did I believe we could afford college. Still, my parents clung to the dream of college for their children and kept raising our expectations, and I and my four siblings all received at least one college degree.

During the years I led the Department of Education, I stressed the importance of parental involvement in the education of their children. I repeated this time and time again and made it one of the major themes of my administration. I often thought about my parents' major involvement in my education during those growing years on the ranch. Time and time again, Dad asked me about how I was doing in school or quizzed me or reviewed my lessons with me. I recall his careful assessment of my report cards and his comments if my grades did not meet his expectations. Mother was functionally illiterate, so she was unable to help me with my studies. However, she frequently asked about how I was doing in school and if I had done my homework, and she took time to meet with my teachers to review my educational progress.

I am proud of my record as secretary of education on academic choice in public schools. Promoting this concept and increasing parental involvement were major efforts of the Department of Education during my leadership. While in Washington, I thought about my parents' decision to make sure my sister Sarita, and subsequently the rest of their children, attended one of the Anglo schools in Kingsville. Sarita and I started in the Santa Gertrudis School on the King Ranch, but somehow my parents managed to have us transferred to the Anglo school in a separate school district. This action was remarkable and unheard of in the 1930s, but to me, thinking about it as an educator, it was also an excellent example of public school academic choice by parents wanting the best possible education for their child.

At our home on the ranch, there were many books. I remember Dad returning from stock shows in Fort Worth and San Antonio with boxes of used books for us to read. At least twice a month, Mother drove us to the small library in Kingsville, and we returned with an armload of books. My parents insisted that reading was the key to learning, and they frequently reminded me about the importance of reading. Soon, my appetite for reading was insatiable. Today, I can look back on a lifetime of reading and the pleasures and information given to me because my parents sustained and nurtured my reading habit. Once, as secretary, while discussing reading education with a gathering of educators, I told them (somewhat facetiously) that the curriculum for the first three years of school should be "reading, reading, and more reading."

So it is apparent to me that the lessons I took from the King Ranch about bilingual education, raising the expectations of children, parental involvement in the education of their children, academic choice in public schools, and a commitment to reading all shaped my service as secretary of education. What is better than to take a series of life experiences imparted by loving parents and use them to shape decisions about education at the national level? How fortunate I have been in my travel from the King Ranch to the White House.

Now, the journey from the King Ranch is almost finished. I am in my seventh decade of life. As I look over my shoulder, I believe I understand the many factors shaping my life of academics and public service. I trust I have made these clear in my autobiography.

I close this memoir with one more story. Dad often said to me, "Son, educate yourself. It is a treasure no one can take from you." I thought he was referring to schooling and learning to read and how to do mathematics. Now, I understand that he also meant that in addition to schooling, there is much to learn from others outside the schoolhouse. I took those lessons taught to me on the King Ranch by my parents and the men and women who lived on the ranch and unknowingly incorporated them into my life. I greatly value what I was taught there. It was as fine an education as the one I received at great universities.

What a wonderful, fulfilling journey through life it has been for me, and it started on a ranch in Texas.

Index

Masters, Wesley, 204
Mayer, Jean, 172–76, 185
Mayes, Wendell, 204
MCV (Medical College of Virginia). *See* Medical
    College of Virginia (MCV)
Medeiros, Cardinal, 168
media treatment of Lauro as education secretary,
    208–9, 210, 235, 255–56
Medical College of Virginia (MCV): appreciation
    of experience at, 147; as job prospect, 126;
    teaching and research at, 130–31, 135, 141,
    144, 145; and William Maloney, 164
medical education career summary, 272
medical schools: Central American problems with,
    157–64; at Texas Tech, 182, 188, 191–93, 203.
    See also Medical College of Virginia (MCV);
    Tufts University School of Medicine
Melampy, Robert M., 116–23, 187
men and women, segregation in church, 73
Methodism, Grandma Panchita's adoption of, 30
Mexico: bandit raids from, 9–14; and *la entrada*,
    14–16; medical education consultation in,
    164; visit as education secretary, 245–46
migrant students, need for educational support,
    260–61
Milford School Bell, 233
minority groups and education, 23, 71–73, 212, 240.
    See also Hispanic Americans
Moore, Carl, 122
Morehead, James, 169, 170
Morganti, Clyde, 185–86
Mosley, Dick, 83–84
Mosley, W. T., 83–84
movies and childhood, 7, 48, 72
Murdock, Jesse L., Jr., 132, 133
Murdock, Jesse L., Sr., 131, 132–33
Murdock, Peggy Ann (Mrs. Lauro Cavazos, Jr.)
    (wife), 27–28, 124, 125–27. *See also* Cavazos,
    Peggy Ann
Murray, Grover, 191
Music Building, Texas Tech, 189–91
music in King Ranch area, 6–7, 64

Natcher, William H., 243–44
National Education Association, 20, 21
National Education Goals, 232–33, 245, 251
National Institutes of Health, 171
Negroponte, John D., 245
Nelson, Sharon, 186, 193
neuroanatomy, training in, 130
New Deal, 60–62
New England Medical Center, 168
newspapers, importance as ranch resource, 61–62.
    See also press

Newton-Wellesley Hospital, 168
New Year's tradition, 134
New York Times, 255
Nicaragua, 158
Norias Division, 8–14, 25, 32–33
Norris, Francis, 212
Northway, J. K., 48
Nuevo León, New Spain, 24
nursing, Peggy's career in, 134–35, 154–57, 188–89
nutrition curriculum, 172, 187

Ochoa, Albert (brother-in-law), 186
Ochoa, Sarita (née Cavazos) (sister), 186, 197, 220.
    See also Cavazos, Sarita
Odessa, Academic Health Center at, 192, 203
Office of Management and Budget (OMB), 235
O'Shea, Elena Zamora, 17–18
Our Lady of Guadalupe shrine, 42–43

Pan American Health Organization (PAHO),
    157–64
parental involvement in education, 241, 257–60,
    274, 275
parents, Lauro's: lessons learned from, 4, 272, 273–
    74, 275; positive example of, 19; relationship
    with, 44–45, 123–24, 139, 195. *See also* Cava-
    zos, Lauro F., Sr.; Cavazos, Tomasa Álvarez
Paris, France, sabbatical in, 165–66
Parker, Carl, 254
Parrish, N. K., 132
Parsley, Bill
peer review of legislation, 236
Pérez, Raúl (uncle), 76
Pfluger, Robert, 180, 181–82, 183, 184, 187
Phelan, Marilyn, 184, 185
physical plant at Texas Tech, 182, 189–91, 203
Pierce, Freda, 178, 179, 180
poaching and King Ranch, 57–60
political pork projects, 235–37
politics: as barrier to change, 230–31; Bush's sup-
    port for Lauro's nonpartisan position, 232;
    and difficulties in making real changes, 270;
    early exposure to ranch, 69–70; and educa-
    tion secretary role, 211–12, 234–38, 254–55,
    266, 267; Lauro's lack of partisanship, 21,
    208–9, 217–18, 234–35, 261, 269
Port Aransas, Texas, 268, 269–71
Porter, John, 116, 117
potential, education of children to fullest, 227, 233,
    274
poverty and educational achievement, 250
Pozo, Maria Augustina de, 16
prayer as central to ranch life, 89
prejudice: and concerns about living in South,

142–43; and elementary school bullying, 83; and Peggy's father, 132–33; and segregation in Kingsville, 71–73, 77–79; during Texas Tech presidency, 193–95

press treatment of Lauro as education secretary, 208–9, 210, 235, 255–56

Price, Dorothy, 122

private schools, vouchers for, 242

public health initiative at Texas Tech, 187–88, 191

public schools: and academic choice, 229, 231, 238–43; funding for Texas, 253–54; Lauro's support for, 242–43; need for restructuring of, 232–33

Punta del Monte Ranch, *103*

Quintanilla, Francisco (grandfather), 18, 39, 40, 41, *108*

Quintanilla, Rita Álvarez, "Mama Grande Rita" (grandmother), 18, 39–41, 43, 72–73

Quintanilla, Rita (Mrs. Rodriguez) (aunt), 18

Quintanilla, Tomasa Álvarez (mother), ancestry of, 14–19. *See also* Cavazos, Tomasa Álvarez

Quintanilla ancestry, 14–16

racism. *See* prejudice

Raimo, Mary, 256

ranch houses, 45–46, 69, 97

Ranching Heritage Association, 202

ranching operations: bandit raid, 8–14; brush control, 70; cattle breeding, 33, 34–38, 59–60, 123, 124, 127–28; daily life, 7, 8, 51; dairy farm, 52, 99–100; dangers of, 53–54, 89–90; father's career progression, 7–8, 32–34; home environment, 47–48, 51–52; King's cattle-buying trip to Mexico, 14–16; poaching problem, 57–60; and Vallejo, 85–100

Rancho Santa Cruz, 39–40, *108*

Raymond, Edward C. (uncle), 6

Raymond, Leonor (aunt), 6

Raymondville, Texas, 49–50

reading, commitment to, 275

Reagan, Ronald, 3, 21, 205, 206, 209, 223–24

regents, Texas Tech board of, 180–81, 198–202, 204, 215–16

regional health centers initiatives at Texas Tech, 191, 192

regional meetings on school choice, 241–42

regional public hearings on Hispanic education, 252, 254–61

religion: and church segregation by ethnicity, 73; and civil marriage ceremonies, 41, 46; First Holy Communion, 46–47; Grandma Panchita's disaffection with Church, 28–31; and Peggy as Catholic convert, 124; Texas Tech church attendance, 118; and Tío Meme, 42–43; Vallejo's spirituality, 89

remediation strategies for students, 260

Republican Party, suspicions about Lauro's political agenda, 21, 208–9

research: improvement in Texas Tech, 203; at Iowa State, 116–19, 121; at MCV, 131, 141; Paris sabbatical, 165; squirrel monkeys, 169–71; and Tufts match, 146

Richmond, VA, 133–36, 138–39, 140, 141, 145. *See also* Medical College of Virginia (MCV)

roadrunners, 91

roads and travel across ranch, 49–50

Robel, Charles, 165

"Robin Hood Plan" for equity in school funding in Texas, 254

Rodriguez, Rita (née Quintanilla) (aunt), 18

Roman, Gilbert, 261

Roman Catholic Church. *See* religion

Roosevelt, Franklin D., 60, 61

roundups at King Ranch, 36–38

Running W brand, 47, 68

sabbatical in France, 164–65

Sáenz, Evaristo, 64

Saint Elizabeth's Catholic Church, 131

Saint Elizabeth's Hospital, 168–69

Saint Gertrude's Catholic Church, 73

Salinas, Lorenzo, 52

Salinas de Gortari, Carlos, 245–46

San Antonio, Texas, 254–55

San Antonio Express-News, 210

Sanders, John Theodore, "Ted," 251, 252, 261

Sanders, Mike, 190

San Juan de Carricitos land grant, 24–25, 59

San Martín's Catholic Church, 6, 72–73

San Salvador, El Salvador, 158–62

Santa Cruz, Rancho, 39–40, *108*

Santa Gertrudis breed, 34–38, 59–60, 127

Santa Gertrudis Division, 8, 32–34

Santa Gertrudis Ranch, 16, 17–18, 69–70

Santa Gertrudis School, 68–71, *111*

Sauz Ranch, 9, 58

Schlafly, Phyllis, 21

school-based management, 240, 242

school choice, 229, 231, 238–43, 274–75

schoolhouse, ranch, 68–71, *111*

School of Allied Health, Texas Tech, 188, 193, 203

School of Architecture, Texas Tech, 202

School of Nursing, Texas Tech, 188, 193, 203

School of Pharmacy at Texas Tech, 203

School of Veterinary Medicine at Texas Tech, 203

schools. *See* education; public schools

security, ranch, 50–51, 57–60